ABOUT ISLAND PRESS

Island Press, a nonprofit organization, publishes, markets, and distributes the most advanced thinking on the conservation of our natural resources—books about soil, land, water, forests, wildlife, and hazardous and toxic wastes. These books are practical tools used by public officials, business and industry leaders, natural resource managers, and concerned citizens working to solve both local and global resource problems.

Founded in 1978, Island Press reorganized in 1984 to meet the increasing demand for substantive books on all resource-related issues. Island Press publishes and distributes under its own imprint and offers these services to other nonprofit organizations.

Support for Island Press is provided by Geraldine R. Dodge Foundation, The Energy Foundation, The Charles Engelhard Foundation, The Ford Foundation, Glen Eagles Foundation, The George Gund Foundation, William and Flora Hewlett Foundation, The Joyce Foundation, The John D. and Catherine T. MacArthur Foundation, The Andrew W. Mellon Foundation, The Joyce Mertz-Gilmore Foundation, The NewLand Foundation, The J. N. Pew, Jr. Charitable Trust, Alida Rockefeller, The Rockefeller Brothers Fund, The Rockefeller Foundation, The Florence and John Schumann Foundation, The Tides Foundation, and individual donors.

Our Country, The Planet

Also by Shridath Ramphal:

One World to Share
Inseparable Humanity
An End to Otherness

Our Country, The Planet

Forging a Partnership for Survival

Shridath Ramphal

Foreword by Seymour Topping

Washington, D.C. ☐ Covelo, California

Library of Congress Cataloging-in-Publication Data

Ramphal, S. S.
Our country, the planet / Shridath Ramphal : foreword
by Seymour Topping.
p. cm.
Includes index.
ISBN 1-55963-165-1 (cloth).
ISBN 1-55963-164-3 (paper)
1. Economic development—Environmental aspects.
2. Population—Environmental aspects.
3. Environmental protection.   I. Title.
TD195.E25R36   1992
363.7—dc20   91-43320
                                      CIP

Printed on recycled, acid-free paper
♲
Manufactured in the United States of America

10 9 8 7 6 5 4 3 2 1

To the memory of Barbara Ward and René Dubos
and to all who continue their mission for
Our Country, The Planet

One touch of nature makes the whole world kin.

Troilus and Cressida

Contents

Foreword

W E   A R E confronted with indisputable evidence that the struggle
to keep our planet habitable for the human race is at a critical juncture.
As Sir Shridath Ramphal, the former secretary-general of the Commonwealth and foreign minister of Guyana, documents in this authoritative study, the debate among experts on the central issues of
survivability has been resolved. Scientists agree and attest that the
progressive thinning of the ozone layer and the effects of global warming will put world civilization at risk unless prompt action is taken to
curb current polluting practices. Without effective worldwide programs to protect the biosphere, those images of our descendants existing in domed communities designed to shield against ultraviolet
radiation or sheltering behind dikes in cities such as New York to
guard against rising seas as a consequence of global warming become
credible.

The call by the scientific community to immediate action to forestall
disaster extends to other ecological threats. We are urged to consider
the impact of population pressures on the shrinking resources of the
Earth, the desertification of much of its surface, and the loss of biodiversity essential to a balanced ecosystem. In 1991 the human race
totaled some 5.4 billion; by the year 2000 the number will be 6.25
billion, leveling off, according to UN demographers, in the middle of
the twenty-second century at 11.6 billion. Sir Shridath reminds us that
3.3 billion hectares of land are under assault by desertification. This
carries immense implications for human hunger and deprivation, especially in the developing world. Researchers estimate that as many as 25
percent of all species inhabiting the Earth in the mid-1980s will have
disappeared by 2015 if current deforestation trends hold. Given this
momentum of devastation we cannot help but ask the question, is it
already too late? Is it too late to expect realistically that the human

race will band together in an effort on behalf of our children and succeeding generations to preserve and restore the planet? Have we already unleashed fatal trends that may be irreversible?

Sir Shridath, drawing on the experience of service with five international commissions on global development and the environment, correlates scientific research to define clearly for us the nature and magnitude of our excesses, and the appalling dangers inherent in them. He catalogues the solutions projected by experts working under the aegis of the United Nations and other international bodies. He appeals for the realization of those solutions during a new era of enlightened change, which would dawn with the heads of government proclaiming an "Earth Charter" at the Conference on Environment and Development in Rio de Janeiro in June 1992. But are the projected solutions, enormous in cost, within reach given the reluctance of nations to sacrifice from the treasury for the common good? Will the peoples of the industrial nations, particularly Americans, whose energy consumption imposes the greatest burden on the environment, be amenable to accepting a more modest lifestyle? Are nations ready to forgo a measure of their sovereignty in the interests of enlightened global governance? The answers will turn on whether political leaders can muster the will and that of their people on behalf of long-term programs designed to both safeguard the Earth and assure equitable access to its resources. A revolution in human consciousness is required, Sir Shridath tells us, if that challenge is to be met and our ethical obligation to succeeding generations fulfilled.

The current search for workable programs that would satisfy present-day needs and meet those of future generations is being undertaken within the conceptual framework of sustainable development, a concept formulated in 1987 by the UN World Commission on Environment and Development, chaired by Prime Minister Gro Harlem Brundtland of Norway. The commission defined sustainable development, accepted now as the guiding principle of environmentalism in the 1990s, as "meeting the needs of the present without compromising the ability of future generations to meet their own needs." The commission judged sustainable development attainable if the nations of the world united without delay behind a sound strategy for the year 2000 and beyond.

Sir Shridath, a leading member of that commission, views sustainable development as based on two crucial components: needs, in particular the basic needs of the world's poor, and environmental limits, which, if breached, in particular by the world's rich, would affect the capacity of the natural world to sustain life today and tomorrow. For Sir Shridath the rich, broadly speaking, are the people of the North making up that quarter of the world's population, most of them living in industrial countries, that accounts for 80 percent of world consumption of commercial energy. The other three-quarters are the poor. They live for the most part in the developing world and account for only 20 percent of commercial energy consumption. Since energy consumption, largely the burning of fossil fuels for transportation and residential and commercial use, is the principal factor in global pollution, the need for restraint rests mainly with the North.

Sir Shridath's book is more than a demand for restraint, it is also an impassioned plea for the North to assist in rescuing the South from the poverty that Indira Gandhi once characterized as the world's worst polluter. He buttresses the case made by the Brundtland Commission that environment and world development are inseparable. Large-scale environmental degradation in the developing world, typified by the clearing of tropical forests for timber exports and farming, is likely to continue until the North joins in mutually beneficial programs of sustainable development in the South. Forests are sinks for the absorption and storage of carbon dioxide, the pollutant that is the principal threat to the biosphere. They are also the primary repository of biodiversity and genetic resources that are essential to the ecosystem and exploited mainly by industrial nations.

When the voices of the North urge that deforestation be halted and that developing countries adopt other ecological restraints, the voices of the South reply: Your consumption is largely responsible for the environmental risks all of us face today; you are the main beneficiaries of the wealth accumulated through processes of economic growth that produced these risks; we are in the early stages of economic growth; we cannot afford to join in measures intended to avert long-term global risks if it means diverting resources critical to the immediate and basic needs of our peoples; it is therefore incumbent upon you, while exercising restraint in your consumption, to provide us with the financial assistance and access to technology needed to relieve our poverty and put our economies on an environmentally sound footing. In the interests of ecological self-preservation and to relieve the unimaginable suffering of the multiplying millions in the developing world, Sir Shridath, regarded by many as the most articulate voice of the South, appeals to the North to come to the rescue on a vast scale.

He proposes a multilateral program comparable to the Marshall Plan, which the United States undertook after World War II for the reconstruction of Europe. The response of the North, beleaguered by its own problems, is hesitant and uncertain.

Engagement between North and South, challenge and response, on the issues of sustainable development is the dynamic that inspired the UN conference in Rio de Janeiro and that is driving ongoing negotiations. The dialogue centers on what programs shall take priority and who shall bear the costs. Those at the diverse negotiating tables, delegates of some 170 nations, are infinitely better informed and far more representative of the global community than the governmental missions that attended the Stockholm conference in 1972 in response to the initial worldwide environmental alarm. This commitment reflects the growing awareness of the threat to our planet that in the last few years has impelled political leaders to take some action. There is reason for hope.

In 1990 the signatories of the Montreal Protocol agreed to phase out, no later than the year 2000, the use of chlorofluorocarbons (CFCs) and the other main substances that attack the ozone. Since then, scientists have found that ozone depletion has accelerated beyond earlier projections, exposing countless thousands to death from skin cancer. New findings reveal a weakening of the shield over the United States and other temperate-zone countries in the summer, when ultraviolet rays are most dangerous, as well as in the winter and early spring. Action to speed up the phasing out of CFCs, halons, and other ozone-depleting chemicals is impending. Substitutes have been developed for CFCs used in refrigeration, air-conditioning, propellants, and the like. In tandem with the ozone alert, another major move to save the biosphere gathered support. Beginning in 1988 at a series of scientific and governmental meetings led by the Europeans, the problem of global warming was attacked seriously for the first time. The Earth is kept at a stable temperature by a layer of the biosphere made up of the so-called greenhouse gases, which retain some of the sun's incoming warmth. The principal greenhouse gas is carbon dioxide, which unfortunately is also the principal pollutant emitted by the burning of fossil fuels. By thickening the natural greenhouse canopy these emissions, 70 percent of which come from industrial countries, warm the Earth and thereby threaten to produce climate changes with such catastrophic results as rising sea levels. Half of global warming is attributable to the burning of fossil fuels. Another quarter stems from the emission of

CFCs. Some of the balance is blamed on deforestation. Since there is agreement on remedial action for the long-term repair of the ozone layer through restriction of CFC emissions, the most pressing problem before the world community centers on the release of carbon dioxide in burning fossil fuels. Most industrial countries have announced action to stabilize, if not to reduce, their output of carbon dioxide during the 1990s.

Ironically, the notable laggard in 1991 was the United States, the worst polluter in this respect. The United States accounts for 23 percent of world carbon-dioxide emissions from fossil fuel use. The other Group of Seven nations together account for 18 percent. One of the seven, Japan, uses only half the energy expended by the United States per unit of production. The United States stood alone at preparatory meetings of the Earth Summit in resisting adoption of a treaty that would impose mandatory cuts in the emissions of carbon dioxide. The European Community and Japan favor reducing emissions to 1990 levels by the year 2000. While generally accepting the recommendation of the National Academy of Sciences that the United States should act to halt global warming, the Bush administration has argued for flexible, voluntary restraints until further research makes the dimensions of the threat clearer. Evidence suggests that administration policy is motivated more by concern over the impact on the American economy of severe restraints than by doubts about the scientific projections on global warming. American officials defending White House policy as adequate cite the numerous actions being taken at the federal and local level to diminish the release of greenhouse gases. U.S. emissions are expected to rise over the next decade, but more slowly because of the Clean Air Act, energy efficiencies mandated by Congress, and stringent vehicle emission controls ordered in some states. There is also renewed interest in turning to clean nuclear power if safety requirements in the development of reactors and the disposal of waste can be satisfied.

The decision of the UN General Assembly to convene the Rio conference at the heads-of-government level indicates how environmental concerns have come to the top of the global agenda. Underlying the multilateral movement, however, and manifest in Sir Shridath's cry for help on behalf of developing countries, are serious tensions. If concrete results do not flow from Rio in terms of aid to the developing world and restraint in consumption by industrial nations, a breakdown in North-South dialogue could ensue. Maurice Strong, secretary-general of the conference and the man who directed the 1972 Stockholm conclave as well as commissioned this book, has said that the Earth Summit poses opportunities that cannot be missed: Failure to seize them might delay needed changes for ten or twenty years and possibly make them impossible.

The ambitious goals envisioned by spokesmen of the South will inevitably evoke questions as to political feasibility, at least in the early 1990s as Western industrial nations struggle with budgetary deficits, recession, and urgent appeals for aid from Eastern Europe and the new nations of the former Soviet Union. The proposed Earth Charter sets forth basic environmental and developmental principles to govern the relationship of states and peoples with each other and with the Earth. An agenda of action, Agenda 21, designed to realize charter principles in all major areas affecting the relationship between environment and development is under negotiation. It is exceedingly complex and sometimes contentious negotiation. The initial focus is on the period following the conference, from 1993 to the year 2000, and then beyond into the twenty-first century. To effect the transition to sustainable development, the South is seeking commitments from the North for major policy changes, economic assistance, and technology transfers.

Whatever the high political visibility of the occasion, it is clear that Rio cannot accomplish all that needs to be done. At their London meeting in July 1991 the Group of Seven declared they were committed to work for a successful conference. The absence of specifics in their statement was an augury of how difficult it will be to rise to all the challenges. Beyond consensus on the Earth charter lies the prospect of hard North-South bargaining that will extend over years. The North, including the United States, Japan, and the European industrial nations, must struggle initially to satisfy at least the minimum financial demands of the South so as to sustain North-South cooperation. The North will be looking in return for stability and democracy in developing countries, conditions not always attainable in the turbulent Third World, to ensure effective use of aid.

Among the nations of the North, only Japan seems to be in a position to make substantial additions to its financial contributions. With the decline of the Soviet Union the United States may rank as the only superpower, but it will be argued that the nation is caught in a budgetary squeeze, with a large deficit in 1992 of about $260 million, and that the "peace dividend" stemming from the end of the cold war has yet to materialize. In the European Community, only Germany has the resources for additional sizeable outlays, but Bonn is committed to a vast program of economic and environmental rehabilitation of East Germany and Eastern Europe. Disabled in the process of political and economic transition, and saddled with a foreign debt of some $68 billion, the disintegrated Soviet Union has become more of competitor for assistance than a donor to developing countries. Its own environmental problems, such as the contamination of the Aral Sea and the aftermath of the Chernobyl nuclear disaster, beg for attention and resources that are in short supply. And yet if we see the challenge in terms of human survival, these economic arguments cannot be a complete answer.

Japan, emerging as the world leader in assistance to developing countries, has indicated interest in extending supplementary financial support in the environmental area. Sizeable contributions would be made on an annual basis. Japanese companies, like some multinational corporations in the United States, are becoming increasingly active in exploring business opportunities in such fields as resource recovery and recycling, development of renewable sources of energy, and pollution control. The Japanese contribution will be substantial but not sufficient in itself to fulfill these enormous needs. The only solution lies in a multilateral approach by the North.

Apart from large financial flows, the Western industrial nations and Japan are capable of providing significant assistance in the areas of debt relief, trade, and technical assistance. At their disposal are the World Bank, the International Monetary Fund, and the General Agreement on Tariffs and Trade. Debt, more than half of it owed to private banks, has been especially crippling to Third World growth. Payments of about $125 billion annually to creditors exceeded in recent years the inflow of aid. Steps to lighten the debt burden are being given priority. Also helpful would be tighter regulation by industrial countries of private institutions, which would diminish the flight of billions of dollars of capital from the South. Much of the other outflow of funds from developing countries stems from military spending, nearly $150 billion annually. Joint action by the Soviet Union and Western countries, the principal arms suppliers, to curb sales would allow urgently needed funds to be diverted to economic development.

The response of the North in the next few years will likely show progress but will it surpass what Sir Shridath regards as "muddling through"? Muddling through is his scenario of ad hoc response by rich countries, well-intentioned but usually limited action, crisis management rather than avoidance. This is a far cry from his visionary

√ scenario of enlightened change in which the North would accept humanity's need for mutual sustenance and finance a new crusade to relieve poverty and bring about sustainable development on a global level. For a program of the kind reflected in Agenda 21, the envisaged cost is of the order of $125 billion a year between now and the end of the century: about the same amount as Third World countries spend annually today in debt repayments to the North. The funds would go largely to energy conservation, retiring Third World debt, stabilizing populations, protecting topsoil on cropland, reducing deforestation, and conserving biodiversity.

Notwithstanding the growing economic power of Japan and the European Community, before embarking on anything approaching such an ambitious program the North would still be looking to the United States for a lead. In the circumstances of 1992, it would be difficult to imagine the United States accepting more than a limited partnership in bearing the costs of such an environmental program. Weakened by the costs of the cold war, suffering a budget deficit that has transformed it from a creditor to a debtor nation, preoccupied with the deterioration of its cities and poverty among some 13 percent of its population, the United States shows no inclination to put the brakes on growth or ask people for new long-term financial sacrifices. A proposal for a broad carbon tax on energy consumption to reduce pollution and fund environmental projects would find little acceptance in a country that steadfastly insists on low-tax gasoline to the detriment of its environment and trade balance.

If there is any prospect of change in that outlook, it will come only when Americans are persuaded of the need to act in their own interest to forestall the environmental disasters consequent upon the absence of concerted action by the North. Almost fifty years ago, Americans responded to a call for sacrifice in a global crusade to stem Soviet communism. The result was the Marshall Plan and military expenditures comparable to the cost of the visionary strategy laid out in *Our Country, The Planet.*

SEYMOUR TOPPING
President, American Society of Newspaper Editors

Preface

T H E dedication of this book is an acknowledgment of the debt I owe innumerable people for making it possible. These caring individuals, many of them mentioned in the bibliography but symbolized for me by Barbara Ward and René Dubos, have had the enlightenment to see our earthly home in its wholeness, the wisdom to recognize how we are endangering that habitation, the humanism to want to sustain it for all, and the resolve to persevere in convincing our self-assured societies of the need to act while there is still time. Among them are scientists, economists, ecologists, demographers, futurists, journalists, and many others, including ordinary folk, concerned with the problems of environment and development. I acknowledge my indebtedness to them all for their vision, their scholarship, their example, their inspiration. In writing this book I have had no higher ambition than to carry forward in a small way that mission to which they have given so much.

When Maurice Strong asked me to undertake a presentation of the issues on the agenda of the Earth Summit that would be both a personal statement out of a varied experience and a worldview that took account of the perceptions of developing countries, I was flattered by the invitation and overawed by the assignment. In the event, writing this book has been an exhilarating, and very humbling, experience for which I express my gratitude to him. I hope that the book might assist in some measure his own heroic efforts for the success of the Earth Summit. I have been conscious throughout, however, that Rio de Janeiro in June 1992 will be the staging post for an onward journey. I have looked to it, therefore, as an important part of a process that will continue beyond it. It is to that longer process as well that I hope this book will contribute.

I have had the special privilege of being a member on each of the five independent international commissions that tried in the 1980s to deal with what are now the main items on the agenda of survival. They were the commissions on international development, security, environment and development, humanitarian issues, and the South. I owe a particular debt to those with whom I worked on those commissions: those who led them—Willy Brandt, the late Olof Palme, Gro Harlem Brundtland, the Crown Prince of Jordan and Sadruddin Aga Khan, and Julius Nyerere—and their members from all parts of the world who were my colleagues. While what I have written does not speak in the names of the commissions, I would have been much more poorly equipped for the writing of this book without the benefit of that shared experience.

I am also indebted to my family and many others too numerous to mention who assisted, facilitated, and tolerated my preoccupation with the book's preparation. To them all I express my gratitude for their unfailing and invaluable support. But there are some I must mention, those whose direct involvement really made the book possible. At a technical level, Martin Holdgate and Howard Irwin read and commented in detail on the entire text. So too, from different perspectives, did Vincent Cable, Maria-Elena Hurtado, Clive Jordan, Raj Ramphal, and M. S. Swaminathan. In addition, Vincent Cable, Maria-Elena Hurtado, Martin Ince, Howard Irwin, and Bishnodat Persaud assisted me specifically with particular chapters. Their many contributions, all in their personal capacities, were crucial. Each brought to bear expertise and judgment of unique quality and immense value. Credit must go to them all for what is best in the book. Each may disagree with some aspect of what I have written, and I must not imply their responsibility for what appears.

I owe a special measure of gratitude to my secretary, Bernie Lee-Dare, for her commitment, stamina, forbearance, and skill in reducing my manuscripts and lap-top drafts to workable documents and an eventual text for publication. Her steady hand and quiet reassurance were critical to the completion of the book. Paul Goodwin helped with the checking of seemingly endless statistics and George Harris with the essential task of reproducing and assembling the text through all its stages. I thank them all for their painstaking work.

Elsa Mansell, Janet Singh, and my London "support group" provided the basic administrative backup without which I could not have managed.

My most abundant thanks are due, however, to Charles Gunawardena, who worked with me from start to finish on the book. He brought to bear on the text his immense editorial skills and his accumulated wisdom and judgment. His guidance no less than his talents have been of inestimable value. It is in character of him, and a sign of how closely he has been involved in this work, that he would not wish to be absolved from responsibility for the outcome.

Finally, this book would not have been possible without the financial support so readily given by the Government of Canada, the Canadian Institute for Sustainable Development, and ECOFUND '92, and the wider encouragement that came from these and other sources. I acknowledge that support with both pleasure and gratitude.

PART ONE

Overview

ONE

A Fragile World

The Universe requires an eternity.
                                    —*Jorge Luis Borges*

A T T H E end of 1988, the *National Geographic* magazine carried
on its cover a holograph of our planet that fractured as it was tilted:
state-of-the-art technology depicting with some irony the fragile state
of the world. The message was clear: Despite human accomplishments, Earth and all it sustains are endangered. It was not a new
message, but it had acquired new authority and urgency with the
recognition that human survival itself could be at risk.

This book is about survival on an endangered planet. It will draw
attention to some of the more portentous ways in which we are
imperiling our human habitation. It will underline our need for awareness that as humans we are a part of nature, not apart from it; that we
should adopt humility, not arrogance, in our dealings with nature; and
that we should resolve to live in harmony, not contention, with nature.
It will argue that changing our behavior, our impact on the planet, is
necessary and ethically right, and is the path dictated by wisdom—the
attribute on which rests all our claims to special status in this world. It
will emphasize how urgent it is to take that path, and why we must do
so in practice, by action, and through performance; not only in perception, by words, or through promises. It will urge that we can do this
only by dealing with causes, not merely with symptoms or effects.
Throughout, it will try to convey how the various environmental issues
appear to the great majority of humans who individually have contrib-

3

uted little to the predicament in which they are placed but who will inevitably be its main victims—two-thirds of the human population, those living in the poorer parts of the world, however described: the "developing countries," the "Third World," the "South."

F R E Q U E N T L Y in the book I use the word *we*; it is necessary to explain who I have in mind. Occasionally, as when I refer to some of the international bodies on which I have served such as the Brandt Commission, *we* has a specific and self-evident meaning. Such use apart, however, *we* refers to all of us, the human species. I acknowledge, particularly in chapter 7, how divided we are; there will be times, therefore, when *we* will refer to particular groups among us—like people in rich countries or in poor ones—but always as part of the whole community of people that I perceive the world to be.

The people of the planet Earth are multiracial, multicultural, multireligious, and multilingual, and as a result they experience all the stresses that variety brings with its riches. But they are also bound together by their common humanity, their common home, the planet Earth, and their common future. Some people are more aware of this than others. Young people are, intuitively; so too are those who work in global activities like communications, or travel, or international business, as well as professionals of many disciplines for whom knowledge can rarely be circumscribed by national frontiers. *We* is beginning to mean not some of us but all of us. Not everyone is convinced that there is a human society to which we all belong; I hope this book will encourage some of them, at least, to change their way of looking at the world.

Another word of explanation: Since differences in various people's quality of life and the relevance of these differences to the human environment are of prominent concern here, it must be acknowledged at the outset that one cannot always measure quality of life in terms of money or material possessions. There are some who want for nothing money can buy whose quality of life is poor; there are others who have nothing the material world values whose quality of life is rich. But these are exceptions. We need to warn ourselves that quality is not only, perhaps not essentially, in the eye of the beholder.

We must also remember that there are poor in the rich countries and rich in the poor countries. In wealthy nations life is a struggle for many who for one reason or another, often unrelated to personal inadequacy, stand outside the mainstream. Members of ethnic minorities live often on the periphery.

Nor does the mainstream in a rich country have great wealth. The large middle class of the industrial world consists of hardworking people buying their homes on mortgages, saving for the annual holiday, contributing to the support of parents and grandparents in homes for senior citizens. They have social security benefits on retirement, the fallback of unemployment insurance of one kind or another, and in most countries, free or heavily subsidized medical care, but invariably they feel obliged to supplement these safety nets with personal insurance. To describe such people as rich may be misleading in a national context; to describe them as rich in a global context, as I do in this book, is a reasonable generalization. Where families enjoy comfortable housing, heated or cooled as the season requires, one or perhaps two cars, quality clothing, frequently changed according to the dictates of fashion, annual vacations, guaranteed medical care, good education facilities, a miscellany of labor-saving devices, power and water on tap, television, and ample recreational opportunities, it is neither inaccurate nor pejorative to describe these people—relative to those in the wider world—as rich. And that is all that I mean.

There are many in poor countries who aspire to the quality of life enjoyed by the comfortable middle class of rich countries. And there are some who attain these standards. At the moment they are a small minority in most developing countries. They are more prominent in some places, such as the newly industrializing Asian countries of Singapore and South Korea and countries where the distribution of income is particularly uneven, like Mexico or Brazil. The rich in developing countries, however, are the inhabitants of an oasis whose prosperity is under constant threat of erosion from the surrounding wasteland of poverty. And there are, of course, the superrich in the oil-producing Gulf states whose feudal structures perpetuate vast inequalities of wealth.

International financial institutions sometimes refer to the extremes of wealth and poverty in a world of some five billion as the top billion and the bottom billion. By the top billion, they mean most of the people of the rich industrial countries—the OECD (Organization for Economic Cooperation and Development) countries of Western Europe and North America, Japan, Australia, and New Zealand—plus the superrich in poor countries. In other words, the top billion is in large part the one-quarter of the world's people to whom this book refers as rich. By the bottom billion, these institutions mean the poorest of the poor, those living on one dollar a day or less, people so destitute they almost fall off the economic scales. In truth, the poor of the world cover a much wider range of people, including the great majority of people in the low-income and lower-middle-income countries of the developing world, from Nepal and China to Morocco and Brazil.

Bearing all these considerations in mind, it remains valid to speak of rich and poor countries and of the rich and the poor within them. All such references of mine should be read in this light.

One final word of introduction to the text. Throughout it you will find references to human survival, in respect of both the threats we face from a degraded environment and the goals toward which solutions must be directed. Human survival implies the threat of extinction, the end of *Homo sapiens* as one of Earth's species. That is, of course, extreme. It would be wrong to suggest that the alternatives before us are existence as we know it or the end of the human race. The dinosaurs may have gone in a cataclysmic bang, and that could happen to humans (though not necessarily) in a nuclear holocaust; but the consequence of persistent unsustainable living is much more likely to be a steady deterioration of the quality of life, leading to an indeterminate end.

That that end will be extinction some would certainly contend. The cumulative consequences of global warming, ozone shield depletion, population explosion, and other emerging critical stresses could lead to extinction. But human survival has another, less literal, implication. Even if total extinction is not likely, it is clear that the fundamental elements of human existence are at risk. Our predicament can be variously described. Steady deterioration of the quality of life, traumatic for the rich, catastrophic for the poor, is perhaps the least dramatic way of describing humanity's future. Climate change and a rising sea level are life-threatening for at least some humans. The prospect of our exhausting the life-giving product of green plants, the gift of photosynthesis, is critical for very many more, perhaps everyone. Deterioration in the standard of living (if it can be called living) of the one billion of the world's poorest is, for them, decidedly a matter of survival.

We need to understand that in respect to both the threat we face and the goal toward which we reach, human survival connotes the critical path of humanity's prospects. It is not just a matter of here today and gone tomorrow—that is not nature's way. More apposite is the analogy of a tree dying from acid rain. For humanity, it is the tree of life that is endangered. Whether it dies altogether, or withers but clings to life, or loses its leaves and branches yet survives to bloom again, depends on our responses to the blight that afflicts it in the form of the crisis of environment and development.

S U R V I V A L is a concept involving time. It speaks of continuity or conclusion. But we cannot begin to address survival without an awareness of beginnings: human origins in the natural order, the place of our species in the vista of time. The magnitudes of time involved are, however, so overwhelming that they can easily distort our perspectives. They need reducing to simpler terms. If we compress geologic time from billions of years to a more readily grasped span, for example a century, we can think of our planet as a garden one hundred years in the making. Ninety-two years to be precise, if we take the formation of the solar system 4.6 billion years ago as the birth of the planet and take one year to represent 50 million years. On that basis, for the first thirty-two of those ninety-two years, Earth remained a barren wasteland spinning endlessly in space like many another planet. Then came the first stirring of life in the Earth's oceans when cells began to replicate. It took another fifty years, by which time the garden was already eighty-four years old, for the first animals and plants to emerge—some seven years ago. And that was well before the human species appeared.

The dinosaurs and great reptiles emerged only two years ago, and well over a year and eleven months were to pass before our first recognizably human ancestors, *Homo habilis*, manlike apes, appeared in the garden. The first of the recent ice ages was to follow—some two weeks ago—displacing the forests and their attendant life forms from the regions around the Earth's poles and bringing changes in the distribution and make-up even of the tropical forests. It was only during and after the last of these glacial periods, within the past 50,000 years—or eight hours in garden time—that modern man, *Homo sapiens*, spread over the planet, reaching into Australasia and the Americas. Earth's garden has been rolled and watered by the elements for ninety-two years; we have been in it for less than a day.

By the time we came, the garden was a bounteous place. Flora and fauna had emerged in wondrous, bewildering, and exquisitely interlocking variety. Humanity is the baby of the family, the newcomer in the garden of Earth. Already, however, we have done more than any other species to change the ancient garden for good and ill. We developed agricultural skills within the last few hours and greatly enlarged the garden's capacity to sustain life. And within the last five minutes we began our industrial revolution, a process of change that was to be at once both wonderfully creative and incredibly destructive.

The crisis of survival we face arises from the propensity for destruction, including self-destruction, our species has displayed in the brief moment of time it has been a guest in the garden of Earth. It is, in truth, a crisis. Many no longer doubt or discount the massive danger confronting our planet and the living things on it. Few assert that such a turn of events is chastisement at the hands of the Almighty. We are our own scourge, threatening the capacity to survive not only of ourselves but of the very garden that gave us life.

IN LATER chapters I shall try to illustrate how we have gone about being such wanton guests, we who believe we are far superior to any species that ever occupied the garden. The point I am making here is how utterly brief our presence has been in the scale of time, and perhaps how transient it will be. It is a point that must not only alert us to the humility becoming of newcomers but also remind us of our duty to the long process of evolution that preceded, produced, and nurtured us. Both acts are important; together they should lead us to acknowledge our obligation to the process of creation, our true ancestor, and to realize that the elements of that process must be nurtured if we are to preserve our earthly home. In his *Historia de la Eternidad*, the Latin American writer Jorge Luis Borges captured all this poignantly: "The Universe requires an eternity. . . . Thus they say that the conservation of this world is a perpetual creation and that the verbs, 'conserve' and 'create,' so much at odds here, are synonymous in heaven." (p. 33) To make them synonymous on Earth as well is a central challenge to *Homo sapiens*.

Life on Earth has taken many forms. Creation did not begin with humanity, and we would do well to remember that not all life forms have lasted. Biologists reckon that over the sweep of geological history many times more species than now exist evolved, flourished for a time, then became extinct as planetary conditions changed and fitter forms emerged to replace them. Survival in nature's garden was never easy; it

demanded adaptation to a continuously changing environment and
success in unending competition, particularly for food. Sometimes
changes were catastrophic, like the uncertain events that ended the age
of the dinosaurs sixty-five million years ago, a little over one year in
our compressed version of time. Nature's basic elements were life
giving, but they were harsh controllers. Life was constantly at their
mercy. Air, water, earth, and fire, often separately, sometimes together, could destroy no less than create. A series of ice ages ravaged
life forms, but, as when fire burns a forest, regeneration followed.
There was both mercy and method in the elements.

It was out of this process of continuous evolution that we emerged
late in time. We were marvelously gifted, more advanced in important
ways than other species, especially and essentially in cerebration, and
by extension, thanks to elaborate neural pathways, in speech. New
and different, we came into a world already teeming with life—in the
air, in the oceans, on the land and beneath it. We too were at the mercy
of the elements; and for us too they were harsh. But over the years that
we have been on Earth, we have used our unique mental gifts to
survive and to succeed in our natural environment, overcoming what
was inhospitable and harnessing what was favorable. Today, we have
much to show for the stewardship of our species.

We developed great civilizations—in Mesopotamia and Egypt, in
China and the Indus Valley, in the Americas, in Greece and Rome
and, later, Europe. Our ancient centers of learning produced our
early philosophers, our first scientists. We showed great courage and
skill in exploring the planet and understanding its wholeness. In more
recent times, our science and technology have made rapid advances in
fields as various as agriculture, medicine, communications, and electronics. The pace has been breathtaking and bewildering. It was not
so long ago that Gutenberg pioneered printing with movable type,
Stephenson built the steam locomotive, and Alexander Graham Bell
invented the telephone. But they are oldtimers now, with printing
revolutionized by computers and lasers, the steam engine superseded
by the rockets of space travel, and the telephone wire overtaken by
satellites and fiber-optic cables. And still we proceed, our science and
technology speeding us ever more rapidly up the hill of progress.

B U T there has been a debit side to progress. In the beginning
as we adapted to the environment we learned to live in harmony with

nature. Some still do, but only a few, and mainly in shrinking rain forest reserves or in the high Arctic. Our conventional wisdom regards them disparagingly as primitive, people not yet risen to our mature condition of civilization. Discoveries and excavations have confirmed that some early peoples established settlements of a high order of sophistication. The monuments of Machu Pichu and the great Zimbabwe ruins are among those that bear witness to such sophistication. The temples and tombs of the pharaohs and what remains of the splendor of Mohenjadaro and Harappa speak to us—as does evidence of civilization elsewhere—of much earlier human achievements. Did these civilizations succumb to the rigors of the elements? Did they fall out of step with nature? Some, it seems, had to learn to live in harmony with nature after suffering the effects of disharmonies of their own creation. The fire they produced altered their habitats. Some great animals—mammoths, mastodons, the giant ground sloths of South America, the giant elk of Europe, the hippopotamus-like Australian marsupials—were hunted to extinction. The moas—the world's largest birds—were exterminated in New Zealand.

And there is reason to believe that some of our ancestors were victims of their own agricultural practices that exceeded the limits of Earth's capacity for regenerative growth. Mismanaged irrigation, for instance, probably led to the decline of our first civilization, in the basin of the Euphrates and the Tigris, in what is now Iraq. Caracol, a Mayan culture recently discovered in western Belize, is believed (although speculation abounds) to have collapsed from lack of potable water. Others were the victims of human aggression, tribal struggles for primacy that continue to this day, the most destructive of all having been fought by the tribes of Europe in the middle of this very century, the last of the passing millennium.

From the beginning there was concern with environmental matters, mainly pollution. In *Pollution Prevention Pays,* Michael Royston cites examples of humanity seeing the need to live in harmony with nature: various references in Hammurabi's edict in Babylon 4,000 years ago, the ancient Chinese I Ching's cryptic sayings, the laws of Moses, the books of Deuteronomy, Hindu classical literature, the precepts of Zoroaster, the sayings of the Buddha, the edicts of the Indian emperor Asoka, Plato's laws for his ideal republic, and Mohammed's teachings in the Koran; the rituals and taboos of many African peoples and equivalent practices in Southeast Asia; the nature ethic of American

Indians; and legislation in the Middle Ages against pollution—in Lombardy in 1236, in London and Venice in 1306, and in Paris in 1501. We have been aware for a long time of the need to protect ourselves by preserving our environment, but from time immemorial other instincts and obsessions have diverted us.

But many indigenous peoples did live in harmony with nature, in ways that were to elude modern civilization. I write this in the Caribbean where we are marking the quincentennial anniversary of the voyages Columbus made in the fifteenth and sixteenth centuries. They were to change the world—not through discovery, which is a notion of dubious legitimacy, certainly for the "discovered," but through the encounters thus begun between Europeans and the first peoples of the Americas. Long before Columbus came in 1492, Native Americans had evolved sustainable lifestyles by adapting to the idiosyncrasies of their environments. They lived, it is true, with much hostility among themselves, but in such harmony with nature that the land the newcomers came to, coveted, and conquered seemed a veritable paradise.

To Europeans overwhelmed by what they perceived as the otherness of those they encountered, the first Americans were savages. Europe's very act of dispossession, however, confirmed that the first people of the New World had pursued a path of development that met their own needs without compromising the ability of future generations to meet theirs. It was a cruel irony that the inheritance these people had nurtured was to be usurped in no small measure because they had nurtured it so well. Five hundred years later we would see that path as the way of survival for all the world, including the dispossessors: the path of sustainable development.

Like other occupations before and since, the European occupation of the Americas was founded on genocide. But the despoliation went beyond our own species. A process of resource extraction was inaugurated that was to produce astonishing contradictions between enlightenment and greed and cruelty. It was not a process peculiar to the New World. In John Masefield's celebration of trade through the ages in his masterpiece of onomatopoeic verse, "Cargoes," we can now discern a picture of plunder through trade and of enrichment through industrial specialization that is more graphic than many tomes of economic history:

> Quinquireme of Nineveh from distant Ophir
> Rowing home to haven in sunny Palestine,

With a cargo of ivory,
And apes and peacocks,
Sandalwood, cedarwood and sweet white wine.

Stately Spanish galleon coming from the Isthmus,
Dipping through the Tropics by the palm-green shores,
With a cargo of diamonds,
Emerald, amethysts,
Topazes, and cinnamon, and gold moidores.

Dirty British coaster with a salt-caked smoke stack,
Butting through the Channel in the mad March days,
With a cargo of Tyne coal,
Road-rail, pig-lead,
Firewood, iron-ware and cheap tin trays.

This was not, over the centuries, the only type of cargo. Some was human.

Nineveh is gone and with it the quinqueremes. Stately Spanish galleons no longer dip through the tropics laden with cargo, and British coasters carrying Tyne coal to the furnaces of the industrial revolution have long been replaced by supertankers transporting Middle Eastern oil. The quinqueremes and galleons of yesteryear are the bulk-loading ore carriers and container vessels of today that still ply the old routes of mercantilism, bearing the primary products of the developing world to the factories and mills and smelters of the developed, and then returning with manufactured goods.

The industrial revolution began in Europe, in Britain more particularly. Its boundaries in time have been described in many different ways. I am attracted to the version that has it beginning with the voyage of Columbus's *Santa Maria* at the end of the fifteenth century and ending with the flight of the Enola Gay, which was used to drop the first atomic bomb on Hiroshima just over 450 years later. That bomb changed the world. It was one marker of the start of the postindustrial era, and a signal that apocalypse was in our own hands.

In reality, the turning of the tables on nature began at the start of the industrial revolution proper. The "dark satanic mills" of which William Blake wrote with such passionate anger over 200 years ago exacted a toll not only of human misery but also of nature. The chimneys of Manchester and Birmingham were the forerunners of the furnaces of the Ruhr and the smokestacks of Pittsburgh. The human species had begun an intensive assault on nature. Natural resource depletion, atmospheric pollution, hazardous waste disposal—all were there in the beginning, though barely recognizable as the first salvos of the assault. They were to develop into the equivalent of genocide—ecocide, the slaughter of nature.

During two centuries of progress we have been our own "horsemen of the Apocalypse," killing not with fire and sword but by unleashing ill-understood and complex chemical and biological processes. Acid rain—rain with the acid content of lemon juice—does not fall naturally from the heavens above. Without humans, there would not be a hole in the ozone layer opening up over Antarctica each September and getting steadily bigger. That Earth threatens to grow warmer and the seas to rise are not acts of God. For the most part, species do not disappear from the face of the Earth each day through natural selection. A nuclear holocaust, by accident or design, could not be explained as Armageddon. All these phenomena are or would be of our making, as are the contradictions of poverty amidst plenty and of hunger despite waste. No longer at the mercy of the elements, we seem intent on being the authors of our own damnation—without of course admitting it. We speak of a threat to the environment as if it were itself an act of nature. We are reluctant to see it as a threat to the human species of our own creation. But, without that admission, we are unlikely to respond effectively to the dangers that face us.

Our assault on nature was driven by what was perceived as the virtue of accumulation, and for a long time we excused it as cruel innocence, a tolerable side effect of progress. But it turned into a culture of consumption and an inexcusable threat to human survival. Adaptation to the rigors of the elements led us gradually away from the goal of harmony with nature to the pursuit of dominion over nature. It was no longer enough to even the odds with nature; we had to render nature subservient to the needs and even more so the desires of our special species. In this century particularly, we have become so sure of our genius, so confident of our mastery over the habitat, that we have actually lost awareness of ourselves as a part of nature. In the large cities of the industrialized West, life is characterized by the nearly complete displacement or exclusion of the natural by the manmade.

Our science, it is true, in many of its forms—anthropology, geology, chemistry, biology, astronomy, all pathways to the past opened up by our genius—confirms our evolution within nature and our dependence on nature for our present existence and future survival. That is what we know in our minds. But how we live, the way we prosper or just survive, what we think and do (or fail to do) about the future, derives less from intelligence than from desire—particularly a compelling urge to prevail and prosper at all costs.

The process of modernization has bred in us not only self-assurance about human achievement but also an assumption of self-sufficiency regardless of the natural order that sustains us. We are justly proud to have "discovered" DNA, the genetic code that is the key to life. But how seldom we acknowledge that before us and our discoveries there was the code itself. The primordial genius was in nature. Long before we became nature's interpreters we were nature's creation.

T H E R E is another downside to human progress: It has decidedly not been progress for most human beings. The material progress of which we are most proud is enjoyed by only a few and, in some respects at least, at the expense of the many. While all of humanity has benefited in some measure, the prosperity that is the bottom line of progress is the privilege of a quarter of humanity, which is using up the planet's resources in an alarmingly selfish way. Prosperity has passed most others by. From the perspective of those who have not prospered, this colossal gap in the quality of human life is the most serious flaw in the record of human achievement. The privileged minority is only just becoming aware that this imperfection is a reality and that it must be removed if in the future life is to be tolerable for anyone.

If we had to use a few words to say what most endangers the environment, they might be "wealth and poverty" or perhaps, more pointedly, "industrialization and underdevelopment." Both phrases are shorthand, of course. We could try a somewhat longer formulation: "excessive consumption of resources by the rich and intolerable destitution among the poor." That, too, is shorthand. We will leave it to later chapters to elaborate on acid rain, greenhouse gases, the ozone layer, global warming, climate change, sea-level rise, species extinction, desertification, disappearing forests, the fuel-wood crisis, nuclear risks, hazardous waste, soil erosion, urban squalor, water scarcity, fish-stock depletion—to mention only some of the more prominent problems. As human society pays attention to them all, it is in danger of missing the bigger picture and the message it conveys. We prefer, perhaps subconsciously, to attend to symptoms and avoid causes. This tendency is inevitably more pronounced among those who have so much that change always seems threatening than for those who have so little that change can only improve matters. Herein lie the seeds of discord that could disable global action for survival.

The question of consumption is central to the issues I am about to address, collectively known as the environmental crisis. It is human impact on the biosphere that is producing environmental stress and endangering the planet's capacity to sustain life. Essentially, that impact is made through the energy and raw materials that people use or waste worldwide. If use was even roughly equal among people, measuring human impact would be a relatively simple matter of multiplying the amount of energy and raw materials each person uses by the number of the world's people. But there is no equivalence in our expenditure of resources. The vast majority who are poor make only a minimal claim on them. The very opposite is true for the rich, who are prodigal in their consumption. Energy, especially the use of fossil fuels, is at the very heart of the matter. A quarter of the world's population, most of them living in the industrial countries, account for 80 percent of world consumption of commercial energy. The other three-quarters, living for the most part in the developing world, account for only 20 percent.

The environmental crisis is a common crisis, facing all countries and peoples alike, but developed and developing countries contribute to it in such unequal measure, and have such markedly different economic experiences and economic capacities, that the crisis itself is perceived quite differently—threatening relations between countries and blocking a convergence of responses to the crisis. By way of illustration, Western industrialized countries enjoyed a period of remarkable and largely unexpected prosperity in the 1980s. Their leaders described it in the communique of the Group of Seven summit in 1988 as "the longest period of economic growth in postwar history." This prosperity and the high levels of consumption it supported led to intensified pressure on the environment in many respects, but it also gave rich countries the resources to tackle environmental problems. Some countries, those with greater environmental prudence, have already achieved measurable results in cleaning air and water and reducing pollution.

A L L this contrasts sharply with the position of a large number of developing countries that regard the same period as a "lost decade" for development. For them, the 1980s brought not greater prosperity but greater poverty. For hundreds of millions of their people, life was a struggle for survival. When the priority for individuals is just to survive, and when for governments it is not much different—in the face of high debt service, low commodity prices, and protectionist barriers—development with due care for the environment tends to be seen as tomorrow's concern, if it is understood at all. Development has to be credible before sustainability can be perceived as a viable option.

Poverty and environment are inextricably linked in a chain of cause and effect. Environmental problems cannot be tackled in isolation from those national and global economic factors that perpetuate large-scale poverty. International economic problems such as oppressive levels of debt service and depressed commodity prices ultimately force countries to exploit their natural resources in an unsustainable way in order to maintain "essential" export earnings. The temptation, for example, to pump oil from its reserves in the Amazon is almost irresistible for cash-strapped Ecuador. Shrimp exports have become an important source of foreign exchange for Bangladesh, one of the world's poorest countries, but the ecological price is high; large areas of mangrove swamp, important for coastal stabilization and fish nurseries, have been destroyed to create the shrimp farms. Some countries have had to look to enhanced exports of tropical timber to pay their import bills and their creditors, depleting ecological capital in the process.

What makes all this so acutely critical is that every sign points to the incidence of poverty growing in many already poor countries. Average incomes, low to begin with, fell in both Latin America and sub-Saharan Africa throughout the 1980s, when economic development was set back in many countries. Excluding China, the number of people in the world without enough to eat, which rose from an estimated 650 million to 730 million in the 1970s, is reckoned to have risen much more in the 1980s. Each year among children under five years old, 180 million suffer serious malnutrition and over 14 million die, mainly from preventable diseases. In seventeen out of forty-two low-income developing countries, the daily calorie supply per capita was lower in 1986 than in 1965. In about fifty developing countries, per capita staple food consumption fell in the 1980s. In most parts of the developing world, the record is of sharply reduced economic activity, falls in real per capita income, rising unemployment, and cutbacks in spending on education and health—all the result of austerity measures in the wake of economic crisis.

Recent arguments over tropical forests and over the environmental conditions that aid donors increasingly demand of developing countries have brought to a head serious anxiety in poor countries. They fear that, despite the privations they have had to undergo, the interests of their people are being given scant attention while, for example, rich countries demand restraint in the use of CFC (chlorofluorocarbon) gases or the cutting down of forests. Worthy and necessary as some of these injunctions are, it seems unfair to poor countries that they should forsake opportunities for economic growth so that problems largely caused by imprudence and profligacy in rich countries can be ameliorated. The injunctions come across as attempts to preserve the global distribution of wealth and power. "Don't do as I do; just do as I say" is not calculated to secure a willing response when it is addressed by haves to have-nots. If poverty is not tackled, it will be extremely difficult to achieve agreement on solutions to major environmental problems. Mass poverty, in itself unacceptable and unnecessary, both adds to and is made worse by environmental stress. Ecology and economy are inseparable.

This is why the global policy dialogue must integrate environment and development. Both rationality and reality compel us in this direction, though there is still resistance, mainly in rich countries and especially in the United States. By development, of course, I mean development in all countries: the progress of rich countries and the lack of progress of poor ones and all the gradations in between. Failures and inadequacies in development have produced environmental degradation that now threatens the planet and life on it. What inevitably it also threatens is the sustainability of development itself. Through the process of development known as industrialization the human species has made its most grievous impact on the environment. Only through fundamental changes in the nature of that impact— through changes in economic behavior, in lifestyle, and in the management of development itself—can a positive synthesis, a symbiosis even, be produced of ecology and economy. The development model responsible for the lifestyle the industrialized world now enjoys is simply not sustainable. That world is too voracious in its consumption of resources. It must yield to a way of life that is sustainable in both economic and environmental terms.

And for the poor as well, viable and sustainable development must be the key to addressing the main environmental problems that afflict their regions: deforestation, desertification, soil erosion, degradation of river basins and coastal areas, the explosive growth of urban areas, air and water pollution, waste disposal, festering slums. Poverty is both a cause and an effect of environmental deterioration. Breaking the vicious circle in which so many of the people of the developing world are caught is imperative—on environmental as well as developmental grounds.

Eradicating the causes of poverty and making wealth creation more benign in its impact on the environment are the essential challenges we must meet if we are to find a path to sustainable development and ensure human survival. What we have done instead is to quicken the pace of environmental degradation. We have made our onslaught on nature more ferocious, our impact on the environment more brutal.

"A s w e enter the global phase of human evolution, it becomes obvious that each man has two countries, his own and Planet Earth." Those were the concluding words of the introduction to *Only One Earth,* the book Barbara Ward wrote with René Dubos to set the scene for the United Nations Conference on the Human Environment in 1972 in Stockholm—the first global effort to come to grips with environmental problems. The vision of one world was not new. It had helped to inspire the League of Nations earlier in the century. Even before that, social and political scientists, philosophers, religious leaders, and others had advanced the idea of the family of man. But the notion of my country, the planet, was different; it looked not only beyond countries but even beyond people. It looked in fact to our earthly habitation and the whole of creation, with new insights of a planetary order founded on the concept of a shared biosphere and secured by strategies for survival. The era of the environment was beginning.

More than a decade later, I was a member of the Independent Commission on Environment and Development, chaired by Norway's Gro Harlem Brundtland. The commission's establishment reflected growing concern about environmental degradation worldwide. In our report, issued in 1987, we put the case starkly: "Environmental trends ... threaten to radically change, to alter the planet ... threaten[ing] the lives of many species upon it including the human species." A year after that, the Toronto Conference on the Changing Atmosphere concluded that "humanity is conducting an unintended, uncontrolled, globally perverse experiment whose ultimate consequences may be second only to a global nuclear war." These were strong words from two independent bodies, both of which brought together countries from east and west, north and south.

If we were to place such warnings in a national context, in a State of the Nation address, for example, they might read: "Environmental trends threaten to radically change our country, threatening the future of all of our people, and many of the other life-forms on which we depend. By the way we live, we are conducting an uncontrolled experiment whose ultimate consequences for our people may be second only to devastation by nuclear weapons." We would not be complacent hearing this. We would declare a state of emergency or at least act as if we faced one. We would see our situation in terms of the survival of our families, our communities, our country. We would mobilize as a nation to save ourselves. We would back away from this calamitous experiment, whatever the sacrifice, whatever the change in lifestyle that demanded. We would have no higher priority because our country's future would be at stake, and our own and our children's and grandchildren's with it.

The central thrust of this book is that today we need to see the planet as we are accustomed to seeing our countries. Astronauts have seen how meaningless our national borders are in cosmic terms—mere markings on turf that have nothing to do with the biosphere, frail partitions in our single planetary home. We allow these lines drawn on the planet for the organization of human society to limit our perception of human society itself and to dominate our view of the planet. Yet the perception of the whole world as our country, as the integral land whose fortunes and whose future are our own, may be the essential first step to survival in any of the lands we now call our own and in the larger country of the planet to which we all belong.

T H E secret of Earth's success in sustaining life, or as some would say, of being a live planet, has been its ability to develop in slow stages mechanisms that protect it from the sun's destructive radiation and yet enable it to use the sun's life-giving energy. Barbara Ward and René Dubos in *Only One Earth* reminded us that "progressively, over billions of years, defences and mediations arose [against solar radiation] to permit the emergence on a lifeless planet of the covering of living things." We have come to call this covering the biosphere.

What industrial man has been doing over the last three centuries is to break down the planet's defenses. We have disrupted the process that changed Earth from a lifeless planet to a life-sustaining one. At first we were unwitting agents of our own damnation. But we are no longer innocents. Against the charge of ecocide, the human species will soon have no defense.

This culpability has drawn from Greenpeace the following sweeping indictment:

> Modern Man has made a rubbish tip of Paradise. He has multiplied his numbers to plague proportions, caused the extinction of 500 species of animals, ransacked the planet for fuels and now stands like a brutish infant, gloating over this meteoric rise to ascendancy, on the brink of the final mass extinction and of effectively destroying this oasis of life in the solar system.

Crusading hyperbole, perhaps, but it makes a valid point about our excesses and their calamitous consequences, and about the arrogance of refusing to admit responsibility.

In no respect is this responsibility more undeniable than in the impact of CFCs, those manmade chemical gases with which we have bombarded the atmosphere and so far thinned the stratosphere's protective layer of ozone that shields us from the sun's fiercest radiation. A virtual hole has opened up over the south pole and more recently over the north pole as well. When the UN Conference on the Human Environment convened in 1972—as delegates talked to the theme of the care and maintenance of a small planet and more directly to the issue of human survival—no one was aware that already this manmade disaster was forming in the upper atmosphere. As an issue, global warming is not dissimilar. When the Brundtland Commission met between 1984 and 1987, global warming and climate change were only small clouds on the horizon—storm clouds, it is true, but not menacing. The first important international discussion among scientists on these topics took place in 1985 in Villach in Austria. There, twenty-nine scientists from industrialized and developing countries concluded that climate change must be considered "a plausible and serious possibility." We warned as much in the commission's report, which came to be known widely as the Brundtland Report. By the time the report was presented to the UN General Assembly in September 1987, that amber warning had turned to a red alert.

Disastrous flooding in Bangladesh (worse was to come) and the inundation of the low-lying Maldive islands by unprecedented waves were signals that could not be ignored; they were reinforced by evidence that such disasters had become more frequent in recent decades. The issues of global warming and climate change had become of immediate and worldwide concern. In the five years since then, major international scientific work by the Commonwealth Expert Group on Climate Change, followed by the UN's Inter-Governmental Panel on Climate Change, has led to a broad scientific consensus, reflected in the conclusions of the Second World Climate Conference in Geneva in November 1990, that if global emissions of greenhouse gases are not reduced the world will probably be 2° to 5° Celsius warmer, and sea levels 30 to 100 centimeters higher, by the end of the next century. The conference noted that this rate of global temperature change would be unprecedented in the context of the past ten thousand years.

When the UN Conference on Environment and Development meets in Rio de Janeiro in 1992, the depletion of the ozone layer and global warming will have been recognized as grave dangers to the planet and its inhabitants only after the Stockholm meeting. That prompts the question: What other horrors lie ahead? What other forms of self-destruction already indulged in wait to confront us?

The quickening pace of our assault on nature has been so dramatic in its impact that it has heightened awareness of the environmental crisis and sped up our response to danger signals. In 1972 Eastern Europe (Romania excepted) boycotted the Stockholm conference, ostensibly on account of the nonrecognition of East Germany. Brazil and some other developing countries attending the conference were vigorous in their opposition to its very concept; they perceived the conference as a conspiracy to prevent developing countries from catching up with the industrialized world. "What we need is some of the pollution of prosperity" was said with more seriousness than cynicism in at least some parts of the developing world. Yet only twenty years later, when the successor conference to Stockholm convenes, it will be hosted by Brazil and attended by Germany, whose restored eastern half is deeply conscious, along with the rest of the former East bloc countries, of being an environmental disaster area. We have come some way. It remains to be seen whether we have the will to press on with the more demanding part of the journey.

"T H E earth is one, but the world is not"—begins *Our Common Future*, the report of the Brundtland Commission. Those words encapsulate our human predicament. In all too many respects, the world is not one. Yet how complacent we are. History taught us long ago that a national society cannot be sustained if power, privilege, and prosperity are the prerogatives of only a few, with deprivation, degradation, and despair the lot of the many—two nations in one state, "the privileged and the people," as Disraeli described them in the nineteenth century. Why should we think world society can be sustained when such disparities prevail within it? Change is now unavoidable, not least because the interdependence of the human condition has acquired sharper focus in many areas—in the world economy, in international security, in the preservation of the environment, in the conservation of the resources of a small planet that our expanding species must share.

It took man in space, especially man on the moon looking at Earth, to testify to this essential unity—one Earth, small and indivisible, one glorious throbbing globe whose precious balance of elements makes life possible. Of course we knew all this; our wisdom affirmed it; our maps and globes proclaimed it; yet we needed that visual proof. Separateness, the sense of otherness that we have made so prominent a feature of human existence—both in how we organize human society in sovereign states and in how we view ourselves and each other—is not the picture from space.

The artificiality of national boundaries is further confirmed by the transnational character of most environmental problems. Hot air masses, ocean currents, and continental rivers do not recognize frontiers. The damage caused by ozone depletion or global warming will not affect isolated communities or countries; both phenomena have a planetary sweep. Norwegian and Swedish lakes have been made virtually lifeless by acid rain from the sulphur and nitrogen oxides emitted by power stations in western and central Europe. Forests in many parts of Europe have been blighted by these gases and by others spewed out by the continent's swelling tide of motor vehicles. Fallout from Chernobyl reached farms as far afield as Ireland. Tree cutting in Nepal has led to flooding in Bangladesh, and the loss of trees in Ethiopia has caused water supply problems in Sudan and Egypt. CFC emissions in the northern hemisphere raise the risk of skin cancer in Australia and Argentina. Gases from the burning of fossil fuels and other industrial activities could be altering the Earth's climate, affecting all regions by moving crop zones, raising sea levels, and disrupting weather patterns.

"No man is an island unto himself" wrote the poet John Donne four centuries ago. The people of the Maldive archipelago lying in the vast expanse of the Indian Ocean are discovering as well that no island is an island unto itself. On the basis of what is known about the accumulation of greenhouse gases, there is consensus among scientists that a rise in sea level, consequent on a rise in global temperature, could submerge the Maldives in a twenty-first-century version of the Biblical deluge. What is endangered is not merely a thousand beautiful islands. The survival of an entire nation, with its distinctive language and culture, has been put in jeopardy by human action elsewhere on the planet. As part of our ocean floor, the Maldives could become a symbol of our failure to preserve Earth as a habitable place for all.

Frontiers may separate nations but do not insulate them from environmental degradation. In the end, they may not even deter massive migrations of environmental refugees. Environmental problems— whether they manifest themselves as global, cross-border, or national phenomena—are ultimately international problems. They simply cannot be solved nationally in any comprehensive sense. Sovereignty, whatever else it connotes, does not imply sanctuary.

Separateness is also challenged by new evidence of the limits of power in relations between nations. In the nuclear age, we reached the threshold of absolute power only to find that across it lay oblivion. The ultimate sanction was that in destroying the enemy's world you destroyed your own. The possibility of extinguishing life on the planet became the shaky cornerstone of human existence. And other mutual desolations threatened. The air we breathe is not ours alone, the seas that wash our shores wash other shores as well—we are made of common clay. So through our separate abuse of the environment we make the seas and oceans a dirty communal pond and the atmosphere a polluted universal sky. And now, as we reach beyond the atmosphere and contaminate outer space with debris, and weapons, we invoke a common destiny only dimly understood—save that it will finally make no distinction among nations or people.

In our contemporary world of excesses—of consumption, of poverty, of population growth—the one constant is our "only one Earth." Since there are limits to our capacity to survive devastation of the planet's life-support systems, we need to come to terms with this reality of one Earth if we are to optimize our prospects of making it secure and habitable for all. On an over-populated planet, as in an over-populated city, human misery cannot be quarantined. We cannot immunize the global environment against the contagion of mass starvation and disease. We cannot inoculate the world against itself.

When Abraham Lincoln said that his country, threatened with disunity, could not endure "half-slave and half-free," he was talking of more than just social and economic injustice. He was talking of the limits of immorality within one state, among one people. It is the same with our country, the planet. More than a century after Lincoln, we have to face up to those limits in our global community and decide what kind of world is tolerable and sustainable.

T H E UN Conference on the Human Environment was a watershed event. Between the establishment of the UN at San Francisco in 1945 and the conference at Stockholm in 1972, there were many international gatherings. The UN provided the setting for extensive dialogue on political, economic, social, and cultural matters. Wideranging debate took place at the annual sessions of the UN General Assembly and in forums such as the UN Conference on Trade and Development (UNCTAD) and the UN Commission on Disarmament. But, increasingly, the dialogue became specialized as people searched for solutions to specific problems. In 1972, for the first time, nations came together to consider the state of the planet Earth, habitually taken for granted, treated as an unchanging backdrop to the human drama. For the first time, we were integrating the scenery into the action of the play. Nothing would be quite the same again, for after Stockholm we were bound to look at ourselves in fundamentally different ways. For a while, however, this was less than obvious.

A principal achievement of the Stockholm conference was heightening worldwide awareness of pollution. It is worth underscoring that, beyond the scientific community, the problem was still widely perceived as physical pollution. It took India's prime minister, Indira Gandhi, to widen the concept with her allusion at Stockholm to "the pollution of poverty." Stockholm, therefore, put the issue of environment on the global agenda and opened up debate about its parameters. But Stockholm did something else that was to be of crucial significance. It led to the establishment of the UN Environment Program (UNEP), with its headquarters in Nairobi. It was a modest institutional beginning, almost grudgingly conceded; UNEP is still not a full-fledged UN agency. It was established as minimal machinery to carry forward the dialogue initiated at Stockholm and, at least in the vision of some, to be the catalyst for global responses to what was quickly unfolding as the crisis of environment.

Stockholm also promulgated the International Declaration on the Environment. This fell far short of the goals of devising "patterns of collective behaviour compatible with the continued flowering of civilisations" and accepting "responsibility for the stewardship of the earth" that the Ward/Dubos study had espoused. But it was the beginning, a foundation on which was to rise if not a monument to human survival at least some essential building blocks for maintaining Earth as a place suitable for human life.

Before 1972, the checklist of environmental literature was relatively modest. Rachel Carson's *Silent Spring* had been a lone, plaintive voice raised against the wide-scale use of pesticides. Many scientists, economists, and other researchers, it is true, were at work. Ecology did not begin at Stockholm. Over 150 eminent individuals served as consultants on the Ward/Dubos study, most of them representing distinguished research institutions. For all that, environment was a largely neglected subject in 1972. It had no place in the high politics of the early 1970s, years that were to be absorbed with the energy crisis. The Stockholm meeting was almost an esoteric occasion. It was certainly not on the agenda of world leaders. Mrs. Gandhi was the only head of government to attend it aside from Sweden's prime minister, Olof Palme. Today the situation is very different. Environment is high on the global agenda. The bibliography at the end of this book points to the explosion of high-quality research and analysis that has taken place over the last twenty years. This is more than just a fad; it reflects genuine and intensifying concern over the dangers facing humanity.

In 1984, when Mrs. Brundtland invited me to join the World Commission on Environment and Development, I was unsure if I should accept the invitation. A few years earlier I had been a member of the Independent Commission on International Development Issues, under the chairmanship of Willy Brandt, which in its report drew attention to grave imbalances in the world economic situation and proposed a program to stimulate global economic activity based on North-South cooperation. Three years later, in 1983, we felt impelled to issue a second report warning of the impending crisis over the loans extended to developing countries by Western banks and suggesting ways of dealing with it before it became unmanageable. In both cases our suggestions received a positive response from people the world over, but not from Western governments, which simply did not want to consider economic issues beyond the next election. The compulsions of democracy seemed to stand in the way of the demands of human survival. North-South relations were to go into recession along with the world economy. And the debt crisis would become chronic.

The governments of industrialized countries had not been ready for Brandt on development. I wondered if they would be ready for Brundtland on environment and development. Would they care enough to pay attention? I am glad I overcame my reservations and joined Mrs. Brundtland's team. Five years after we issued our report, the interrelated issues of environment and development rank with world peace and democratic freedom as the dominant concerns of our time. In the intervening period, politicians began zealously to proclaim their "green" credentials—from Mikhail Gorbachev to Margaret Thatcher; so did financiers—from the president of the World Bank to the managers of mutual funds. Britain was one of the few major countries not to contribute to the costs of the Brundtland Commission, but by 1987 it was ready to host the presentation of the commission's report; it has since been a leading campaigner for action to arrest the depletion of the ozone layer. France, which was competing with Britain for the environmental wooden spoon, became similarly active in efforts to halt global warming.

How did this transformation come about? I like to think that the Brundtland Commission and its report had something to do with it. But perhaps as important an influence on public attitudes was the succession of environmental disasters that took place around the world even as the commission was going about its work: the chemical leakage in Bhopal (1984), the liquid-gas explosion in Mexico (1984), drought and famine in Africa (1985), the mud slide in Colombia (1985), the nuclear accident in Chernobyl (1986), the Rhine chemical spillage (1986). In the wake of the Brundtland Report came disastrous floods in Bangladesh and the inundation of the Maldives. There followed in the first half of 1989 four oil spills in U.S. coastal waters, the largest from the *Exxon Valdez* as she grounded on a reef in Alaska's Prince William Sound. Oil covered some 2,600 square kilometers of coast and nearby waters, bringing enormous destruction to wildlife, including over thirty thousand birds. With the incidence of such disasters increasing in recent decades, political leaders began to accept that they were not purely random or one-time events.

But, while this series of calamities heightened awareness of mounting environmental stress, less immediately dramatic trends became in many respects more troubling. In 1989, I was at York in northern England to speak at the centenary of Britain's Royal Society for the Protection of Birds, one of the world's oldest conservation bodies. I felt it appropriate to point out to the audience that we were only a few miles from Drax, the site of a giant power plant whose gaseous emissions had rained down on and killed Scandinavian forests and lakes. I also spoke of York Minster, the city's exquisite medieval cathedral that has withstood the ravages of climate, political upheaval, and civil war, even the Luftwaffe, only to have its ancient stone succumb to modern industry's corrosive fumes.

But underlying everything I said was the notion that people are as important as monuments or trees, pandas or parrots—that we are endangered too. My point was that we have to care more than we seem to do for the preservation of life in all its forms; that, as the society's work over one hundred years of conservation had established, the protection of birds is not so far removed from the protection of the human species; that our fate was one with theirs. It is to some of these matters that we will now turn.

I T W A S the wisdom of the ancients that four elements constituted the universe: air, water, earth, and fire. Each was vital to life, and each was revered, even deified. Earth was the goddess Gaia to the Greeks. Fire was Agni in the pantheon of the Hindus. Many rivers were considered holy; the Ganges still is today. Shakespeare had Cleopatra say, "I am fire and air" to suggest her sense of self-importance. Since ancestral days our knowledge of the cosmos has been greatly enlarged. We know that the air is a mixture of many gases; we can name their properties and reckon their proportions. Yet our new learning has not devalued the wisdom of our ancestors.

The status of the four primal elements remains uneroded and unchallenged. It is we who have changed in our relationship to them. With our new knowledge and our new technology, veneration has faded. Ceasing to worship, to propitiate, even to wonder, we have sought to govern and to manipulate. We have been cavalier in our use of the primal elements, inordinate in our demands on them, uncaring about those who will need them in the future. We have altered the composition of the air, fouled the water. We have raided the fossil fuels that have stored the sun's fire for millennia. We have made the earth yield ever more to feed our increasing numbers, and in the process made it less fertile, in many places even barren, and diminished the diversity of the living biotic.

The four elements of the ancients seem separate, but are tightly linked. In disturbing the balance of the air, for example by pumping gases into it, we may have changed how and where water falls as rain and snow and so altered the bounty of the crops the earth nourishes. The problems we have thus made for ourselves have many names: air pollution, acid rain, ozone depletion, desertification, global warming, deforestation, species loss, and freshwater scarcity, to name only a few.

In our drive for material betterment we have become so indifferent to our roots in nature that we are in danger of tearing them out, leaving our human species to wither on the vine of progress. Though the elements threaten to destroy some of us through climate change and sea-level rise, we cannot be described any longer as being at the mercy of the elements. It is our supposed mastery of nature and dominion over the elements that has led to this crossroad. We have ravaged the elements, defiled, defouled, deflowered them. But the elements cannot really be mastered, only harnessed in a creative partnership. In view of the way we have treated them, we should not be surprised if the elements now appear unmerciful. We have put them at *our* mercy, and they suffer.

> Think how the crown of earth's creation
> Will murder that which gave him birth,
> Ripping out the slow womb of earth

wrote Vikram Seth in his novel *The Golden Gate*. He was describing a nuclear holocaust, but the imagery is relevant to our environmental onslaught. Yet, in truth, it is not simply a matter of destroying Earth. The quintessential reality of our position as humans has not changed, for all our pretensions at dominance. We are part of nature. As we approach the third millennium, our predilection to ecocide puts us at the mercy of ourselves.

PART TWO

Ravages

TWO

Air and Water

>...Where's the King?
> Contending with the fretful elements;
> That things must change or cease...
> Strives in his little world of man to outstorm
> The to-and-fro conflicting wind and rain.
>   —*King Lear*

"A s I live and breathe"—an everyday expression implying that we live because we breathe. So, indeed, we do. Plants and animals, among them humans, were able to emerge because of the supply of oxygen generated by the earliest marine organisms over many billions of years. Called vital air by earlier generations, oxygen is essential to the life of all animals and plants, through its role both in respiration and in the formation of the ozone shield that protected life from what would otherwise be unendurable solar radiation. Oxygen is elemental.

Fresh air is the phrase we use to suggest healthy living. Today, air is nowhere as fresh as it was eons ago. There is a threshold of impurity beyond which it loses its life-sustaining property. How near are we to that threshold and where? Nearer and in more places, perhaps, than we think. Today, in Los Angeles, in Mexico City, in Beijing, even in London it is becoming commonplace to see people wearing nose masks. The fact that they filter out only particles of dust and soot simply adds to the poignancy of our urban predicament. We are defiling the environment by contaminating the air that is fundamental to our being, and therefore to our continuing to be.

In a very basic sense, pollution is caused by all living things, whether animals in their habitat or leaves falling in a pond. But at normal levels of activity, nature itself recycles waste, copes with pollution. It is human excess that tips us over the edge of the acceptable into calamity. It is not our use of fossil fuels to generate electricity that is the problem; it is the magnitude of the generating capacity required by inefficient use of energy and inattention to conservation. It is not the internal combustion engine that is evil; it is the almost total lack of moderation with which we allow its exhaust fumes and lubricants to pollute our cities. It is not cities themselves that destroy the environment but rather the combination of burgeoning populations and spiraling poverty. At the heart of the issue of pollution is the disaster threshold. We are finding it difficult to recognize when that threshold is crossed, and all too frequently, we seem to be trying to convince ourselves that because some pollution is always present, even its worst excesses need not be fatal.

T H A T easy conviction will be denied us, because pollution is beginning to be fatal. It is estimated, for example, that as many as six times more people die in Greater Athens on heavily polluted days than when the air is relatively clean, and that 150 million U.S. citizens breathe air officially designated unhealthful. The World Health Organization (WHO) has alerted us to the dangers; it has set global standards and guidelines. The UN sponsors the global environmental monitoring system (GEMS) to check on countries' performances in relation to these (and other) standards. But in our world of inverted priorities, many governments do not permit international monitoring of their cities, regarding them as hallowed areas of territorial sovereignty, not the pockets of pollution they are.

National myopia cannot change global reality save for the worse. Smog has been described as a cocktail of pollutants; it is the product of the shaker of industrial hardware that is so much our image of progress: the power plants, refineries, petrochemical plants, smelters, incinerators, and so on. There has been improvement in some parts of the industrialized world, but the cities of many newly industrializing countries are smog-ridden. It is hardly surprising that smog alerts, like nose masks, are no longer exceptional in many cities. The air of Mexico City is contaminated by over 2.5 million vehicles and 130,000 factories—the "pollution of prosperity" developing countries longed for in Stockholm twenty years ago. Breathing that air is thought to be as damaging as smoking two packs of cigarettes a day. In 1988, smog levels in Mexico City exceeded WHO standards on 312 of the year's 366 days. In January 1989 levels were so high that schoolchildren were given the whole month off. Periodically, people are advised not to jog.

In 1991 the inevitable stage was reached: Since people no longer have access to clean air, it must be brought to them, packaged. *Casietas de oxygiena,* cabins like telephone booths, were installed in the city so that residents may buy lungfuls of oxygen. Is this what is in store for all of tomorrow's cities? Have we so defiled our inheritance from nature that we will die, not live, from the air we breathe?

Sulphur dioxide, the belch of many industries, is a major pollutant of the atmosphere. The great march of the industrial revolution is marked by ballooning sulphur-dioxide emissions that swelled from less than 10 million metric tons in 1860 to 160 million in 1980. Eighty-five percent of world industry is concentrated in rich countries; more than half of the rest is in only nine countries of Asia and Latin America. The poorest countries share a little more than a fifth of 1 percent (0.21 percent) of world industry. As the global cost of industrialization spreads, the poor will remain hapless victims while paying a higher and higher part of the price.

O N   T H E S E as on other matters, rich countries speak to poor with many different voices. Some, environmentalists among them, urge, "Don't do as we do." Others, among them medium-sized enterprises without the constraints of global multinationals, say, "Let us help you to modernize by shifting industry here; but please, no environmental hassle." Still others, ideologues included, sing the marching song of market forces and the enterprise culture, calling on the developing world (and Eastern Europe) to "travel with us down the pathway to progress through modernization." There is a catch in each message and developing countries know this; so the voices themselves are off-stage when decisions are made. The trouble is that what passes for the freedom of developing countries to make decisions is more and more the compulsion to follow the leadership of power.

The result of following that lead is that Tehran, Seoul, and Rio de Janeiro had, in the period from 1980 to 1984, more than twice the level of sulphur-dioxide emissions stipulated by WHO as safe, while

Delhi, Beijing, and Shenyang had six times the recommended safety level of "suspended particulate matter"—soot, ash, and dust. On China's border with North Korea is Benxi, a city of over four hundred factories that pump out some 87 million cubic meters of polluting gas every year. Benxi is earning the dubious reputation of being the world's most polluted city. A few years ago this city of a million people became so impenetrably submerged below its industrial pall that it disappeared altogether from satellite photographs. Malaysia's Kuala Lumpur, certainly one of the world's most attractive cities, now has pollution levels, mainly from vehicles, that are two to three times as bad as in the worst U.S. cities.

Eastern Europe suffers the worst air quality in the industrialized world—just how bad is only now being fully revealed. Over a third of Hungary's 10.3 million people endure air and water pollution levels that are officially acknowledged "inadmissible." Every seventeenth death, and every twenty-fourth disability, has recently been shown to be due directly or indirectly to air pollution. Pollution-related illness and death will cost Hungary almost $400 million over five years, says Budapest's National Institute of Public Health. In cities like Krakow and Leipzig, and in many parts of the former USSR, the situation is worse.

Tackling air pollution is not a major technological problem. The technology for cutting sulphur-dioxide emissions from power stations, for example, is available and widely enforced in industrial countries. So is the technology for making the exhaust fumes of motor vehicles less poisonous. In the case of rich countries, the problem is substantially the will to change behavior patterns in fundamental ways. In the case of poor countries, it is basically a matter of economics and finance. Anti-pollution technology raises costs; cleaning up industrial processes requires heavy outlays. When we begin to recognize that such costs, and many others like them that reflect the impact of human activity on the biosphere, simply have to be factored into the economics of production, we will have begun in earnest the process of saving ourselves.

For developing countries the dilemma is acute. In the interest of sustainability they cannot afford dirty technology, yet without development they cannot afford cleaner. Correspondingly, the rich cannot afford to leave the poor with technology that is "cheap and nasty." From a global perspective, that means that vigorous economic growth must help to raise poor countries to a level where they can afford cleaner technology. But if matters are to get better, such vigorous growth must be consciously assisted by a world community that recognizes sustainability as a universal credo and helps nations materially to achieve it.

F O R wealthy countries, which have far outstripped all others in polluting the planet, the duty to clean up the dirt of the industrial revolution could hardly be more compelling. There have been some responses, usually under the pressure of disaster, and generally without acknowledging a duty beyond national borders. The London smog that killed more than four thousand people in December 1952 led to a series of clean air acts that reduced Britain's smoke emissions by 85 percent, but its sulphur-dioxide emissions still exceed WHO safety standards, and much was left undone by not curbing emissions that carried death to nature on the northeast winds. Western industrial countries are taking action to reduce air pollution caused by smoke, sulphur dioxide, and nitrogen oxides. The problem is that their targets are unlikely to reduce acid deposition below the critical load ecosystems can take.

Perhaps the most ambitious antipollution program to date has come appropriately from the city that has for long been the symbol of air pollution—Los Angeles. Although the city led the way with catalytic converters to clean up the exhaust gases from motor vehicles in the 1970s, by 1988 southern Californians were in much the same crisis of pollution as residents of Mexico City. On 232 days that year, air quality fell below acceptable standards; on as many as seventy-five days schoolchildren and persons suffering from respiratory and heart problems were advised to stay indoors. The next year saw the introduction of the Air Quality Management Plan, designed to cut air pollution steadily over the next twenty years.

Los Angeles's plan will involve some 150 stringent regulations and cost some $3 billion a year to implement. Seventy percent of air pollution in the area derives from motor vehicles. Under the plan, 40 percent of southern California's cars, 70 percent of its trucks, and all of its buses must have abandoned gasoline for cleaner fuel by the year 2000. And there will be curbs on other polluters as well, from barbecues to power stations.

Will other cities in the United States follow the lead of Los Angeles? Will other countries? The answer must almost certainly be yes. Japan has already heavily cut sulphur emissions and eliminated lead from gasoline, and Europe has followed it. With some problems being solved, however, others are being revealed. As nitrogen-dioxide emissions go down, we become more aware of carbon dioxide. As lead goes down, we become aware of particulates. Thus several other measures are going to be needed to reduce air pollution. Some indicators of what might lie ahead are the daylight restrictions on traffic in central Florence and Rome. In Santiago, a fifth of the cars are kept off the road each day in a rotation system.

Smog has always seemed to be a local problem. People nearest the toxins are still the most endangered, but no one now minimizes the cross-border implications of domestic excess. One of the realities that most helped to bring this home to industrial countries—essentially because they were inflicting damage on each other—was acid rain.

Though the term acid rain entered the popular vocabulary only within the last few decades, the phenomenon was first detected and given this name, according to British records, in the nineteenth century. An early member of Britain's pollution inspectorate reported, in a scientific journal in 1852, that he had found sulphuric acid in rain falling in the area around Manchester. He used the term acid rain when he wrote in greater detail about his investigations in 1872.

H I G H L Y corrosive sulphuric and nitric acids are formed when oxides of sulphur and nitrogen combine with water vapor in the air. These oxides are spewed out as gases mainly by electricity-generating plants, smelters, and industrial boilers that burn coal and oil. Nitrogen oxide also comes from automobile exhaust. The acids return to Earth in rain, snow, and fog and are also deposited directly from the air onto trees. The pollutants travel long distances on prevailing winds, taking no account, of course, of national frontiers, so that the sulphur dioxide produced in one country becomes the sulphuric acid that poisons fish in another. The countries may be neighbors; more than half the acid rain received by eastern Canada comes across the border from industrial centers in the United States. Or they may lie farther apart; much of the acid rain in Norway is bad breath from Britain's industrial heartland.

A proliferation of lakes is one of nature's gifts to Scandinavia. When in the early 1970s trout and salmon in many Scandinavian lakes were found to be mysteriously dying, the suggestion that it could be due to acid rain coming across the North Sea was scornfully received in

Britain. Strong doubts were expressed and alternative explanations offered. Ultimately it was agreed that a joint research program employing multinational teams of scientists should be carried out under the auspices of the principal scientific societies of three countries, Britain, Norway, and Sweden. The final report on these investigations was not issued until 1990, but the scientists made an interim report three years earlier in which they confirmed that Britain was exporting acid rain to Scandinavia. An immediate sequel to this interim report was action by Britain's power generation authority—which had agreed in advance to accept the scientists' finding—to fit expensive equipment that would reduce sulphur emissions at its giant Drax power station.

The southern parts of Norway and Sweden, parts of central Europe, eastern Canada, and the eastern United States are the areas most severely harmed by acid rain. The main impact is on lakes and waterways, forests and the soil. Thousands of lakes have died, losing their capacity to support fish, chiefly in the two Scandinavian countries and in North America. Millions of trees have suffered; the impact on Germany has been so great, with over half of its forests including the famous Black Forest affected, that *waldsterben* (forest death) is a common word in newspaper headlines. Forests in Switzerland and Austria and in several East European countries have also been blighted. Alkaline soils and lime-rich areas can offset acids; this explains why some parts of Europe and North America have escaped the ravages of acid precipitation.

W H E N I was growing up in Guyana we collected rainwater in glass jars. Rainfall is in fact naturally acidic, but we could rely on ours being naturally "distilled"—as acid-free as rainwater can be. There is a scale for measuring acidity which goes from 0 to 14, the pH scale; this places distilled water at the halfway point of 7, and the lower the pH value, the higher the acid level. In ascending order of acidity are milk, apple juice, lemon juice, vinegar, and finally battery acid. According to the OECD, polluted areas in Scandinavia, Japan, central Europe, and eastern North America have annual pH values that can fall as low as 3.5, somewhere between the acid content of apple juice and lemon juice. Most fish die at pH levels below 5, which is why thousands of lakes in the eastern United States—including at least a tenth of all those in the Adirondack Mountains—have no fish. Sweden has added lime to three thousand lakes at a cost of $25 million to neutralize the acid and bring them back to life.

But even so substantial an effort as Sweden's does not, of course, get to the basic cause: the use of coal and oil in power stations, industrial boilers, and vehicles. These fossil fuels are the culprits—they, and we who use them with disregard for their impact on the biosphere. Norway each year has some rainfall that is as acidic as lemon juice. In the United States, precipitation as acidic as vinegar has fallen in Pennsylvania, and rain with a pH value almost equivalent to battery acid is reported to have once fallen on Wheeling, West Virginia. Even at pH 3.5, which is now the OECD norm, we are talking of rain that is a hundred times more acidic than it should be. Is it any wonder that trees are dying and fish disappearing from lakes and rivers and streams? There is something particularly threatening in this assault on life in the water from which all life first came. Yet we have been slow in admitting our responsibility, and slower still in acting to end our misconduct.

P R E S S U R E from the countries most severely affected has, of course, prompted efforts to limit the offending emissions. The UN Economic Commission for Europe (ECE) provided the auspices for the drafting of the Convention on Long-Range Transboundary Air Pollution, covering both Europe and North America, in 1979. The convention itself produced no binding provisions, but a protocol later negotiated obliged signatory countries to cut sulphur-dioxide emissions by 1993 to 30 percent of their 1980 level; a second protocol set somewhat less stringent controls on nitrogen oxide. So far, only twenty out of the thirty-four countries to whom the convention applies have ratified the first protocol; eighteen have agreed to the second. The European Community has set targets for larger reductions through its Large Combustion Plants Directive. While a few countries, Sweden, Germany, Switzerland, Austria, and Japan, have gone far in reducing sulphur-dioxide emissions—Japan has cut emissions by 90 percent—overall progress has been disappointing, and it has not been possible to get polluter countries to pay for damage caused to other nations. Two of the world's largest polluters, the United States and Britain, have been dragging their feet. Neither country has become party to the 30 percent protocol on sulphur dioxide under the ECE convention, though Britain has taken action toward satisfying the European Community directive.

While there has therefore been some progress by industrialized countries in addressing the pollution that causes acid rain, there is still a long way to go. What is disturbing is the defensive attitude of major countries. They have been slow in admitting responsibility except in the face of the most overwhelming evidence and scientific consensus. As the vice-chancellor of Oxford University, Professor Sir Richard Southwood, said in his Linacre Lecture in 1990, "The polluter pays principle is not so easily applied in practice in an international context." If this is so between fellow members of the OECD community, what difficulties are likely to be encountered at the global level?

> . . . just as the origins of life remain mysterious, so does its forward movement. What is certain is that life might have remained at a very primitive stage if a new kind of shield had not begun to build up. The starting point was the release from the planet of a protective atmosphere, containing oxygen and ozone, which intervened between the waters and the sun's lethal radiations. Below this shield, a new life-expanding process, photosynthesis, began to enable living things— bacteria, algae—to use the sun's radiance for the creation of organic matter and for the release of more oxygen. (p. 77)

As noted in chapter 1, Barbara Ward, René Dubos, and the members of the world scientific community who worked with them to produce *Only One Earth* in 1972 did not know that the primordial shield of life they were describing, in the lines quoted above, was already being ruptured. That shield is the ozone layer; the rupture is the hole in it of which we have heard so much in recent years. Without that stratospheric shield, humankind would not be here. To weaken it is to put human survival at risk. Again it is a question of threshold. Scientists are cautious about the level of ozone depletion that will imperil life on Earth; they are not in doubt about there being such a threshold or about man having moved much too far toward it.

O Z O N E is a Jekyll and Hyde type of gas. In the lower atmosphere it is an unwelcome presence, contributing to city smog as well as to the greenhouse effect. In the upper atmosphere, 20 to 40 kilometers above the Earth, (the Concorde flies at a height of 17 kilometers), it is a lifesaver. A thin layer of ozone screens us from the malign ultraviolet rays of the sun. But for this shield, radiation would cause many more cases of skin cancer, including malignant melanoma, and of cataracts. Light-skinned people are more likely to get skin cancer. Australia has the highest incidence, and over ten thousand people a year are killed by it in the United States alone. Ultraviolet rays also affect life on Earth in other ways. They can destroy certain forms of aquatic life, including phytoplankton, the microscopic organisms on the ocean's surface that make up the crucial first level of the marine food chain and that absorb carbon dioxide for photosynthesis, controlling the buildup of greenhouse gases. Ultraviolet radiation also harms food crops by reducing yields.

It was in 1974, not long after the Stockholm conference, that two U.S. scientists first suggested that CFCs were attacking the ozone layer. It took several years of argument, many more scientists, and a converted U2 spy plane to confirm the depletion and to put the finger firmly on CFCs. A crucial development was the actual discovery of the ozone hole in 1984 at Halley Bay in Antarctica by ground-based British Antarctic Survey scientists, who measured the ozone in the air column above them.

CFCs are highly useful chemicals, nonpoisonous, nonflammable, stable, and inexpensive. Developed in the 1930s as coolants, they replaced ammonia in refrigerators and helped to make refrigeration and air-conditioning more widely available. They were later used for propellant in aerosols, first to spray pesticides on mosquitoes that spread malaria and then for everything from furniture polish and air freshener to deodorants and medical inhalers. CFCs were also used to blow foam into upholstery and between walls (as insulation) and to clean computer circuits. These versatile gases, unleashed at ground level, slowly drift upward, taking about eight years to reach the stratosphere where, it has recently been found, ultraviolet rays attack them, releasing chlorine. The chlorine in turn reacts with the ozone it meets, converting the ozone into oxygen. This conversion thins out the ozone shield that protects Earth from ultraviolet radiation. CFC gases remain in the stratosphere for about a century.

UNEP started trying to get international action on the ozone layer in 1975, but it required more convincing evidence of the extent and causes of its depletion to persuade the world's nations to take any meaningful action. Western governments were at first skeptical and

CFC manufacturers wholly unconvinced. Though a few nations, notably the United States, Canada, and the Scandinavian countries, restricted the use of CFCs in aerosol spray cans in the 1970s, it was not until 1985 that the Vienna Convention for the Protection of the Ozone Layer was negotiated. The convention was only ground-preparing action; it did not lay down any specific measures to limit the use of CFCs.

Two years later, a protocol to the convention drafted in Montreal took matters further, with countries agreeing to reduce the use of CFCs by 50 percent by 1996. Scientific investigations providing further disturbing evidence of the loss of ozone then gave more urgency to international efforts. And in yet more steps, the latest in London in June 1990, the countries that had signed the Montreal Protocol committed themselves to phasing out the use of CFCs entirely by the year 2000. The 1990 meeting also decided on action to phase out the other main substances that attack the ozone layer: halon, carbon tetrachloride, and methyl chloroform. Thirteen countries were in favor of moving the deadline for CFCs forward to 1997, three large producers of CFCs among them. But three other major producers—the United States, Japan, and the Soviet Union—resisted this. However, in February 1992 the Bush administration agreed to greatly speed up phase out plans.

T H E convention on ozone and the action taken as a result of it nevertheless represent a significant advance in global efforts to deal with environmental matters on the basis of partnership. Ozone loss is the first important environmental issue on which developed and developing countries have found common ground and shown a readiness to accommodate each other. It is necessary to note that while CFC use is set to rise with economic growth in developing countries, they now account for only about 16 percent of current global use of CFCs. They were justifiably wary in the negotiations of entering into commitments that would have the effect of impeding their development, for their geography clearly dictates an extension of refrigeration and air-conditioning. Chemical firms in the North have developed substitutes for CFCs that are said not to carry environmental hazards, but they are more expensive than CFCs, and some are also greenhouse gases. Poor countries adopting the safer technology face a relatively stiffer burden than rich countries, where the increase in cost of a domestic refrigerator, for instance, would be much less felt, and also where refrigeration is less necessary to food hygiene than in many developing countries.

Special arrangements for developing countries whose annual consumption per head of CFCs is less than 300 grams (U.S. consumption is 1.3 kilograms, or more than four times that level) include a ten-year grace period for reducing the use of CFCs and other ozone-destroying products. Some help was given to developing countries under the Montreal Protocol, with a fund of $160 to $240 million to ease their move away from ozone-depleting technologies. However, even the larger amount of funding, to be activated when India and China sign the protocol, is marginal to real needs.

The history of international efforts regarding the ozone layer, encouraging as it is on one level, is cautionary on the other. From the time UNEP's governing body decided to alert the world community by convening an international conference, it took nine years to get to the Vienna Convention. Another four years passed before the Montreal Protocol came into effect. During that time the volume of CFCs in the atmosphere is reckoned to have nearly doubled. It is a delay we—or future generations—may have cause to regret. A skin cancer expert in Sydney has warned that Australians will have to wear space suits and live in glass-domed cities in the next century unless scientists find a way to stop the erosion of the ozone layer. Few doctors or scientists accept so stark a prospect, but most would agree that complacency is unwarranted.

In July 1991, as the summit of the Group of Seven was being held in London, conservationists were holding "The Other Economic Summit," TOES. The Group of Seven virtually ignored environmental issues that the previous year's summit at Houston had promised would remain on their agenda. However, British scientists were not silent. The head of the United Kingdom Stratospheric Ozone Review group, Dr. John Pyle, warned that ozone depletion over Britain and Europe was double previous estimates and was now worse than that over Australia and New Zealand; the risk of skin cancer, of blindness from cataracts, and of crop damage had increased in the region between southern Spain and London. Dr. Pyle expected ozone levels to drop 15 percent from 1980 levels by the end of the 1990s. "We know that the hole in Antarctic ozone occurred quite quickly," he said. "We just don't know what is going to happen over Europe."

I F A C I D rain is an example of the cross-border consequences of our
environmental transgressions, ozone depletion is testimony to the
global implications of our conduct. The immediate consequences, it is
true, seem likely to have a greater effect on the northern temperate
zone between 30° and 64° latitude, covering most of Europe, the
former Soviet Union, almost all of populated North America, northern
China, both Koreas, and Japan. And those at greatest risk of skin
cancer from increased radiation are persons with fair skin, a large
proportion of the residents of the industrialized countries of the
North. Such considerations demand from their governments a serious,
urgent response, and by and large that is now forthcoming. The full
implications of the weakening of Earth's ozone shield, however, remain unknown, and there is already growing concern that human
immune systems will be weakened and the food chain damaged.

There is another danger from CFCs. They have not just contributed
massively to ozone depletion; they have also helped to force climate
change through the greenhouse effect. All countries and people, indeed
all of nature, are the victims of CFCs.

Consideration must be given to responsibility. Much effort has gone
into bringing China and India, with a third of the world's population
between them, into a universal pact to end the production of CFCs and
to develop and use safe substitutes. That was both right and necessary
to protect our future. We must remember, however, that it is the
industrial countries that have been responsible for 95 percent of the
CFC gases released into the atmosphere so far. Quite apart from
the implications this has for burden sharing, there is a clear need
for vigilance to ensure that the use of CFCs will indeed end.

It was Dr. Joe Farman, a member of the British Antarctic Survey
since 1956, who led the team of scientists that produced the first
conclusive evidence of ozone depletion in 1984. In 1990, he gave this
further warning in *Sustaining Earth,* a compilation of writings on
environmental topics:

> Everyone in the West has said that they have stopped making carbon
> tetrachloride [one of the oldest and more damaging halocarbons
> used to produce CFCs and having a life of up to 140 years], and
> indeed it has been banned, yet it is still growing in quantity, with no
> known natural sources. F-113 [a modern CFC] is mainly used in the
> electronics industry. The world's largest market for electronics is the

United States military, who insist on using cleaning agents like F-113, even though it may now be the case that high-pressure water will suffice. . . . The continued release of long-lived halocarbons can no longer be tolerated. Safe substitutes must be found, and large-scale production of substances which can carry chlorine and bromine to the stratosphere should cease. Only when this has been achieved will the atmosphere begin to return to a safer state. (pp. 75–76)

In 1991 a report for the Commonwealth, "Sustainable Development: An Imperative for Environmental Protection," also sounded a note of caution: "It will . . . be essential to ensure that CFC substitutes now being developed . . . do not exacerbate global warming. There is mounting concern that the HCFCs and HFCs currently being developed by chemical industries will do more damage to the ozone layer and the atmosphere than was thought previously." (p. 75)

"W A T E R , water, everywhere, nor any drop to drink." For many millions of people worldwide, the fate of Coleridge's Ancient Mariner is not a tale of yore, it is the reality of daily existence on our planet, 70 percent of whose surface is covered with water. From the perspective of space, Earth is a planet of water. On the ground, in relation to human needs, the reality is very different; only 3 percent is fresh water, and most of that lies frozen at the poles or inaccessible underground. Still, there is plenty for human needs, or at least there should be. The fresh water that falls on land each year as rain and snow is estimated to be enough to flood the continents 80 centimeters deep.

The trouble is that it falls very unevenly across the continents. It helps vegetation to burgeon in some countries and leaves only deserts to thrive in others; it provides plentiful supplies of drinking water to Iceland but very little to the Middle East. As a result, about two billion people in eighty countries live with water shortages. They are constantly on the threshold of drought, but even those countries blessed with freshwater resources face the looming problem of scarcity.

For marginal countries the situation will inevitably worsen as human and animal populations increase. The supply of water on Earth is a constant. With the rise in the number of humans, and the volume of water each requires, rising scarcities are inevitable. By the year 2000 Egypt is expected to have a third less water for each of its inhabitants than it had at the start of the 1990s; Kenyans will have half as much. The picture is bleak for many countries of east Africa, the southern Mediterranean, Israel, Poland, and arid parts of the United States. Climate change will introduce many imponderables. Evaporation, for example, certainly increases with temperature. Rainfall patterns are likely to be severely disrupted as the Earth heats up. There will be some gains, but clearly some setbacks too. One study suggests that the entire western United States, already short of water, could find supplies cut by between a quarter and a half of present levels.

F A R M I N G accounts for some 70 percent of global water use. In its *State of the World 1990* report, the Worldwatch Institute gave a stark warning of water scarcity looming in a number of regions where irrigation is critical to farming. Ten African countries are likely to experience severe water shortages by 2000, with Egypt losing vital supplies from the Nile as other nations develop the river's headwaters. In China fifty cities already face acute shortages. The water table beneath Beijing has recently dropped between one to two meters each year, and there is an additional threat of farmers losing up to 40 percent of their supplies to domestic and industrial users. In India tens of thousands of villages face shortages, while many parts of the capital, New Delhi, have water only a few hours a day. In Mexico, 40 percent more water is pumped from the valley containing Mexico City than is replaced, causing the land to subside and introducing the possibility of having to import fresh water. In the Middle East shortages are imminent: Israel, Jordan, and the West Bank are expected to use up renewable sources by 1995, and Syria will lose vital supplies when Turkey's Ataturk Dam comes on line in 1992. In the former Soviet Union, depletion of river water for irrigation and other needs has already caused the Aral Sea to drop by two-thirds since 1960, and tens of thousands have had to leave the area. In the United States, one-fifth of the irrigated land is subject to excessive groundwater pumping. As a result, four million hectares could eventually go out of production.

"In much of the world," says the Worldwatch Institute report, "falling water tables signal that groundwater withdrawals exceed the rate of replenishment." That is the crucial factor; we are drawing down the planet's freshwater capital wherever it is accessible, and at an alarming rate. Between 1900 and 1950, the world's irrigated land area almost doubled to 94 million hectares—an increase of nearly 50 million hectares in fifty years. In the forty years between 1950 and 1990, the irrigated area expanded by over 150 million hectares, to about 250 million hectares, resulting in heavier demands on groundwater supplies. Today, some 3,300 cubic kilometers of water—six times the annual flow of the Mississippi—are removed each year from Earth's rivers, streams, and underground aquifers to water crops. It is a massive tragedy that after all this, the world's irrigation systems are believed to be functioning at less than 40 percent efficiency. And there are big losses from salt accumulation.

Using water more efficiently by reducing waste is obviously the way forward. It has been estimated, for example, that if water waste around the Indus in Pakistan could be cut by just one-tenth, another 2 million hectares of cropland could be irrigated. Fortunately, the world is becoming conscious of the dangers of water scarcity and the need to make freshwater resources go farther. Improving the flow of irrigation canals and using capillary-tube irrigation to deliver water directly to roots are two of the techniques being considered; recycling is another. But with capital costs high, choosing crops best suited to a region's soil and climate patterns is often the most rational approach. Cutting the use of fresh water in industry, which accounts at present for about 20 percent of use, is another partial solution. Between 1965 and 1974, Japan increased the proportion of recycled water in its industries from one-third to two-thirds, and between 1978 and 1983 the United States cut its water intake for industry by nearly one-quarter, even though the number of factories grew.

Reducing consumption in the United States is immensely important, and crucial to that in turn is realistic pricing. The enormous waste of water in the western United States, for example, owes much to the unwillingness of politicians to force farmers, householders, and even golfers to conserve water. Of all the world's people, Americans use the most water, about 2,300 cubic meters per capita per year, half of it in factories and power plants. This consumption compares with 1,500 cubic meters for Canadians and 1,210 for Australians. People in Japan, Spain, Portugal, Belgium, and the Netherlands use over 900 cubic meters; the British use only 225 cubic meters a head and the Swiss under 110. Developing countries on average use 20 to 40 cubic meters per person each year. The average American accounts for as much freshwater use as seventy west Africans. Not only is there freshwater scarcity worldwide; supplies are very unevenly distributed, and even more unevenly consumed. Freshwater distribution around the world is largely an act of nature, but its consumption is a matter for which we cannot shirk responsibility.

T H E S E differentials clearly pose problems and dangers, not only because economic development and standards of living are affected, but also because peace and stability are threatened. Fresh water is often a shared resource. Most of the world's largest rivers flow through more than one country, and about 40 percent of the world's people get their water—for drinking, irrigation, generating power—from shared rivers. Some countries that depend on shared sources are experiencing shortages that seem set to get worse.

The potential for conflict over water may be highest in the Middle East, an area not short of tripwires for conflict. The rising scarcity of water is accompanied by rapid population growth. In 1979, only a short while after he had signed the peace accord with Israel, President Sadat of Egypt was saying, "The only matter that could take Egypt to war again is water." It was a reminder that Egypt's lifeline was the Nile, a river that flows through eight other countries before it reaches the Mediterranean through Egypt. The Nile provides 85 percent of Egypt's water, and the country depends on the river not only for producing half its food but also for generating a fourth of its power and a large part of its tourist revenue. Egypt can be gravely affected by what countries upstream do.

Israel's water policy has long been a sore point with the Palestinians of the West Bank, and as late as 1990, King Hussein of Jordan was warning that a dispute over water could lead to war between his country and Israel. The source of contention between West Bank Palestinians and the Israelis is the use the latter make of the aquifer straddling their two respective areas. The proportion of the aquifer lying under the West Bank is itself disputed, and Palestinians claim that, while domestic and industrial needs are catered to, its agricultural expansion is blocked. The Iraq-Kuwait conflict had much the same genesis, if you substitute oil for water.

Jordan has had problems with Israel over the waters of the Yarmuk River, and the distribution of water in the Euphrates and Tigris river basins, which nurtured man's first civilization, has often caused friction among Syria, Iraq, and Turkey. In the mid-1970s, the Ath-Thawrah Dam by which Syria sought to use water from the Euphrates was a flashpoint in its relations with Iraq, which charged that the diversion of water was harming agriculture there. More recently, Turkey's massive South East Anatolia development project, involving dams on both major rivers, has caused pronounced tension in both Iraq and Syria. A few years ago Turkey claimed to have come across a Syrian plot to blow up the mighty Ataturk Dam that is a part of the Anatolia project.

Though the risks to peace from discord over the allocation of water are greatest in the Middle East, it is by no means the only area where countries could come into conflict over who gets how much water. More than two hundred of the world's river systems serve two countries or more. At first glance, it might appear that the issues should be susceptible to resolution on the basis of mutual interest, but the history of disputes over water confirms that they do not lend themselves to easy solutions. Not only are there long-nursed suspicions and tensions to be tempered; an equitable distribution of benefits often requires large investment in schemes for exploiting and managing shared water.

The scale of investments in dams, reservoirs, and power plants is such that they can rarely be readily raised by the countries themselves. Significant international involvement becomes indispensable. The danger to global security that unresolved water issues are likely to pose amply justifies such involvement. Since water disputes tend to be local or at most regional rather than global, they do not command worldwide attention. However, the signs are clear that the world community must elevate the issue of water to a position of higher priority; it is an environmental issue with important implications for security. Development agencies, including the World Bank, have a role. Joyce Starr, who as chairman of the Global Water Summit Initiative, an American-based NGO (nongovernmental organization) pressure group, has been active in mobilizing support for cooperative action to defuse friction over water, has recently warned, "Water security will soon rank with military security in the war rooms of Defense Ministries."

N o t only has human activity depleted the planet's supply of fresh water in quantitative terms, it has also been wanton in relation to the quality of water. The one wrong is as ecologically damaging as the other. Were we fully sensitive to the importance of water, we would use what we have in the most efficient manner possible and preserve its quality. We are doing neither. The result is that surface waters are being polluted everywhere by a poisoned broth of human, industrial, and agricultural waste. And today's polluted surface water is often tomorrow's contaminated groundwater. Every year in North America, the excessive use of phosphates for green lawns leads, with rapid runoff, to phosphate contamination of groundwater. In 1990, several Ontario rural townships actually closed wells supplying water to their communities because of the seepage of industrial waste.

W E S T E R N industrial countries have made some progress, establishing controls on industrial pollution in particular. But massive problems remain. Most people would find it surprising that in the twenty-one OECD countries, with the world's greatest financial capacity to counter freshwater pollution, little more than half of the people are served by sewage treatment plants. Inevitably, the ratio varies greatly among countries, from almost 100 percent in Sweden to only 20 percent in Belgium and Spain.

The Rhine drains one of the world's most highly industrialized regions. It has been the focus of major European efforts to improve sewage and industrial waste treatment. Some of these efforts have been effective. For example, fish have returned to some parts of the river from which they were absent for decades. But pollution from toxic chemicals and mineral waste is still high, the danger of contamination ever present. We were at work on the Brundtland Commission addressing these very questions when the massive chemical spill occurred in 1986. As a result of a warehouse fire in Switzerland, agricultural chemicals, solvents, and mercury flowed into the Rhine, killing millions of fish and threatening drinking water in West Germany and the Netherlands. It called to mind the trenchant verse of Samuel Taylor Coleridge's "Cologne" over a century and a half ago:

> Ye nymphs that reign o'er sewers and sinks,
> The River Rhine, it is well known,
> Doth wash your City of Cologne;
> But tell me, nymphs, what power divine
> Shall henceforth wash the River Rhine?

One of the biggest problems in the Rhine now comes from salt washed from agricultural land and mining operations. The pattern of success in controlling pollution from such point sources as factories combined with continuing pollution from a variety of other sources, including accidents, seems typical of many rivers in industrial countries. Runoff from agricultural lands heavily laden with pesticides and fertilizers and wastewater flowing from cities and towns add a continuous stream of contamination. The wastewater is a witch's brew of sewage, heavy metals, oils, hydrocarbons, garbage leachates, chemicals for de-icing, organic waste from animals, dust, and other harmful ingredients. The runoff from city streets in Florida, for example, is thought to account for more than half of the state's water pollution and nearly 85 percent of the heavy metals found in its rivers and swamps. In nearly 60 percent of the polluted lakes surveyed in the United States, nutrients from fertilizers and animal waste were found to be the main contaminants.

T H E situation in industrialized Eastern Europe is much worse, because economic output was put well ahead of environmental concerns and the costs of pollution were never factored into prices. Pollution has been extensive and water courses are fouled by all manner of waste and debris. It is said that the River Vistula, which flows through the heart of Poland, is so sullied that most of it is unsuitable even for industrial use. Most rivers in the former Soviet Union are notoriously polluted. Effluents from industries along the River Volga are believed to make up 10 percent of that river's average flow at Volgograd, three-quarters having received no treatment whatsoever.

The situation in some Third World countries is even worse. Most of India's rivers are little more than open sewers carrying untreated waste from urban and rural areas to the sea. About 70 percent of the subcontinent's surface waters are polluted. In general, Asia's rivers are perhaps the most degraded in the world. Out of seventy-eight rivers monitored in China, for example, fifty-four were seriously polluted with untreated sewage and industrial waste. So much industrial and agricultural waste—from oil palm and rubber processing, and from sewage and chemical industries—pollutes Malaysia's main rivers that more than forty of them are said to be biologically dead.

The worldwide freshwater situation is grim. Only integrated management strategies that prevent pollution in the first place and help to clean up water courses seem to hold out hope of reviving freshwater supplies. Individual countries can do much, and some are making imaginative efforts, though, inevitably, these are mainly rich countries where resources are available and problems often less acute. Sweden, for example, has pointed the way with legislation introducing a system of renewable permits to ensure that industries comply with stringent safeguards regarding effluents to water (and to land and air as well). Safeguarding the quality of the world's fresh water is now a matter of considerable urgency. International action, including support for regional efforts, is critical, but we are unlikely to tackle the problems unless we see ourselves as citizens of the planet. The time has passed when we can throw our dirty waste into the nearest pond, lake, river, or ocean and forget about it. We have treated the primal element of water with scant respect, and nature is striking back.

D I R T Y water has become the world's most dangerous killer. At least twenty-five thousand people die every day from their use of it, nearly four thousand in India alone. Diarrhea alone kills at least 4.6 million young children each year. About 200 million people are victims of schistosomiasis (bilharzia), caused by contaminated water on the skin. Five hundred million people have trachoma, one of the main causes of blindness, because of dirty wash water. About half of the people living in developing countries, some two billion members of the human species, do not have safe drinking water. In some countries the proportion is much higher. In Ethiopia, 94 percent are in that deprived, vulnerable category, and that is in years when war and drought have not wrought further havoc.

The lack of clean water is invariably accompanied by the lack of sanitation facilities. Each need bears on the other in a vicious circle. Where there is no proper sanitation, human waste pollutes the wells, rivers, and lakes from which people draw their water. Without water supply schemes, municipal sewage systems cannot be installed even if there are financial resources to do so; in rural areas the option does not even arise. For much of the developing world, chronic contamination of fresh water means that sanitation remains primitive.

The many who endure such conditions are denied basic human needs, a fact the rest of the world, the few who enjoy a better life, cannot ignore. Central to the issue is the intolerable and wholly disproportionate burden that falls on women: women who must bear children and watch as they suffer and die; women who walk miles every day, and farther and farther each year, to collect water for the family; women whose own basic needs remain unfulfilled as they give their lives to drudgery so that their children may have a chance to survive. Until we find a way to provide clean water and adequate sanitation for all, we will leave human civilization blighted with indefensible inequities.

B E L A T E D recognition of this yawning need prompted the UN to mount a special effort in the late 1970s. The 1980s were declared the International Water Supply and Sanitation Decade, with WHO as the agency coordinating activities. The goals set for the decade were not excessively ambitious when measured against the world's needs, but they proved too ambitious in the light of resources that were not forthcoming. Many would not think it inaccurate to write off the decade as a failure. In a general sense, all of us share the responsibility. The UN's worthy goal of "clean water and adequate sanitation for all" can be realized in the Third World—as can many other environmental objectives—only with a robust pace of economic development that will generate resources.

Overall, the global freshwater situation is approaching the threshold of collapse—overconsumption in rich countries, underconsumption in poor ones, scarcity and pollution of supplies in many countries, rich and poor. For some, neither rich nor poor exclusively, the point of collapse is not far away. We tinker with the symptoms but shy away from the causes, refusing to confront and remove them.

O U R record in relation to the planet's supply of fresh water is not a creditable one. Are we doing any better with respect to seawater? With 75 percent of the Earth's water in the oceans, one would hope that human impact in this area would be more sensitive to sustainability, acknowledging as we must how much oceans contribute to sustaining life on the planet.

In truth, for most of human history, the matter of the sustainability of the ocean's resources has hardly entered our minds. When the poet Thomas Gray wrote in the eighteenth century of "the dark unfathom'd caves of ocean," he reflected our basic assumption about the limitless resources of the sea. Certainly we have behaved as if the sea's bounty is limitless, its capacity to absorb maltreatment infinite. In its relationship with the oceans, as in so many other relationships with nature, *Homo sapiens* has been neither *sapiens* nor *sentiens*, neither wise nor caring.

Throughout his history man has used the ocean as he pleased. It has been both highway and harvest ground. Some of his early accomplishments entailed voyaging across the ocean, even though, more often than not, he was an unworthy visitor at journey's end. With mastery of the skills of navigation, he began the era of dominion over the ocean. He was not just a traveler; he was a hunter-gatherer as well. The "fishes of the sea" were his abundant prey, and his taking of them was but part of the natural order of depletion and replacement.

We have however been overvoracious in our hunting the bounty of the seas, and we have ravaged them in other ways as well. Now, as we intensify our aggression, we are at a threshold that we cross at our peril—the exhaustion of what has been over centuries a significant and reliable component of the human food supply, and despoliation that threatens to diminish the ocean's capacity to be life sustaining. Not for us Byron's circumspection from his work "Childe Harold":

> Roll on, thou deep and dark blue Ocean—roll!
> Ten thousand fleets sweep over thee in vain;
> Man marks the earth with ruin—his control
> Stops with the shore.

A G A I N , it is the scale and pace of our exploitation that make the difference. The oceans were being fished before Columbus voyaged five hundred years ago. It took all that time, until 1950, for annual commercial catches to reach a level of some 20 million metric tons. Yet, in less than forty years since 1950, according to the UN's Food and Agriculture Organization (FAO), commercial catches more than quadrupled, reaching 92 million metric tons in 1987. And that excludes some 24 million metric tons harvested by local fishermen working in coastal regions. The crucial factor, however, is that FAO estimates that the world's fleets cannot catch more than 100 million metric tons of the fish currently being taken without critically depleting stocks. In other words, we are moving rapidly to the limits of sustainability of the ocean fish resources on which we have relied.

In some respects, we have already exceeded the limits. In the northwest Atlantic, for example—a fishing zone dominated by the United States, Canada, and Iceland—all fish stocks have already been overharvested. Catches have slumped by over 30 percent since the early 1970s. Stocks and catches of northeast Atlantic fish have also declined significantly under the impact of European fleets. The same fate seems to await Japan in the northwest Pacific, where harvesting is proceeding at a frenetic pace beyond the sustainable yield.

D E V E L O P I N G countries have entered the ocean fishing stakes, and eight of them—China, Chile, Peru, India, South Korea, Indonesia, Thailand, and the Philippines—are now among the dozen nations with the biggest catches. China apart, however, Japan and the former Soviet republics are far ahead of any other country. By the time developing countries reach a capacity for significant shares in fish harvesting, the fish resources of the oceans will have been massively depleted, mainly through overfishing by others.

The Law of the Sea Convention concluded in 1982 was the world's most ambitious and enlightened attempt to manage what ought to be the heritage of all for the benefit of all. It offered a chance to end the fishing free-for-all by giving all countries Exclusive Economic Zones (EEZs) extending 200 miles from national shores. Coastal states have sovereign rights over all fishing in these zones, including that by foreign vessels. This means a great deal to small island states, for example those in the South Pacific, but conflicts and disadvantages continue as deep-water fleets from Europe, Japan, and the United States continue to harvest tuna and other migratory fish within declared South Pacific EEZs in defiance of the convention.

Recently, Japanese fishing fleets have outraged the international conservation community and small countries particularly by their recourse to drift nets. Up to 50 kilometers long, these "free-floating walls of death," as they have been called by Greenpeace, trap not only fish but hundreds of thousands of sea birds and marine mammals as well. Even without drift nets, some commercial fishing like shrimping is conducted with utter disregard for the depletion of fish stocks. Marine life is crudely scooped up, and fish not sought after are simply discarded. We have become indiscriminate predators of the oceans with no thought for others, or for our own future.

O V E R F I S H I N G is not the only culprit. Fish stocks are being endangered by other human encroachment. A particularly pernicious trend is the destruction of mangroves, coral reefs, and seagrass, among the world's most endangered ecosystems. These all shield the coasts and provide vital breeding grounds and habitats for fish. Nearly two-thirds of all fish caught in the world are hatched in mangrove and tidal areas. In my own part of the world, the Caribbean, some 90 percent of all commercial species of fish and shellfish depend on mangroves, coral reefs, and seagrass at critical stages in their life cycle. Yet everywhere, mangroves are in retreat, coral reefs are being degraded, and sea-grasses are threatened. Mangroves are cut for firewood or to make way for fish ponds, poisoned by pesticides from agricultural fields, or simply smothered by sediment from riverine and coastal development. As mangroves fail, coral reefs become more vulnerable to silt. Reefs are also victims of the construction of hotels or even of tourists themselves. From all this devastation they recover very slowly. Awareness of the serious damage being done to ocean habitats is growing. UNEP has an Oceans and Coastal Areas Program Activity Center in Nairobi whose work demonstrates in an outstanding way what can be done, but resources are scarce and other priorities overwhelm the fate of these often overlooked habitats.

A s I F all this were not enough, saltwater pollution has now emerged as a serious problem. Until recently, it was relatively localized in river estuaries and harbors; now it is spreading around the world's coasts and beginning to affect the open ocean. Nearly half of this pollution is discharged either directly to the sea or via rivers. It is remarkable that in as prominent an industrial country as Britain, three-quarters of the sewage from coastal towns and cities is discharged raw, without even minimal treatment, into the sea. Not surprisingly, Britain's beaches regularly fail European Community safety standards. Elsewhere, medical waste, including syringes, washed up on beaches in the northeast United States in 1988, and the following year on the French and Italian rivieras. Publicity from these incidents has at last prompted action.

A further third of saltwater pollution comes by way of fallout from air pollution, a reminder of nature's unity, and of the degree to which all countries and all people are ultimately the victims of everyone else's pollution. What most captures the headlines and dramatizes marine pollution is the damage caused by oil spills. These, however, account for only a small fraction of saltwater pollution. Many will remember that, well before the major oil spills, Thor Heyerdahl collected water samples on the voyages of the *Kon-Tiki* and *Ra* in the Pacific and Atlantic oceans and issued early warnings of seawater pollution after finding globules of oil floating in midocean. However small in relative terms, oil spills do cause real if transitory damage to the marine environment, as was all too vividly demonstrated by the *Exxon Valdez* accident in 1989 in Alaska. In that year, there were twelve major accidents involving oil spills around the world.

Genuine accidents are, at worst, the result of negligence. What can be said of the fact that each year more than one million metric tons of oil is deliberately discharged by tankers as they pump out oily water and wash out their tanks before taking on new cargo? Although the worst of this pollution floats on the world's shipping lanes, the damage to marine life, especially plankton and larvae, is real and inexcusable. Even worse is the dumping of industrial waste, supposedly being phased out, and radioactive material, which was supposed to have ended in 1983. But so cynical has been the behavior of major polluters that constant vigilance is clearly required. In 1990 UNEP warned that "the marine environment could deteriorate significantly in the next decade unless strong, coordinated national and international action is taken now." Such action is not being taken. The marine environment, for all its vastness, remains at our mercy.

O V E R A L L , the global air and water picture is one of unsustainable demands on the planet's natural resources. As Mahatma Gandhi once said, "There is enough in the world for every man's need, but not for every man's greed." We tend not to see our demands on water as an example of greed because we are oblivious to the limits of this supply. We assume that with water and air nature has been generous. The water of the oceans and the air of the skies are global commons not owned by any government, and this seems to induce irresponsibility. In the absence of cooperative global management, there is no call on us to be prudent and circumspect in our use of nature's resources. Our perspective is essentially one of the right of the human species to take from the elements all there is to be had, without any countervailing duty to live in harmony with nature and preserve what it provides in a manner that will sustain us into eternity.

THREE

Earth and Fire

> A great and strong wind came . . . but the Lord
> was not in the wind: and after the wind an earth-
> quake; but the Lord was not in the earthquake:
> And after the earthquake a fire: but the Lord was
> not in the fire: and after the fire a still small voice.
> —*The First Book of Kings*

F O U L I N G the air and poisoning the water are not our only tres-
passes against the elements. Nor were they the earliest. Man's first
onslaught was against Earth itself. It came with progress, a result of
one of those great leaps forward man has made over the millennia. Ten
thousand years ago our species tamed the land and domesticated
plants and animals to produce food in a systematic way. This transformed human prospects. No longer merely hunter-gatherers taking
from nature what it offered, we would make the soil yield what we
determined, and in what quantities we willed, by dint of effort. We
were assuming dominion over the earth.

How we were to exercise that dominion through a hundred centuries that lay ahead would depend in large measure on how we saw
ourselves in relation to nature and to Earth in particular. Our early
ancestors stood in awe of nature; they showed both reverence and
caring for it. The traditions of every society acknowledge that in all
flora and fauna there is sacred life.

> Earth's crammed with heaven,
> And every common bush afire with God

was how Elizabeth Barrett Browning expressed it in the last century. Chief Seattle, who commanded the Indian tribes in the Pacific Northwest of the United States, conveyed the same message with no less poignancy in his letter of 1855, replying to the American president's request that he "sell" his people's land to the government:

> How can you buy or sell the sky, the warmth of the land? The idea is strange to us. If we do not own the freshness of the air and the sparkle of the water, how can you buy them?
>
> Every part of this earth is sacred to my people. Every shining pine needle, every sand shore, every mist in the dark woods, every clearing and humming insect is holy in the memory and experience of my people.

And to this day the Aboriginal people of Australia hold fast to their legends of the Dreamtime when the earth was sung into life; songlines give sanctity to the ancestral places on their island continent.

Many early cultures shared these values and insights and evolved ways of life that were in harmony with nature. Yet even these cultures did not always show wisdom in managing the earth. A propensity for misuse of nature's bounty has been a chronic flaw in the human character. We know that now, but it persists with such tenacity that it could yet be our Achilles' heel, the fatal flaw endangering the very survival of our species.

"O U R land, compared with what it was, is like a skeleton of a body wasted by disease." What Plato said of Attica in the fourth century B.C. could well be a description of desertification, the main environmental problem in the modern world's drylands, arid, semi-arid, and dry subhumid areas totaling about 5 billion hectares. UNEP estimates that to some degree desertification now affects over 3.3 billion hectares of dryland, an area the size of North and South America combined. Like many diseases, desertification advances in stages from its first onset to its final ravaging. Alan Grainger described the phenomenon well in the opening words of his authoritative book, *The Threatening Desert*:

> Large parts of the dry areas that cover more than one-third of the earth's land surface are being degraded, with serious effects on the

environment, food production, and the lives of millions of people. Desertification, characterised by the degradation of soil and vegetative cover, can occur in any dry area, not just on the fringes of natural deserts. It is a global phenomenon, affecting both developed and developing nations, and is a particular problem in Africa, the Middle East, India and Pakistan, China, Australia, the USSR, the USA, Latin American countries such as Brazil and Chile, and European countries such as Greece, Spain and Portugal. (p. 1)

As with freshwater supplies, the planet's drylands are not evenly distributed. More than 80 percent of their total area is in three continents: Africa, Asia, and Australia. Together, they account for all thirty-four of the countries with 75 to 100 percent of their land area arid or semiarid and for four-fifths of the planet's land area that is at least moderately desertified. Eighteen of these countries are in Africa and fifteen in Asia, mainly the western half. Australia's drylands are sparsely populated; it is in Africa and Asia that countries and people are most threatened by desertification.

The point that desertification is not mainly the expansion of existing natural deserts is important. Ever since the Sahelian drought in the early 1970s focused world attention on the process of desertification, there has been a tendency to think of it as the encroachment of desert. Sahel derives from the Arab word meaning "edge of the desert." As such, it is an apt description of the especially vulnerable arid zone of western Africa just south of the Sahara desert. But desertification is more than desert enlargement.

An example of this came in 1988 with a remarkable disclosure from the Soviet Union. Since 1956, to assist the raising of cotton on marginal land, irrigation water had been diverted from one of the main rivers feeding the Aral Sea, then the fourth largest lake in the world. The diversion progressively reduced it to a third of its size, and the exposed lake bed turned into a vast salt desert of several thousand square kilometers. The salt, driven hundreds of miles by wind, has in turn degraded vast tracts of farmland in a process of desertification.

The causes, of course, are to do with dryness and climate. But the experts are at odds over the degree to which climate, and in particular drought, is a decisive factor in desertification. The continuing debate now must accommodate concerns that prolonged drought in the Sahel, for example, may be a sign of long-term change to the climate as a consequence of the greenhouse effect. In this context, climate is a manmade factor in land degradation—one made by others than those who use the land.

T H E role of drought apart, there is wide agreement over the causes of desertification, which have to do with the way we have used the earth. They range from overcultivation of poor soil, overgrazing on fragile rangeland, excessive cutting of wood on dry land, and deforestation of upland watersheds to mismanagement of irrigation. None is wholly new. A notable example of manmade desertification comes from the beginning of human settlement. Mesopotamia, the once fertile region around the Tigris and Euphrates rivers, is known to us today as the cradle of civilization. The Sumerian civilization, the first recorded in the world, was nurtured there, as were the Assyrian and Bablyonian. They produced some of the world's first cities and combined urban development with a sophisticated system of agriculture through irrigation.

Few traces exist of those ancient cities. The transition from fertile crescent to desert landscape was one of progressive degradation caused by overuse and misuse of land, siltation of rivers as upland forests were cut down to meet the needs of urban populations on the plains, salinization of the soil from irrigation, and eventually the breakdown of the irrigation system itself. In *Far from Paradise: The Story of Human Impact on the Environment*, John Seymour recounts his visit in 1983 to the excavated remains of the ancient village of Magzalial, above the plains where the great cities were to rise, on a site in the high country of northern Iraq:

> I tried to imagine the countryside as it must have looked 9000 years ago. . . . It would have been wooded, with oak, pistachio, almond trees and probably many others; the ground would have been green beneath the trees because the mini-climate of a wooded area favours grass and herbaceous plants. It would have been comparatively cool and humid because the not-inconsiderable rainfall of that country, instead of all running away to the sea in gulleys and rivers, would have sunk into the well-covered ground and been taken up by the plants and trees and transpired back into the atmosphere. The river below us, instead of being virtually dry, would have been steadily flowing with clear water. . . . The people of the village would be engaged in collecting nuts and other tree fruit, hunting wild animals,

fishing in the river. Some of the women would have been hoeing small clearings of land to sow the seed of newly domesticated wheat and barley. Much of their stored grain would have been from wild grasses. Maybe some of the men and little boys would have been caring for small flocks and herds of newly-domesticated animals. Those people could never have imagined the howling wilderness, with its drought and dust storms, in which their successors drag out a miserable existence today. (p. 37)

Eight years later, in the aftermath of the Gulf war, the world was to catch a glimpse of that howling wilderness as Kurdish refugees sought escape beyond Iraq through that barren, desertified land.

So desertification is not new; yet something about it is. The process that turned a wooded countryside into a wilderness took thousands of years. There was time for other civilizations to rise; for the development of other ways to harness the earth's bounty. But, as with our treatment of the elements of air and water, so with our treatment of the earth: In a very short time we massively intensified our impact and quickened the pace of our assault. Once more, it is a matter of crossing the threshold of sustainability, with implications of worldwide significance.

The Fertile Crescent was a large area extending around the Tigris and Euphrates in a semicircle from Israel to the Persian Gulf. Now it is desert, and desertification is accelerating across the continents: in sub-Saharan Africa, the Middle East, west and south Asia, the western United States, and parts of South America and Mexico. Over the last fifty years some 65 million hectares of Africa south of the Sahara have turned to desert. In Mali, the desert has advanced 350 kilometers south in twenty years. In the Sudan it has spread 100 kilometers in seventeen. Over 100 million people in Africa are affected by desertification. Ten years ago the World Bank found that the northernmost region of west Africa was already unable to supply enough fuel wood and agricultural land to its people, and that seven entire countries there were approaching the limits of the earth's carrying capacity.

It bears remembering that the Sahel drought, which in the opinion of most experts continues to this day and will go on, killed between 50,000 and 250,000 people, about 3.5 million cattle, and countless sheep, goats, and camels. It is now even suggested that the drought signaled a return to the region's normal conditions after an unduly wet period in the early decades of this century. Despite unfavorable conditions, agricultural production has been rising in several Sahel countries, but—due to Sahelian poverty—population growth has been faster. The pressure of people on the vulnerable land has led to erosion, and at the height of the dry period, three times as much dust as normal, African topsoil, blew as far away as Barbados, 4,700 kilometers across the Atlantic. This is all now largely forgotten because it was yesterday's disaster. The Ethiopian famine is perhaps not yet forgotten, because of the visual impact it made on us through television. Ethiopia seems set to replicate Mesopotamia's fate. Its highlands, once rich and fertile, supported agrarian societies for millennia; in this century, more than 90 percent of the highland forests have been cut down. Every year, almost a billion metric tons of topsoil is washed away; an area of 20,000 square kilometers (the size of the state of Massachusetts) has already lost so much that it can no longer grow crops.

Desertification affects all three main types of dry land: rangeland (pasture), rain-fed cropland, and irrigated cropland. Nearly three-fourths of the world's rangeland is subject to desertification, and a significant amount turns to desert each year. A third of the total area of rain-fed cropland is dry land, and nearly half of this, amounting to over 200 million hectares, is also affected by degradation of various kinds. Nearly two-thirds of the world's irrigated area of 240 million hectares is also dry land. The productivity of over 40 million hectares is being reduced by the deterioration of the soil, mainly through waterlogging, which leads to salinization and/or alkalinization. An estimate made in 1991 reckoned that over 3.5 million hectares of rain-fed dry land and over 1 million hectares of irrigated dry land are going out of production each year because of soil degradation. It is believed that an area larger than these two combined of pastureland is lost each year.

F E W detailed estimates have been made of the costs to countries of dry-land degradation, but an idea of the impact it has on the economies of poor countries is given in a study of Burkina Faso, formerly Upper Volta, one of the Sahel countries. Made for the World Bank in 1990, the study reckoned the annual cost to the country in terms of fuel wood, crop, and livestock losses to be as high as 8.8 percent of its gross domestic product (GNP). Nearly two-thirds of the loss could be attributed to the reduced availability of firewood.

This information points to the place of firewood not only in domestic life but also in national economies in the Third World. In several African countries like Burkina Faso, wood supplies 90 percent of the total energy consumed. It is the main domestic fuel used by nine out of ten households for cooking and heating on cold nights. It is also the source of energy for several small village industries, used, for example, to burn bricks, bake bread, cure tobacco, brew beer, and dry tea. It is truly the fuel of the poor. Diminishing supplies of firewood bring discomfort to consumers and portend more acute hardship for those people in the dry lands for whom its collection and sale are the sole livelihood.

Overcultivation, overgrazing, overcutting of fuel wood, deforestation, land-use mismanagement—all explain why the land degrades to a desertlike state. But there are, at least in some cases of desertification, deeper causes, and they bear as well on responses and solutions. They will be explored in later chapters and are only mentioned here. A trio of interrelated factors—chronic underdevelopment, intractable poverty, and overpopulation—often lies behind the human conduct that brings on desertification. A UNEP survey in 1984 showed that desertification affected 70 percent of dry land in developing countries but only 40 percent or less in developed countries. No survey is required to demonstrate that the countries that suffer most from desertification are among the poorest in the world, far down the ladder of global influence. And within these countries, the people who suffer most are the very poorest. Desertification contributes to the growth in the number of the world's "absolute" poor, our planet's marginal people.

In the geography of hunger, the most prominent area is the Sudano-Sahelian region, which includes the dry zones of both west and east Africa and some of the world's poorest countries. It is no coincidence that desertification and related problems have affected the land and people of such countries so severely. Per capita GNP in Chad, Ethiopia, and Somalia was less than $200 in 1988. In Mali, Burkino Faso, and Niger it was between $200 and $300. In Mauritania and Sudan it was approaching $500, and only in Senegal was it higher. (In contrast, the U.S. per capita GNP was almost $20,000.) What such low average incomes mean is that large numbers of people live in extreme poverty and deprivation. With the number of people rising in the vicious spiral of poverty and population, the poor simply lack the means to increase food production without degrading land, for the only land they have is of the poorest quality and vulnerable to desertification. These GNP figures also indicate that the countries lack the economic resources to make an adequate response to such threats to human survival. Capital for investment in productive, sustainable agriculture is just not available, nor are the human resources, the skilled men and women to plan and carry out remedial land-use programs.

Compare this situation of helpless governments and powerless people with that in a rich economy. Poor land management of the vast dry lands of the Great Plains in the United States was a major factor in the Dust Bowl disaster of the 1930s, when much of the topsoil of Oklahoma and surrounding areas was blown into the Atlantic Ocean, as the Sahelian drought was to blow the topsoil of West Africa into the Caribbean forty years later. What followed in America, however, to the nation's credit, was massive mobilization of manpower and funds. The federal government's Soil Conservation Service and the Civilian Conservation Corps advised farmers and undertook soil conservation work, including the planting of shelter belts. The wheat yields of the Great Plains did eventually recover, and their recovery has been to the benefit not only of America but the world. But the cost of recovery was high, and no poor country could have afforded it.

Desertification need not be a terminal scourge. The knowledge and the resources, both human and financial, exist to prevent it being so. Until each of us pledges allegiance to the planet as we do to our own country, however, we are unlikely to mobilize as a world community to protect those 3.3 billion hectares of land under assault by desertification.

The world has gone through the motions of trying to mobilize. UN-COD was the unlovely acronym for a global conference that took place in Nairobi in 1977. The UN Conference on Desertification was prompted by the world's distress over the loss of life in the Sahelian famine of the early 1970s. The delegates to UNCOD adopted a plan of action whose goal was to end desertification by the close of the century. With nearly two and a half decades to go, this would not have seemed too ambitious a target. Indeed, given the extent of human suffering already visited upon the Sahel region, the conference could hardly have supported a more leisurely pace of action. But seven years on, UNEP's head, Dr. Mostafa Tolba, told a meeting of the organization's governing council that desertification had increased rather than diminished since UNCOD. He added that the goal of ending desertification by the year 2000 was no longer feasible. Today, seven additional years later, there is no reason to think the position has improved.

The well-intentioned plans drawn up in Nairobi have not been implemented. Starvation in Africa, though it has continued to evoke generous support for relief measures, has failed to bring about the action necessary to deal with its fundamental causes. The situation remains as Alan Grainger pointed out: "While the rich pay an economic price for their lack of diligence in taking care of the land, the poor (and their livestock) pay with their health and sometimes their lives." How many millions of our species have so far paid this price? How many more must join them before human society learns its lesson?

"THE sky is held up by the trees. If the forest disappears the sky, which is the roof of the world, collapses. Nature and man then perish together." These are the words of an Amerindian legend. The first people of Guyana, where I was born, are the Amerindian tribes, now 6 percent of the population and increasingly integrated into that country's multicultural society. Their age-old culture is precious to them and to Guyana, though the rest of us have been slow in acknowledging it. Like indigenous people everywhere they have enjoyed a close relationship with nature and still do. The legend about the sky and the trees is theirs. Their ancient culture was keenly aware that, in relations with nature, there are thresholds we must not cross.

Forests are a precious link in the life systems of our planet. They are a part of those vital ecosystem services without which Earth would not have been habitable by the human species in the first place and would almost certainly have become uninhabitable again. Forests have crucial roles in the carbon, nitrogen, and oxygen cycles that nourish and sustain life on Earth. They protect the watersheds that support farming and influence rainfall and climate. They save the soil from erosion. They are home to most of the world's species. They are home as well to hundreds of thousands of forest peoples whose lives, not just livelihoods, depend on an environment in which they have learned to live in harmony. They supply timber for construction, pulp for paper, ingredients for medicine, and raw materials for industrial products. They provide fuel for cooking in half the world's homes. One of the planet's life-sustaining assets, forests are now disappearing too fast for either our comfort or our safety.

Deforestation is as old as agriculture. We started to clear forests when we began to plant crops, herd animals, and lead a settled existence as farmers some ten thousand years ago. Clearing forests and planting and pasturing enabled populations to grow. With the rise in numbers and in demand for food, the rate of deforestation increased. Then further pressures arose: Trees were cut to provide timber for homes, for ships, for fenceposts, and for pit props in mines. When the industrial revolution started there was demand for charcoal for use in metal smelters, boilers, and ovens. So deforestation is not new; what is new is the total extent of Earth's forest cover we have now removed and the pace and manner of its current depletion, set alongside the vast increase of warming gases in the atmosphere caused by the use of fossil fuels. It is the question of thresholds again.

When we think and talk today of disappearing forests we tend to focus on the loss of tropical rain forests. This is understandable, for the clearing of tropical forests—which really began on a large scale only in the 1950s—is a modern phenomenon documented by the media and staggering in scale. According to *World Resources, 1990–91,* recent studies suggest that about 550 square kilometers of tropical forest are being lost each day. That is an area a little smaller than that of Singapore. There are technical difficulties in monitoring—and serious disputes about—how fast tropical forests are disappearing, but even the most conservative estimates place the scale of loss at a level that spells danger. Yet it needs to be recognized that limiting the focus to tropical forests distorts the wider picture of deforestation. That picture is relevant to charting a sustainable way forward.

The central element of that wider perspective is that, to date, by far the greatest destruction of forestland has taken place in the temperate regions of the world. Britain was covered in forest when the Romans conquered it some two thousand years ago. The elephants with which Hannibal crossed the Alps came not from central or southern Africa but from a forested area of north Africa that would be threatened not just by deforestation but by desertification as well. The United States is reckoned to have had nearly 950 million acres of forest when the first settlers came from Europe. By 1920, more than a third of that vast tract had vanished. Today, as much as 85 percent of the primary, old-growth forest has disappeared. While 70 percent of the original forest area remains tree covered, it is mostly with new-growth forest, a second-best successor. Most of today's cultivated and inhabited lands were once clothed in forest since appropriated to human use.

Well before the current onslaught, therefore, people in temperate countries had cleared their forests to expand agriculture and later for other purposes. And the loss of temperate forests, including rain forests, is far from over. In addition to the extensive destruction of trees caused by acid rain and other forms of air pollution in parts of North America and Europe, there is continuing clearance of forestland for farming as well as for logging, urban and suburban development, new highways, and mining and industrial expansion. According to data from the U.S. Department of Agriculture, the area under forest in the United States has shown a continuous decline since the early 1950s. Despite much expenditure and several programs to encourage reforestation, there was a net loss of 254,000 square kilometers of U.S. forestland for the ten years ending 1984.

The chainsaws of logging companies are particularly busy in the great temperate forests of Alaska and the Pacific Northwest, notwithstanding the vigorous efforts of American conservationists. Alaska's Tongass National Forest is the last significant area of temperate rain forest in the northern hemisphere. Home to the grizzly bear and the bald eagle, it is drained by rivers rich in salmon. The forest is their protective and bountiful habitat. It is so lush that acre for acre, the Tongass stores more carbon than the rain forest of the Amazon. The paradox is that even as voices are raised in the United States in strident condemnation of the Brazilians for allowing the Amazon to be exploited, American taxpayers are subsidizing the felling of trees in the Tongass. Many are several hundred years old; our chainsaws humble these magnificent specimens in a matter of minutes.

T H E reduction of forestland poses two main environmental dangers. Forests are great natural repositories of carbon. Trees breathe in carbon dioxide and store it, acting as carbon reservoirs or sinks. As such, they are invaluable agents in keeping the level of carbon in the atmosphere stable. As forests, whether in the Tongass or in the tropics, are destroyed, especially by burning, carbon dioxide is released into the air, adding to the stock of greenhouse gases that are now warming our planet and changing its climate. The obverse of this negative effect of forest loss on climate is the positive role of forests in regulating the atmosphere and climate through their life-support services.

Forestland is also the world's main storehouse of species—of the myriad kinds of plants, animals, birds, and insects with which Earth is blessed. Here there is a major difference between temperate and tropical forests. Tropical forests, in the central global band between roughly 10 degrees north and 10 degrees south of the equator, cover less than one-tenth of the world's land surface. But they teem with life and are host to nearly half Earth's biological species. They are the habitat of a bewildering profusion of plant life: trees and shrubs; climbers and lianas; epiphytes and parasites; lichens, moss, algae and fungi; ferns and orchids.

Alwyn Gentry of the Missouri Botanical Garden recorded 283 species of trees and 17 of lianas in just one hectare of forest in Peru and (with Calaway Dodson) counted 365 species of flowering plants on one-tenth of a hectare of forest in Ecuador—over 20 percent of the entire flora of Britain in 0.1 hectare of tropical forest. Ghillean Prance, director of the Royal Botanic Gardens at Kew in England, found 179 species of trees 15 centimeters or more in diameter in a single hectare of forest in the Manaus region of Brazil. As with plants and trees, so with other forms of life. Harvard biologist E. O. Wilson collected forty-three species of ants belonging to twenty-six genera from a single tree in Peru, almost as many kinds of ants as there are throughout Britain. Perhaps most crucial of all, tropical forests contain innumerable endemic species, species not found anywhere else on the planet.

Tropical forests are, therefore, treasurehouses of nature, as are the air and water and earth in general. They can exist only in a setting that values nature in all its diversity. To seek the preservation of tropical forests while continuing to harm the environment in other areas is to treat them not as treasurehouses of nature but as warehouses of carbon waste—industrial countries' waste.

Today the Third World hears a message from industrial countries about tropical rain forests that goes something like this:

> We consider that our essential role is to make our people more and more prosperous through industrial and post-industrial economic activity. With present systems and technologies, that means that we will have to go on using fossil fuels at least at today's level. We know that this can have serious consequences for all countries because of carbon dioxide's contribution to global warming; but we also believe strongly that it is in the interest of the whole world that we remain prosperous.
>
> It is necessary, therefore, that your role should be to preserve the tropical rain forests in your countries as storehouses for carbon.

Otherwise, there will be just too much carbon dioxide in the biosphere to avert major environmental disasters. In order to sustain our prosperity and protect the livelihood of those affected, we will, of course, continue to exploit our own temperate forests, including rain forests. All the more reason that yours should be preserved.

We have another interest in your not touching the tropical rain forests; we need to be able to exploit their rich biodiversity for the benefit of mankind as a whole.

We have given this matter much thought; we feel we must insist on the roles we have outlined above being strictly adhered to.

This is the message, sent in more convoluted language of course, that is reaching the developing countries at a time when prospects for their prosperity are receding. It is the injunction of the rich to the poor, and it is not being well received.

There are related signals received with equally little enthusiasm: that tropical forests should be considered global commons, an undefiled part of mankind's green treasury, and that the laws governing intellectual property should make it possible to secure patents for genetically modified plants (and animals), the genetic wealth of the forest commons becoming the private property of foreign biotechnology firms. There is invariably a postscript to this message: a reminder that failure to meet debt-service payments strictly on time can lead to serious consequences, as if there was no connection between export earnings from timber sales and debt servicing.

The problem lies, of course, in the failure of our world society to take a holistic view of the crisis of environment. In part, this is perhaps our intuitive recoil from multiple problems. We think it much better if somehow we adopt a case-by-case approach and then, from our narrow and selfish perspective, be selective in what we tackle, choosing first those problems that involve sacrifice or change mainly from others. As we found with the debt problem, however, in an interdependent world case-by-case solutions are largely illusory. Each case must be resolved within the framework of an overall solution. Such a policy framework is going to be essential to success in tackling the intertwined issues of environment and development, and nothing makes this more evident than the issue of tropical forests.

It would be tragic if, through failure to pursue it in a wider context, the problem of tropical forestland was to become a North-South issue mired in a bog of suspicion, recrimination, and ultimate stalemate. The alternative is for genuine understanding, mutual accommodation, and shared effort to lead to agreement on the question of deforestation within a framework of convergence on the wider survival issues posed by the environment-development crisis. Such an agreement is imperative, for the massive clearing of tropical forests could end in irreversible environmental damage too terrible to contemplate. One result would be large-scale species loss.

N o   o n e knows how many species of plants and animals there are in the world. So far, scientists have named and documented 1.4 million. Educated guesses of the total number range from 5 million to 30 million. It is part of the natural order that species become extinct; but we have by human action now speeded up the process by a factor as high, perhaps, as ten thousand. There is evidence of a few cataclysmic extinction spasms in the evolutionary past in which vast numbers of species were wiped out. The last of these, 65 million years ago, carried off the dinosaurs. There are fears that today's wave of species deaths may be even more sweeping than earlier ones. Some scientists believe it could result in the disappearance of one in four species by the middle of the next century. British ecologist Norman Myers thinks that in just ten "hot spots"—all tropical regions with high rates of deforestation— half the endemic species could disappear within a decade.

The diminution of Earth's biological diversity through species loss must concern us, primarily because wild plants are a vast genetic store we can tap to improve our food supply, extract new medicine, and develop other useful products. Our main foods—wheat, rice, maize, potatoes, sugar, and cocoa—were all first developed from wild species. We continue to turn to their wild relatives to raise the yields of cultivated grain species and make them more resistant to disease. Maize farmers have benefited immensely from *teosinte,* a wild species growing in Mexico that was found to resist most common diseases affecting maize. A wild coffee plant from Ethiopia has provided the genetic material to improve resistance to coffee rust in Latin America. Peanut farmers have profited from a disease-resistant gene found in a wild species of peanut native to the Amazon.

Wild plants have also aided in the fight against human disease. WHO estimates that 80 percent of people in the developing world, or 60 percent of the human race, rely on traditional medicine based largely on the use of medicinal plants. In the Indian subcontinent, for instance, the ancient practice of *ayurveda,* with its extensive range of plant-based medicinal preparations, continues to be widely popular. Forest-dwelling people are even more regular users of plant-derived medicinal products. In the last few decades the West's pharmaceutical industry has turned to tropical plants, including many used by traditional physicians, to extend its pharmacopeia. In the case of as many as three-quarters of the plant-derived drugs currently in wide use, it was forest dwellers who first discovered the medicinal value of the plants.

Examples abound of medicines, including some lifesaving drugs, whose ingredients have been taken from wild plants. The antimalaria drug quinine is made from a substance found in the bark of the cinchona tree of equatorial South America. The heart stimulant digitalis and the painkiller morphine come from plants. At the University of the West Indies in the Caribbean, the drug canasol, produced from the cannabis plant, has been successful in the treatment of glaucoma; this pharmaceutical development results from local knowledge of the plant's properties. The rosy periwinkle, native to Madagascar off the east African coast, has provided the main component of vincristine and vinblastine, drugs that have saved the lives of many sufferers of childhood leukemia and Hodgkin's disease, respectively. These two preparations are reported to have earned their manufacturer $100 million in income in 1985 alone. A University of Illinois researcher found that as many as a quarter of the drugs sold by prescription in the United States contain ingredients taken from plants. These medicinal preparations are said to bring in over $50 billion in worldwide sales annually. The U.S. National Cancer Institute has identified three thousand plants as having anticancer potential; two-thirds of them are in the tropics. So far, scientists have tested barely 1 percent of wild plants for medicinal properties, but the benefits have been enormous. How much greater must be the potential of the other 99 percent!

NEGOTIATIONS for an international convention to protect biological diversity have produced fundamental disagreements between industrial and developing countries. Differences revolve around the concept of access: access by high-technology Western companies to the plant and animal wealth of developing countries, and access by developing countries to the biotechnology needed to make commercial use of that wealth. Western governments maintain that they cannot force private companies to part with the technologies they own. "Neither can we ensure access to biological diversity from privately owned lands," developing countries reply. UNEP's Dr. Tolba has no doubt that the issues are connected. "Free access does not mean a free lunch," he says, "rather, it means fair compensation to the private sector holding intellectual property rights when it comes to technology transfer, and fair compensation to owners of genetic resources for providing their natural resources for the benefit of humanity."

The truth is that a convention that does not respect both the rights and the needs of the gene-rich but economically poor developing countries would constitute yet another inequity. For hundreds of years, industrial countries have benefited from the work of countless generations of farmers who have nurtured and improved plants and animals. Recompense for this invaluable service to humanity should be beyond haggling. But not only recompense is involved. Resources should be made available to help to maintain areas of extraordinary biological wealth and to assist developing countries in growing wild varieties essential for our food security. That would be an act of enlightened self-interest on the part of the few countries of the world that can afford to pay for it—an investment in survival.

In 1974 the director of the Max Planck Institute of Limnology in Germany, Harald Sioli, who devoted much of his professional life to Amazonia, wrote a preface to a technical volume on that subject that is, as he describes it, "a desperate supplication to save Amazonia and the last surviving aboriginal cultures in it." Its authors are Robert Goodland and Howard Irwin, both of whom share with me a Guyana connection and therefore an Amazonian one. At the beginning of their book, *Amazon Jungle: Green Hell to Red Desert?*, Sioli writes, "The evident destiny of our modern materialistic, mechanistic, technical, commercial civilisation, which began in Europe and thanks to cheap energy spread all over the world in an unbelievably short time, is to impoverish and destroy the diversity of life forms and life styles, natural as well as cultural, which have appeared and developed on earth during its long history." (p. v) There are many lessons here for us to learn and many insights to guide us as we forge a partnership to preserve Earth's biodiversity and ensure human survival.

THERE is another aspect of our behavior toward nature that has a bearing on the issue of biodiversity in its widest context, beyond the matter of species loss through deforestation. The trend of human modification of the biological world is toward simplification. The object of agriculture is to grow pure stands of crop plants to be eaten directly by us or by animals that in turn can be eaten. The logical result of this trend would be the removal of all life that competes with crops, leaving the planet inhabited only by people growing food. Efficient perhaps, but both dismal and lethally dangerous. A great principle that has emerged from scientific ecology is that the more complex the biological community, the more stable it is. The bewildering diversity of species in a rain forest and the intricate checks and balances among them may look inefficient and messy, but they ensure the stability and continuity of the system overall and thus contribute to the survival of each component kind. This understanding of scientists is being shared with ordinary people everywhere as television brings to the global public the story of nature in peril.

Just as the health of a nation is in the long run promoted by a diverse economy, so the health of the biosphere is promoted by a diverse ecology. The single-crop system is always precarious. It must be maintained and defended by a relentless barrage of chemicals and machinery, this artificial system hobbled with uncertain artifacts. Epidemic catastrophe always looms. A return to the Neolithic age with its stone tools and primitive farming is not the answer, for obviously the number of humans now on Earth and soon to come requires efficient agriculture and resource use. But long-term stability calls for compromises with nature, for instance hedgerows and wood lots next to fields and orchards, the promotion of a variegated land-scape leaving some leeway for the exercise of nature's checks and balances. It requires some surcease from the relentless man-only, bottom-line, price-tag perspective of economists and engineers; from the view that anything that might affect productivity in unknowable ways, or upset users of the playground, is a liability to be resisted; and from treating any process outside strict economic functions as an externality, however fundamental it may be to the stage on which the human drama is acted out.

Ethical, aesthetic, and practical reasons all argue for diversity as a paradigm, as a fundamental support for the platform of sustained yield. To promote ecological diversity and sustained-yield economics is morally the right thing to do. It is a formula proven over millions of years of natural evolution, the very process that brought mankind onto the world scene, and must replace once and for all the sanctified image of the human species as the all-conquering power.

T R O P I C A L forests are diminishing rapidly at the hands of mankind. Loggers, shifting or slash-and-burn farmers, ranchers, commercial agriculturists, firewood gatherers are all responsible, with their relative contributions varying from region to region. But a common factor is economic pressure, on individuals and on countries. Poverty drives the landless to cultivate land under forest, or forest just logged; the poor have no choice but to use firewood to cook their food and, in some countries, to keep warm. At the national level the need for foreign exchange to pay for imports of essential goods (and debt service in many cases) while adverse terms of trade squeeze export earnings forces countries to maximize income from their forests. When foreign exchange is desperately needed, timber or beef exports offer relief for a hard-pressed treasury. In a world that puts many obstacles in the way of poor countries, the threat to tropical forests cannot be separated from the economics of development.

No approach to the future of tropical forests will be successful in securing for the planet their life-sustaining ecological services unless it secures at the same time economic benefits for development. This calls for prudent, environmentally sensitive patterns of maintenance and management of forests as a source of timber, minerals, medicine, industrial raw materials, ecotourism, and so on. The challenge to both developing countries with tropical forestland and industrial countries that are the largest consumers of their output is to work out management principles that integrate ecological sustainability and accounting with economic, social, and cultural viability. It is a challenge that ought to engage us in a serious and sensitive search for the path to true conservation of tropical forests.

Since rural poverty, unequal distribution of land, and lack of export alternatives are behind most deforestation, the demand pressed by some well-meaning conservationists—though by no means all—for a ban on the import of tropical timber is hardly an enlightened approach. It ignores the harsh consequences for many communities. It ignores the scope for introducing programs of sustainable forestry with controlled exploitation of forest resources so that the interests of conservation are reconciled with the need to combat poverty. It also ignores greater causes of forest depletion: the cutting down of trees for fuel and slash-and-burn cultivation. These pressures cannot be eliminated by one sweeping gesture such as a blanket ban. Relieving them involves coming to grips with the fundamental question of poverty—reconciling the claims of economy and ecology. A call for a ban on timber imports by rich countries has a militant ring; it could be, however, a way of dodging the really hard issues that must be faced by rich and poor countries alike if we are to bring deforestation under control. We will be able to do so only through arrangements to share costs and benefits equitably over the whole field of environmental degradation. As the Intergovernmental Panel on Climate Change says in its 1990 report "Potential Impacts of Climate Change," "The forest crisis is rooted in the agricultural sector and in people's needs for employment and income. Deforestation will be stopped only when the natural forest is economically more valuable for the people who live in and around the forests than alternative uses for the same land." (p. 24)

IN THE book *Sustaining Earth*, to which both Professor Ghillean Prance and I contributed, he recounts a personal experience involving the "bush Negroes" of Suriname, Guyana's neighbor to the east. They are the descendants of escaped African slaves who resumed tribal life in the forests of Suriname and have maintained many of their ancient traditions. During an expedition a scientist asked one of these Surinamers to cut down a large tree for botanical specimens. He demurred, and eventually did so only after chanting a prayer that made it plain that he was not cutting the tree willingly and that the white man who had ordered it should take the blame for its destruction. Professor Prance commented in *Sustaining Earth*, "The trees of the forest have a spiritual value to the people and are not their own property to destroy. This attitude leads to better protection and a more prudent use of resources than in our society." (p. 59) Those were values from African culture, not so different from the Amerindian values that assert that the sky is held up by the trees and that man and nature will perish if this roof of the world disappears. Chico Mendes, the Brazilian rubber tapper who was murdered for his militancy in protecting Amazonia's "trees of life," was a part of both these cultures.

At the end of the last century, the naturalist James Rodway wrote a book about the rain forest that was called *In the Guiana Forest: Studies of Nature in Relation to the Struggle for Life*. In it is the following passage:

The interdependence of one animal on another, and these again upon the seeds of trees and even on flowers, is so close, that we can hardly conceive of their existing apart. Changes of environment in past ages have undoubtedly caused the extinction of numberless species, and from the naturalist's point of view it would no doubt be a great catastrophe were the South American forest even partially cleared. (p. 55)

How right he was, and not only from the naturalist's point of view. We need to live in harmony with the forests of Amazonia as we draw on their great resources in a sustainable way. That insight of "catastrophe" a century ago should motivate us still.

Nearly one hundred years later, in 1990, an internationally prominent Guyanese writer, Wilson Harris—born in my home town of New Amsterdam, in what was then British Guiana—wrote a mystical novel entitled *The Four Banks of the River of Space*. Here he envisions himself in a dream world revisiting the rain forest of Amazonian Guyana in the 1950s:

I came upon a Macusi woodman with an axe on his shoulder. He was—in the circumstances of my invisibility—unable to see me but I possessed the outrageous liberty of scanning his features and inspecting him from top to toe. There was a faint sweat in his eyes like a spider's web or the distilled breath of the river upon glass. He was sturdy as rock. His employment was to fell several acres of rainforest timber. A mere drop these were on my canvas of space that invoked the mid-20th century into which I had come. But one wondered how it would spread in the future. The rainforests were the lungs of the globe. Trees needed to be felled, yes, but the breath of the rivers and the forests was a vital ingredient in space. It was an issue of living contrasts interwoven by the soul of the dance through every monstrous desert that lay hidden in the coarse soil of place—deserts that had not yet happened in South America but which we could inflict on ourselves if we were not watchful and capable of attending to the voices of the dead in our midst. (p. 12)

Those monstrous deserts lie in wait for us if the forests of Amazonia are not given the security of sustainable development. In the sustainable development of the rain forest lies its health and the vitality of the people in it and around it—health and vitality that in turn will guarantee sustainability for the world. That will call for much imagination; for new concepts of paying for preserving the planet's life-giving services; and for what may now look like generosity but is in reality only recompense.

T H E ancients understandably saw the four elements as great forces of nature holding humans at their mercy. The elements were equal in the fury with which they asserted their dominion, whether it be fierce winds or tempestuous seas or upheaving earth or raging fire. But there always was a difference between fire and the other elements. For unlike air and water and earth, fire was inherently destructive; never inert, it could be humanity's benefactor only when its energies were controlled. Therefore harnessing the power of fire was crucial to human progress. Mobilizing energy to assist human activity has been man's primordial preoccupation for eons.

Some of the earliest records of human activity, like the fossils of Peking man that go back half a million years, are also among the earliest records of our use of fire. Some early peoples are believed to have used fire to help them hunt and probably to improve pasturage. Human use of fire certainly changed the pattern of Earth's vegetation over broad tracts of land in prehistoric times. In Greek mythology, Prometheus was the Titan who stole fire from Heaven for the human race. In the pantheon of the Greeks themselves, there was Hephaestus, the god of the furnace, of crafts, of industry, the god the Romans were later to call Vulcan. Human effort to harness energy to sustain life and make it progressively more tolerable and fulfilling has been a pursuit from time immemorial. But, as with so much else that we have considered so far, the energy story turned a new page when Europe embarked on its industrial revolution over two hundred years ago.

Coal, oil, gas, and nuclear power, in turn and together, have all been made to serve the objectives of industrial man and to contribute to some of his most notable achievements. Once again, there was no intrinsic wrong in our drawing on nature's resources to advance human welfare. We have sometimes used them, it is true, prominently so in the case of nuclear power, in ways that raise basic questions of legitimacy or at least of wisdom. In general, though, it is not a matter for complaint that we have turned the energy resources of the planet to human advantage. It is how we are doing so that is now profoundly disturbing, and increasingly inconsistent with our claim to superior intelligence. Quite apart from the question of depletion of nonrenewable energy resources, on which there is continuing argument, the scale on which we are using fossil fuels raises serious concerns for life on the planet, human life in particular. The consequences of that use for sustainable living on Earth compel us to pause and adjust in the interest of survival. Once again, it is a matter of going too far, too fast in our onslaught on nature, this time through the unconstrained use of fossil fuels: coal, oil, and natural gas.

G L O B A L warming is one of the few environmental concepts that readily tells its own story: The planet is getting warmer. But how, and why? And for those in colder countries, would the move toward longer summers be such a bad thing? The answers lie in understanding scientific codewords like *greenhouse effect* and *greenhouse gases* and less heavily coded ones like *climate change* and *sea-level rise*.

Greenhouses in which tropical plants are grown in temperate countries are artificial, protected, controlled environments; but some are less artificial, more effectively protected, and better controlled than others. The biosphere, the integral planet with its atmospheric canopy, has always been that better kind of greenhouse. We have seen that life forms were able to emerge on the planet only when the ozone shield developed in the stratosphere and filtered out the sun's malign radiation. But more was needed for life to flourish, something like a double-roofed greenhouse system to allow Earth to receive the life-giving energy of the sun passing through the stratosphere and to retain sufficient amounts of its warmth. This is precisely what our lower atmosphere does. It contains a mixture of gases that allow the sun's rays to pass through to the surface of Earth and, like the glass walls and roof of a greenhouse, keep much of the warmth in. Scientists believe that without this atmospheric greenhouse system Earth's temperature would probably be as low as $-18°$ Celsius, like the temperature on Mars, which has a negligible atmosphere and no life.

The water vapor and carbon dioxide naturally present in Earth's atmosphere absorb and block just enough escaping warmth to keep the planet at a comfortable average of $15°$ Celsius. These carefully balanced greenhouse gases act as the planet's finely tuned temperature control. If there were more greenhouse gases trapping more heat, the planet would get warmer, just as the greenhouse would if one closed its vent.

The principal greenhouse gas is carbon dioxide; that is also the principal gas emitted when we burn fossil fuels. As we burn more and more fossil fuel, we produce more and more carbon dioxide. We also add new greenhouse gases, like CFCs, which are compounds of our own making. Together these two groups of emissions, produced mainly by industrial countries, account for some 80 percent of global warming (what scientists call radiative forcing): carbon dioxide for 56 percent, CFCs for 24 percent, according to IPCC calculations. The concentration of greenhouse gases in the atmosphere is increasing and turning up the planet's temperature control.

S V A N T E Arrhenius was a Swedish scientist who won the Nobel Prize for chemistry in 1903 for his work on electrolysis. Environmentalists remember him, however, for having warned in 1896 that burning coal might release enough carbon dioxide to heat the planet. He predicted that a doubling of carbon dioxide in the atmosphere would lead to a rise in Earth's surface temperature of 4 to 6° Celsius. It was Arrhenius who coined the phrase the greenhouse effect.

The level of carbon dioxide in the atmosphere is generally calculated in terms of parts per million (ppm). For a thousand years prior to the industrial revolution the level of greenhouse gases was relatively constant. The increase thereafter was dramatic. When Arrhenius raised the first alert in the 1890s, the proportion of carbon dioxide had risen from its preindustrial level of 280 ppm to about 300 ppm. By 1950 it had risen to about 310 ppm. Over the last forty years, it has risen to about 350 ppm. If carbon dioxide emissions continue at present levels, its concentration in the atmosphere is estimated to rise more than 150 ppm above the preindustrial level by the end of the next century.

Carbon dioxide has been responsible for over half the enhanced greenhouse effect to date; there is every likelihood that it will be so in the future. For one thing, much of the damage is only reversible over very long periods. Carbon-dioxide emissions, like CFCs, are removed slowly from the atmosphere. The Inter-Governmental Panel on Climate Change in its report "Climate Change: The IPCC Scientific Assessment" warned that "even if all human made emissions of carbon dioxide were halted by the year 1990, about half of the increase in CO_2 concentration caused by human activities would still be evident by the year 2100." The longer the emissions continue to increase, the panel added, "the greater would reductions have to be to stabilise at a given level." (p. 11) The panel concluded "with confidence"—an unusual expression from scientists—that in order merely to stabilize concentrations of long-lived gases like carbon dioxide and CFCs at today's levels would require us to make "immediate reductions in emissions from human activities of over 60 percent."

Carbon dioxide accounts for half of global warming, and fossil fuels account for about two-thirds of manmade carbon dioxide. The consumption of energy from fossil fuels—coal, oil, and natural gas used for industrial, commercial, residential, transportation, and other purposes—results in such large emissions of carbon dioxide that the energy sector alone accounts for nearly half of global warming, 46 percent. Industry, through CFCs, accounts for almost another quarter, 24 percent. The remaining quarter or so of the blame is shared by forestry, through deforestation, and by agriculture, through methane from livestock and rice cultivation. With action to phase out CFCs already spurred by alarm over depletion of the ozone layer, it is clearly on the consumption of energy from fossil fuels that attention must focus if *Homo sapiens* is to face up to the implications of global warming.

AS NOTED earlier, fossil fuels contribute to other human assaults on nature, from city smog and acid rain to oil spills. Using fossil fuels more cleanly, efficiently, and sparingly, reducing our dependence on them, and turning to alternative sources of energy should all be human priorities even if there was no global warming to worry about. That there now is that worry is a clear signal of urgency that simply cannot be ignored, particularly by the world's largest consumers of fossil fuels: the industrial countries that, with less than a quarter of the world's people, burn 70 percent of its fossil fuel. The next chapter will address this question of the need for affluent societies, which have reaped most of the rewards of the industrial revolution, to set an example by accepting major adjustments in their economic behavior, adjustments that the very process of industrialization has now made the precondition of a tolerable future, if not indeed of survival.

Yet the problems of the rich in limiting wasteful consumption are nothing compared to those of the poor in overcoming underconsumption in a world bereft of ecological capital. Until quite recently, political leaders everywhere could indulge in the pretense that environmental issues were for tomorrow's agenda. That is what they all did after Stockholm twenty years ago. But that pretense will no longer hold. Tomorrow is here, rather sooner than expected, and environment and development have been pushed to the very top of the human agenda, which is why Rio de Janeiro will be the Earth Summit.

It remains to be seen whether realism and resolve, or piety and further pretense, will prevail at the summit.

Accustomed to seasonal weather changes of one kind or another everywhere on the planet, from summer heat waves in temperate countries to scorching spells of dry weather in the tropics, we may be tempted to dismiss global warming as another of the perennial quirks of nature. We would be as unwise to do so as those were who scorned Noah's biblical warnings about the flood. This time scientists have spoken out as seldom before, warning of the dire consequences of business as usual. They have been cautious in their judgments and circumspect about uncertainties; they have acknowledged gaps in their knowledge and the need for continuous monitoring and research. But they have asserted their basic conclusion about the reality of global warming with certainty, produced their basic calculations with confidence. And they have spelled out the consequences of our conduct to date and of its continuation.

Who are these scientists, and how have they come to speak out? Earlier I recalled that while the Brundtland Commission was working in the mid-1980s, global warming was still a small storm cloud on the environmental horizon and far from prominent on the commission's agenda. But scientists were beginning to worry. In October 1985, ninety years after Arrhenius's predictions of global warming, twenty-nine of his successors, scientists from industrialized and developing countries, met at Villach, Austria, to make "an assessment of carbon dioxide and other greenhouse gases in climate variations and associated impacts." They had been brought together by the World Meteorological Organization (WMO), UNEP, and the International Council of Scientific Unions (ICSU). A year later, in a report published by WMO, they estimated that if prevailing trends continued the combined concentration of carbon dioxide and other greenhouse gases in the atmosphere would be equivalent to a doubling of carbon dioxide from preindustrial levels, possibly as early as the 2030s, and could lead to a rise in global mean temperatures "greater than any in man's history." Global climate change, they concluded, was a "plausible and serious probability." In 1987 *Our Common Future* drew attention to these warnings, and the world, including governments, began to listen.

In 1989 a group of experts that I assembled at the insistence of Commonwealth governments, under Dr. Martin Holdgate, now director general of the World Conservation Union (IUCN), concluded in its report "Climate Change: Meeting the Challenge" that "global mean temperatures are increasing. By 2030 the world is likely to be warmer than at any time in the past 120,000 years. A best guess is that sea-level will rise by 17–26 cm by 2030. Tropical storms could increase." (p. 3)

In 1988, while the Commonwealth group was working, UNEP and WMO set up at the full international level the Intergovernmental Panel on Climate Change. The IPCC was required to examine how climate and sea level might change, what the impact of those changes might be, and what the most appropriate response to them was. Separate IPCC working groups tackled each of these three tasks. Altogether, some three hundred of the world's leading scientists convened in an unprecedented effort to bring the knowledge and intelligence of man to bear on the issue of survival of life on our planet. The results of the IPCC inquiry released in 1991 represent a massive scientific consensus on the danger of global warming and climate change, and on the action we must take to save ourselves. By then, the six warmest years in recorded human history had all been in the 1980s.

ON CLIMATE change generally, the IPCC's report "Climate Change" stated that in its best judgment if emissions of greenhouse gases continue to grow as currently projected (the business as usual scenario), global mean temperatures will increase at the rate of about 0.3° Celsius each decade over the next century, a rate of increase "greater than that seen over the past 10,000 years." (p. 2) This will result in an increase of about 1° Celsius above the present mean average by 2025 and 3° before 2100. One consequence would be a rise in the global mean sea level at a rate of about 6 centimeters a decade, about 20 centimeters by the year 2030 and of 65 by 2100. One of the possibilities would be a cooling effect from ozone depletion (despite increased radiation), which could provide "a small offset." Other possible side effects, like a decrease in carbon-dioxide absorption by warmer oceans, could worsen the scenario. Already the IPCC has noted that national forecasts of carbon-dioxide and methane emissions up to the year 2025 give 10 to 20 percent higher rates than in the business as usual scenario.

There are still skeptics, scientists among them; they cannot simply be dismissed. But most governments worldwide, no doubt on the advice of their own scientists, are now taking the threat of global warming seriously. The governments of the Western industrial countries, with the exception of the United States, have announced action to stabilize if not reduce their output of greenhouse gases over the 1990s. The need to save the ozone layer has prompted separate action to phase out CFCs.

Predicted changes in temperature may seem small, but in fact they are of a magnitude that could gravely affect the future of life on the planet. With the climate changes forecast for the middle of the next century, in the lifetime of many already born, and with global mean temperatures on the planet higher than they have been in the last 150,000 years, we are entering the danger zone. A rise of even a degree or two could have sweeping repercussions, altering patterns of rainfall, intensifying drought, raising the sea level, causing floods and storms, and affecting farming, the availability of food, and health. As worrying as the rise is its speed. Nature's way has been to bring about changes in world temperature of 1° to 2° Celsius over millennia; we have telescoped the period to a mere four decades. The change will be too sudden for ecosystems to cope—too fast, for instance, for trees to adapt to new climatic conditions or "move" to more congenial habitats.

Unless the effects of the accumulation of greenhouse gases are offset by other factors, the resultant warming will soon have unpleasant consequences for most, perhaps all, countries, and disastrous consequences for some. At some stage, for some regions, the impact would not be wholly adverse; warming could even create favorable conditions in some countries. Japan may be able to step up its output of rice and Britain to grow grapes that rival those of Bordeaux across the English Channel. But the process of warming would continue; neither Japan nor Britain, nor any other country, would be able to arrest climatic conditions at an acceptable level. In the long run there would be no winners.

Nor would the total worldwide effect be benign. In *Climate Change and World Agriculture,* Professor Martin Parry of Britain's Birmingham University, chief author of an assessment of the impact of climate change on agriculture made for the IPCC, says that with a temperature rise of 1° Celsius by the year 2030, total grain output from today's main producing regions would decline, with production in the United States being reduced by 10 to 20 percent. U.S. consumers would not run short, but as the United States is the world's largest exporter of cereals, the one hundred or so countries that depend on its surpluses to feed their people would be more vulnerable. Under such tight conditions, prices would surely shoot up. Where will that leave the poor countries? Professor Parry, in the clinical language of the scientist, writes of "the most severe negative impacts probably occurring in regions of high present-day vulnerability that are least able to adjust technologically." We can take this to mean that areas like the Sahel in Africa, whose people have suffered so long from drought and famine, have not seen the last of their troubles. The survival of many communities is on the line.

T H E future of other societies may also be placed at risk, not because global warming cuts food output but because of the rise of sea level as ocean waters expand with warming. A higher sea would threaten low-lying areas in many countries, rich and poor. If the sea continued to rise, even such cities as New York, Tokyo, Leningrad, and Melbourne would soon need to build expensive sea defenses. But well before that many countries far less able to take protective action would have large tracts of their most fertile land under water. China, Egypt, and Bangladesh, all populous countries, are among the most vulnerable. To the threat to Bangladesh from floods can be added the danger of cyclones, whose virulence was again demonstrated in May 1991. A rising sea level provides a higher base from which storms can unleash their fury. The cyclones and hurricanes of the future may still be called acts of God, but industrial man will have done much to render them more calamitous.

But it is smaller countries, particularly island countries, whose very existence is threatened by rising seas. Countries like Tuvalu and Kiribati in the South Pacific and the Maldives in the Indian Ocean may well disappear under the sea. If they do, if like many species they become victims of ecocide, it will be no fault of their own. Their contribution to the greenhouse effect and global warming is minimal. Their leaders have striven to alert the world community to the dangers that face them. I recall with what cogency President Abdul Gayoom of the Maldives, at a meeting of the leaders of the Commonwealth in Vancouver, British Columbia, in 1987, drew attention to the situation in which his country and its 200,000 people could find themselves. A week or so later, he articulated his fears to a wider assembly at the UN. Few of the Maldives' nearly 1,200 islands would be left if the sea rose more than 2 meters. To President Gayoom must go a large measure of the credit for the decision by the Commonwealth to commission a study on the likely impacts of climate change. The group's report, to which I referred earlier in this chapter, was one of the first authoritative contributions to the international dialogue about global warming.

Being submerged by a rising sea is the direst but by no means the only environmental calamity that could befall small islands. They are particularly vulnerable to environmental problems such as contamination of freshwater resources, saltwater intrusion, marine pollution, damage to coral reefs, mangroves, and fisheries, mismanagement of sewage and other waste, and mushrooming populations on limited land. Global warming could inflict a host of problems on such countries. Those dependent on one or two crops, as many are, would be highly vulnerable to climate change, and the costs of adapting would be extremely high. The loss of land and salinization would increase dependence on food imports. Tourism, which is predominantly shore-based, would be an early casualty of sea-level rise. Many islands in the Caribbean and the Indian and Pacific oceans are already susceptible to hurricanes that cause massive damage, and warming could make them more frequent and severe. One disability of being small is the difficulty of effective representation in international organizations and negotiations, and it is therefore encouraging that, in an effort to protect their interests on environmental matters, thirty-six countries have joined forces under the Alliance of Small Island States.

Another country that faces the prospect of enormous dislocation in the event of a sea-level rise is my own, Guyana, on the northern edge of the South American continent. Almost as large as Britain, Guyana has only 750,000 people. Most would be at risk if the sea were to rise even half a meter. The Dutch and later the British who colonized Guyana used thousands of African slaves and Indian indentured laborers to protect low-lying land from the sea before planting the sugar that made Guyana an imperial asset. It would be a cruel twist of fate if the dilapidated seawall of Guyana's polders were now to overflow because in Holland and Britain, and elsewhere in the industrialized world, the affluence to which sugar contributed introduced patterns of fossil fuel consumption that eventually caused the seas to rise in the distant Caribbean. Guyana's legacy from the forced labor of our ancestors would be lost forever.

We must choose the kinds of responses that would counteract such tragedies. The world needs energy consumption that moderates global warming while enabling per capita income to grow in the Third

World. As the Commonwealth report on climate change concluded, "If room is to be left for adequate economic growth, particularly in developing countries, effective action to halt the greenhouse effect requires a much more stringent approach to energy conservation and a greater emphasis on non-fossil fuels." (p. 102)

I N T H I S matter of energy, the human species has played with fire and is finally getting burned. When the ground offensive in the Gulf war started, I was in the Caribbean. Historical continuities were inescapable in the context of the 1992 commemoration of five hundred years since the first people of America found Columbus on the beach at San Salvador, which is how many people in this hemisphere insist on projecting the occasion. In their obsessive exploitation of the riches of the Americas, Europeans believed that they had a right to the region's commodities, which they considered vital to the prosperity of their countries. That same obsessiveness was there in Saddam Hussein's grab for Kuwaiti oil and his self-righteous assertion of entitlement to it. A not dissimilar sentiment lies behind Western preoccupation with the oil resources of the Middle East, considered by the West to be vital to its prosperity and, therefore, to be secured from jeopardy at all costs. And long before the Gulf war there was the Suez crisis, which also had its origins in the obsession with oil. The obsession was there even earlier in history, with other commodities in place of oil. In the post-Columbus era, European powers went to war with each other over the gold and silver and sugar of the Americas. The irony is that the black gold on which we have predicated national prosperity is the commodity above all others that in man's hands threatens his survival.

Which raises an intriguing point: In the pantheon of the ancient Greeks, Hephaestus, the god of industry, was the only one who was physically flawed. He was the lame god. That suggests something about the record of human industrial activity, mighty as we like to think we are, and in no respect more so than in our sequestering of nature's bounty of energy. "After the fire, a still small voice," says the First Book of Kings, concluding its description of elemental upheaval. At this hour we ought to see ourselves as entering a time of crisis, and to listen closely for that still small voice of truth.

PART THREE

Causes

FOUR

$$\dot{\nmid}$$

The Profligate Rich

The world knows that the few are more than the
many.   — *Rabindranath Tagore*

R A B I N D R A N A T H Tagore's collected aphorisms were first published under the title *Fireflies* in 1928. The line quoted above could
have been composed much earlier, at the turn of the century, and yet it
continues to portray reality even as the twentieth century moves toward its close. This chapter is about the rich on our planet who are
few, yet in so many ways more than the many. It is about what the few
have done in their majorities of wealth and power to endanger Earth
and the habitation it provides for rich and poor alike—the few and the
many.

This chapter, like the others in Part Three, is more about people than
their countries. When we think about the profligacy of the rich or the
powerlessness of the poor, when we explore the implications of population growth or the relations between rich and poor countries, people
must be at the center of our thoughts. Countries are the social, political, economic, and cultural settings in which people function, yes.
They provide governance for societies and for relations among those
societies. And inevitably national labels dominate the statistics that try
to convey a comparative picture of the state of the world. Our mold in
the twentieth century is the nation-state. Yet that mold could be a trap
locking us into a mind-set of separateness no longer as relevant to the
issue of survival as it once was to the issue of subsistence.

Nowhere are separate worlds more evident or of greater significance

89

than in the division between people who are rich and people who are poor. It is the impact of people on the planet and its resources that is the cause of environmental stress. If we are to relieve that stress, our responsibility is to change the lives of people, the lifestyles of both the rich and the poor. In an increasingly democratic world, moreover, it will be people more than governments that make governments act; and among the rich everywhere there are many friends of the Earth who swim against the tide of consumerism and reach out toward a vision of one world.

"Caring for the Earth: A Strategy for Sustainable Living" is an authoritative report on the current crisis of environment and development by three respected organizations: the World Conservation Union, UNEP, and the World Wide Fund for Nature. It sends a stark message about the challenge that lies ahead:

> We depend on the resources of the Earth to meet our basic and vital needs; if they are diminished or deteriorate we risk that our needs and those of our descendants will go unmet. Because we have been failing to care for the Earth properly and living unsustainably, that risk has become dangerously high. We are now gambling with the survival of civilisation. (p. 4)

In urging on all people a strategy for living sustainably rather than gambling with survival, the statement emphasizes that civilization is at risk because we are misusing natural resources, disturbing natural systems, and pressing Earth to the limits of its capacity.

IN THE last hundred years alone, industrial production has risen more than one hundred times over, and in that time the world's population has grown fourfold. The more we are, the greater is our impact; whether we will be too much for Earth to bear depends on how much each of us adds to the total load, particularly how much each of us contributes over and above an acceptable norm. Human impact on the planet is the sum total of the energy and raw materials each person uses or wastes.

The Oxford English Dictionary defines the word *consume* as follows: "To make away with, destroy, as by fire, evaporation, decomposition, disease; to waste, succumb; to use up, esp. to eat up, drink up; to take up, spend, waste (time); to waste away, to burn away." *Consumption* is most apt for describing human activity's impact on the biosphere. While it is the industrial process that visibly degrades the environment, the root cause of degradation is the demand for the products of that process. Consumption fuels demand, demand drives industry, even though industry is what initially gives rise to the culture of consumption. In looking at Earth's threatened environment, therefore, we must pay greatest attention to patterns of consumption. It is as consumers preeminently that the world's few are more than the many.

The statistics tell a revealing story, particularly about those aspects of human consumption that cause the most grievous damage. The consumption of energy is the most crucial, and it illumines the wider picture. Poor people whose only source of energy is firewood obviously use far fewer resources and have a much smaller environmental impact than those who can afford fossil fuels. Today, as few as 25 percent of the world's population account for 80 percent of its consumption of commercial energy—a quarter of the world's people consuming four-fifths of its energy from fossil fuels and hydro, nuclear, and geothermal power. The remaining 75 percent, living in 128 countries, consume only 20 percent of commercial energy. The rich in a high-energy country consume eighteen times the commercial energy used by the poor in a low-energy country. It is those few high-energy consumers, by and large in industrial countries, that account for the bulk of the environmental destruction caused by the use of fossil fuels. Each North American causes the emission of at least ten times as much carbon dioxide as someone living in Asia, excluding Japan.

It cannot be too strongly emphasized that the people of affluent societies impose these massive pressures not only on national but also on global environmental resources, and not because they are numerous but because they are prodigal consumers. Their impact on the biosphere can be lowered only by reducing their per capita consumption of energy and other resources. Unless this distortion is acknowledged as the unacceptable face of twentieth-century civilization, we will waste much precious time attending the symptoms of the disease and fail utterly to come to grips with its real cause.

The broader pattern of resource consumption is as skewed as the statistics for energy indicate. In *Far from Paradise: The Story of Human Impact on the Environment,* Herbert Girardet paints a graphic picture of the imbalance. Reflecting on "the amplification of man" by industrialization, Girardet writes:

Without fossil fuels we would be different creatures. The harnessing of fire in the steam engine, the steam turbine and the internal combustion engine put at our disposal a motive force which has transformed human impact on this planet. A man with a pick and shovel is a different creature from a man who operates a bucket-wheel excavator. Standing next to each other without their equipment they may look the same but in ecological terms they are as different as a mouse and a dinosaur. . . .

In 1980, every American consumed nearly 26,460 lbs, or 12,000 kilograms, of "coal equivalent." West Germans consumed about half that amount, Kenyans used 440 lbs and Ethiopians consumed 55 lbs per capita. An American uses a thousand times more oil than a citizen of Ruanda. . . . These figures do not only reflect different living standards but also different scales of ecological impact.

If all countries in the world were to reach the production levels of the USA or West Germany, the global ecological consequences would be ruinous.

The overall demands of an American throughout his lifetime are sixty times greater than those of an Indian.

Americans consume nearly a ton of grain per capita per year, Africans eat one eighth that amount. Every German has as much land at his disposal in another country to yield food for him as he has in his own country. Cassava is imported from Thailand, maize from the USA, groundnuts from Niger where hunger and starvation are rife—most of this is used for feed in pig and chicken units. . . .

Around 40 percent of world cereal production is used to feed livestock and in the richer countries this figure can be as high as 75 percent. In fact, in the USA 90 percent of cereals used in the home market go into animal feed. (p. 157)

What such inequalities reveal is the degree to which the rich have sequestered resources over a wide geographical range. Wherever humans toil beyond the needs of their own subsistence, they are probably toiling to satisfy the vast appetite of the rich. Women plucking tea leaves in Sri Lanka, farmers loading bananas in Jamaica, loggers cutting forests in Indonesia, miners extracting copper in Zambia, fishermen trawling for tuna in the Pacific—they and their companions who garner Earth's bounty labor in the vineyards of the rich. Granted, there are vineyards in the rich countries as well, and their people also labor to feed that appetite. Even without urging ethical judgments, some conclusions are inescapable.

Our distorted consumption patterns threaten the future of the human species, not to mention other life forms. It is an obscene proposition, but it is no exaggeration. If that is not to happen, if human survival is to be secured, the big consumers must curb their appetite. There will be obligations of many kinds on all people, but this is the precondition of a sustainable future for humanity and its central mandate. So let us look more closely at some aspects of consumption by the few that have a particular bearing on environmental degradation and the survival of us all.

Identifying the most clear and present dangers that threaten sustainable living is not difficult. Nor need it be contentious, unless one is dealing with those who say there is no danger at all. The main drawback to making a priority list of environmental problems is the ever-present possibility that other hazards lurk undetected in the wings, like ozone depletion and global warming when the first UN Conference on the Human Environment was held in 1972. Today that list must include, besides global warming and depletion of the ozone layer, Earth's endangered biodiversity, industrial pollution in its many forms, and the crisis of poverty with the related issue of population. Poverty is inextricably linked to the imbalances in global consumption. But first we should explore other threats to sustainable living and examine to what extent it is valid to complain of the profligacy of the rich.

T H E pressure of the rich on the resources of the planet is comprehensive but perhaps most intense in relation to global warming. Over three decades of detailed measurement at a carbon dioxide monitoring station in Mauna Loa, Hawaii, have established the continued and now accelerating rise of atmospheric carbon dioxide levels, which have grown by more than 25 percent since the industrial revolution, with half this increase occurring in the last thirty years alone. Seventy percent of the global output of greenhouse gases comes from the industrial world. Industrialization is obviously the main source of greenhouse gases; but it is instructive that among industrial countries per capita emissions vary considerably. In Canada and the United States, two of the most energy-intensive countries in the world, the rate is twice that of Japan and Europe.

As indicated in the previous chapter, the IPCC concluded that merely to stabilize long-lived greenhouse gases at today's levels requires "immediate reductions in emissions from human activities of over 60 percent." That is itself a measure of how profligate the industrial world has been in its consumption of resources, especially energy. But the real profligacy is in the consumption of the wide range of goods and services that energy is used to produce.

Much of that consumption has a direct impact on the environment. The extracting of natural resources, the generation of waste, pollution of many kinds—these are some of the culprits, but it is the decisions of people in what is called the final consumption phase that ultimately drive them. The people of the OECD nations—Western industrial countries, including Japan and Australia and New Zealand— constitute most of the 25 percent of the global population who consume most of the world's commercial energy. From 1970 to 1988, a period that was one of economic decline for the people of many developing countries, average consumption spending in major OECD countries increased by almost 80 percent. It is expected to continue growing. The consequences of this "massive and ever increasing consumption"—as the OECD itself describes it—is there to be seen in the impact on the planet's resources.

According to OECD calculations, the average person in a rich country now consumes natural resources at an annual rate up to twenty times higher than the average person in one of the poorest countries. He or she consumes around 120 kilos of paper compared with 8 kilos in a poor country, and around 450 kilos of steel compared with 43 kilos. Energy consumption in OECD countries is twelve times the Third World average.

W O R R Y I N G as all this is, it is the love affair with the automobile, whose numbers are rising faster than the human population, that leads to the most damaging excesses of consumption. Today, motor vehicles account for about a third of global oil consumption. In OECD countries they represent over 40 percent of oil consumption; in the United States, which pioneered the automobile revolution and leads the world in oil imports and carbon-dioxide emissions, over 50 percent. Not surprisingly, motor vehicles account for a quarter of all carbon dixoide arising from the use of fossil fuels in the United States. It is worth noting that the United States, Canada, Western Europe, and Japan together consume well over half the oil produced in the world each year, but themselves contribute less than a quarter of the world's supply.

While their own petroleum deposits get smaller, industrial countries are recording steadily rising consumption levels. Over the period from 1970 to 1988, motor vehicle fuel consumption in industrialized countries increased by 61 percent, bolstered by a rise in road traffic of 86 percent and a growth in the number of vehicles of 94 percent. Road transport, which accounted for 34 percent of oil consumption in 1970, was responsible for 48 percent by 1988. The growth in the number of cars is a key indicator of consumption trends. In the eighteen years between 1970 and 1988 the number of passenger cars in use doubled in Western Europe, multiplied by one and a half times in North America and by three and a half times in Japan.

The increase was slowest in North America; but in this region that has always had the highest distribution of automobiles to people, it was enough to bring the ratio up to 56:100, or more than one car for every two persons. The average for the whole OECD group was 39 cars per 100 people, or three in five households having a car. At 8 cars per 100 people, the world average for automobile ownership is about one-fifth that of the developed countries.

And now, despite all the evidence of the role of carbon dioxide in global warming, projections for the future give no indication of any real constraint in consumption. In 1950 there were 53 million cars on the world's roads, 76 percent of them in the United States; by 1988 there were over 400 million. By 2010, the number is expected to rise to 885 million and by 2025 to exceed 1.1 billion. Two-thirds of those vehicles will be in Europe and North America. A graphic description of the result in terms of energy use was given in the *Toronto Star* on 3 October 1991: An average of 33.4 million liters of gasoline was consumed each day in the province of Ontario alone, equivalent to the amount of water flowing over Niagara Falls every twelve seconds.

One would expect the low rate of population growth in affluent countries to have a moderating influence on this particular example of expansion, but that expectation is being neutralized by two trends. One is that now many moderately wealthy families have more than one car; everywhere in the developed world the number of multicar households is increasing, and the three-car garage is no longer rare. The proportion of multicar households is highest in the United States.

France occupies a middle position in the car ownership league of industrial countries, and there it is estimated that as many as one in five households has more than one car.

The other trend is that while human numbers may be steady or rising very slowly in rich countries, the number of households is definitely increasing. The trend is toward smaller and more numerous households, with one-parent and one-person households becoming a significant part of the social profile. This phenomenon, which appears to be intensifying, has implications for sales of most durable goods and certainly of motor vehicles. Inevitably it is leading to a faster rate of growth in per capita automobile ownership. And the multicar family is not a phenomenon confined to the developed world, whose consumption patterns and lifestyles are models for the rich in developing countries. Public policy must make it possible to meet transportation needs in such a way that this compulsive drift to automobile proliferation is arrested worldwide.

That there can be a measure of constraint, a brake on profligate consumption, was demonstrated in the mid-1970s, which many in the West remember as the period of the energy crisis. From an environmental perspective, it would have been better had the situation been seen as an environmental catalyst. In reaction to oil price increases in 1973 and 1979, and the security and economic risks they underlined for nations heavily dependent on Middle East oil, significant technological improvements were made in the energy efficiency of motor vehicles. As a result, average energy consumption per car was markedly reduced. As the oil market eased, however, and the sense of crisis and dependency receded, the drive to raise efficiency and conserve oil was abandoned. Growth in road traffic and in the stock of motor vehicles soon wiped out the gains made in the 1970s through improved efficiency. This experience was repeated in industry generally. Improvements in energy intensity, that is, the amount of energy used to produce one unit of gross domestic product, markedly slowed down during the 1980s, and the use of energy continued to climb. Over the period from 1970 to 1988, although the index of energy intensity fell 25 percent in the industrial countries as a group (with significant national variations), aggregate energy consumption went up 25 percent.

In *Driving Forces,* their important study for the World Resources Institute, one of the conclusions James MacKenzie and Michael Walsh draw from the experience of the 1970s and 1980s in the United States and Europe is that "the dual goals of improved fuel efficiency (and therefore lowered carbon dioxide emissions) and lowered pollution emissions are complementary rather than antagonistic." But it seems necessary for rich countries to return to a climate of high crisis before they recognize the need to suppress their appetite for oil. Today there are noticeable shifts in car buyers' preferences for larger models in Japan and Europe. The passion for large cars is, of course, a distinctively North American trait. Time was when this could be looked at as a pardonable eccentricity, like ten-gallon hats and other such indulgences beloved of frontiersmen in a wide-open country. But times have changed, and the sooner that is recognized and reflected in lifestyles the better for our planet.

Meanwhile, the U.S. predilection for large vehicles seems to find its most extreme expression in the recreational vehicle (RV). This is proliferating at a faster rate than the conventional automobile. RVs are motorized homes on six wheels in which more and more American families are taking to the road, and adding to congestion. They cost more, and are perhaps more comfortable and better equipped, than some American homes. The number of RVs on U.S. roads is expected to top ten million soon, with almost half a million being bought each year. Sales are helped by the fact that RVs are taxed at a lower rate than some cars costing much less. Additionally, because they are considered homes, RVs qualify for tax relief on interest payments.

The World Resources Institute report recommended specific approaches to reducing threats to the environment from petroleum-powered vehicles. It called for further improvements in fuel efficiency and efforts to encourage such improvements, including mandatory fuel standards and carbon taxes on fossil fuels. Other recommendations were to make transport systems more fuel-efficient through greater reliance on van and car pools, buses, trolleys, and trains; to develop nonfossil energy sources for vehicles by building on promising technologies for auto engines powered by electricity and hydrogen; and to reduce other greenhouse gas emissions from motor vehicles, for example by eliminating the use of CFCs in automotive air-conditioners.

"CARING for the Earth," the report I referred to earlier in this chapter, also made recommendations for action to reduce excessive consumption and waste of resources. Going beyond motor vehicles, it emphasized the development of resource-efficient methods and technologies, the imposing of taxes on energy and other resources in high-demand countries, and the encouragement of green consumer practices and movements. The resource taxes (including a carbon tax) it proposed are designed to replace existing taxes and to be consistent with the "user pays" principle: the more you consume, the more you pay. The tax would really then be a tax on profligacy. Particularly in the context of global warming, which threatens human survival, it is difficult to think of a more appropriate impost.

We know in our minds what we ought to do; what constraints, in particular, the world's big consumers of energy ought to accept; what changes they ought to make in lifestyles that endanger future generations and life itself. And action produces results. In the 1970s, when the United States, Canada, and Scandinavian countries took unilateral action to ban the use of CFCs in most aerosol spray cans, they did what they knew needed to be done, even though others were not yet ready to follow. It has now been estimated that had they waited for universal action, CFCs would now be a larger cause of global warming than carbon dioxide—besides, of course, causing far graver damage to the ozone shield. That is the kind of leadership that is needed from rich countries, consistently and over a wider field of resource and energy issues.

Heavy consumption, besides putting pressure on resources of all kinds, produces monumental amounts of solid waste: more than 30 million kilos in Tokyo, 14 million kilos in New York, and 9 million kilos in Paris every single day. CFCs in aerosols, additives in food, lead in gasoline (now almost eliminated in the United States and Canada) are but a few of the harmful substances unleashed at the stage of final consumption, with escalating impact on the environment. And consumption patterns are changing generally for the worse. In the last two decades, for example, the use of prepared food increased to such an extent that packaging now accounts for almost half of household waste in industrial countries. It has meant an increase in metals, plastics, and other synthetic materials that are difficult to dispose of, to collect, or to recycle. Western consumption of packaged products found artistic expression in pop art. Its arch-apostle, Andy Warhol, made icons out of American household objects such as soup cans and steel-wool cartons—images that were themselves "consumed" at sky-high prices by the consumption society's upper crust. It is significant that pop art spanned the boom years of the 1960s and early 1970s, before consumer confidence was punctured by the rise in oil prices.

The most conspicuous consumption, increasingly being mimicked by the rich in poor countries, is of what economists call durable goods: refrigerators, washing machines, television sets, video recorders, microwave ovens, and so on—all consumers of energy. Not only is their stock growing, so is the rate at which they are disposed of. Obsolescence—encouraging waste—has long been pressed into the service of marketing. Now, as state-of-the-art products succeed each other at dizzying speed and with serious implications for waste disposal, it is assuming alarming proportions. An article by Victor Lebow in the mid-1950s, quoted in *It Is a Matter of Survival* by Anita Gordon and David Suzuki, gives sobering credibility to the concept of "forced consumption": "Our enormously productive economy demands that we make consumption a way of life, that we convert the buying and use of goods into rituals, that we seek our spiritual satisfactions in consumption. . . . We need things consumed, burned up, worn out, replaced and discarded at an ever-growing rate." (p. 186)

Waste, therefore, is not merely industrial; it is engendered by the everyday life of home and office. The Nobel Prize–winning German author Heinrich Böll has brilliantly satirized the culture of waste in his story "The Thrower-Away," about a man whose bourgeois appearance hides the fact that he is employed simply to dispose of the huge quantity of surplus envelopes and paper received daily in an office building. The thrower-away estimates that, in the useless waste of the globe, "energies are dissipated which, could they but be utilized, would suffice to change the face of the earth."

The disposal of waste is becoming less and less manageable, with worldwide consequences. The early 1980s saw the NIMBY ("not in my back yard") syndrome in full swing as industrial countries tried to export their hazardous waste, usually to poor countries. The 1989 Basel Convention on the Control of Transboundary Movements of Hazardous Wastes and Their Disposal, spurred into being by deplorable clandestine attempts to dump hazardous industrial waste in developing countries, has begun the process of addressing the problem as a global one. But it is only a beginning; there is a long way to go before this offshoot of the consumption culture is effectively capped. Meanwhile, the scale of the waste problem is seen in the figures. In 1990, there was 9 billion metric tons of solid waste to be "managed" by OECD countries. Of this, 420 million metric tons was municipal waste and 1.5 billion industrial waste (including over 300 million metric tons of hazardous waste); the remaining 7 billion metric tons included residue from the production of energy and from agriculture, mining, demolition, dredging, and sewage. And this is to say nothing of non-solid waste released into water and the air.

W H I L E waste on Earth, at least, has received considerable attention, waste in outer space, particularly manmade space debris, has been neglected. That form of pollution, apart from the emissions caused by putting satellites into orbit, is considerable and rapidly accelerating. Many satellites with a restricted operational life will remain in space for hundreds of years. Of some eighteen thousand objects launched by 1986, over six thousand are uncontrolled, free-floating debris. In their study *The Pollution of Outer Space, in Particular of the Geostationary Orbit,* G.C.M. Reijnen and W. de Graff make the following point:

> A very serious form of space debris has been formed by the practice of the major space-faring nations to launch nuclear-powered short-lived satellites (about three months' life-time), which after comple-tion of their mission are manoeuvred into a special "storage orbit," highly radioactive as they are, and remain there, in principle for-ever. . . . Present and future space operations are, therefore, threat-ened by space debris of many sorts.

It sounds absurd to talk of congestion in space, but this is now the reality in at least one respect. The geosynchronous orbit is the band of space above equatorial countries. It is now heavily occupied by the satellites of those technologically and financially equipped to place them there. Substantial questions of equity are arising; but by the time these are resolved, or today's developing countries acquire the capa-bility of using the orbit above their heads, all the available slots will have been preempted by the satellites or debris of others. Already, as seen from outer space, the crowded geosynchronous orbit is producing an Earth version of the rings of Saturn, only less benign.

T H E truth is that genuine conservation of resources through a reduc-tion in consumption by people who have the financial capacity to consume much has scarcely ever been attempted, except by societies whose resources were diverted to a war effort. Diversion was accepted as necessary because the alternative was capitulation to a worse fate. Today, rich countries have courted that worse fate because they have the resources to head it off.

Reducing per capita energy and resource consumption in countries where it is high is absolutely essential, and it must begin now. There has been some reduction in per capita consumption of commercial energy, but mainly in the poorest countries in sub-Saharan Africa and Latin America. To appreciate just how absurd such a situation is we must understand how little energy their people use to begin with. Commercial energy is measured in units called gigajoules; the average annual per capita consumption in the world is 56 gigajoules. This global average hides vast differences among countries. To take a sample of countries, average per capita consumption in the United States is 280 gigajoules; the Netherlands, 213; the former USSR, 194; Britain, 150; France, 109; Brazil, 22; China, 22; India, 8; Nigeria, 5; and Tanzania, Ethiopia, and Mali, 1. It is in countries like Ethiopia and Mali, where energy use is startlingly low, that consumption has been reduced. It has been reduced, in other words, because of their poverty.

Energy is the driving force of industrial civilization. As the figures cited above demonstrate, there is a clear link between a country's level of energy use and its prosperity. Energy is crucial to promoting economic growth, increasing national wealth, and improving the quality of life. The expansion of agriculture and industry requires energy. Energy is needed to move goods from farms and factories to markets and consumers. Energy is also a vital ingredient in programs to provide housing, spread education, raise standards of health, and even moderate population growth. The extent of energy use is therefore reflected not only in a country's economic vigor but also in the well-being of its citizens as measured by such indicators as life expectancy. Countries whose use of commercial energy is low are invariably chained to the bottom rungs of the development ladder. Developing countries should be able to increase their use of energy and thereby end deprivation for millions of their people. At the same time, the health of the planet requires that growth in the world's consumption of fossil fuels, the main source of commercial energy for the foreseeable future, be restrained. If both objectives were fulfilled, the consumption of energy in the industrial countries would obviously decline. Population growth complicates the issue. In the best possible scenario—not the likeliest—

world population will stabilize at around double its present size, that is, at around 11 billion. At that level of population, if all the people were assured of, say, 75 gigajoules, half the average consumption per person in Britain today, global consumption would rise nearly three times the present level. That gives a measure of the problem.

An average consumption of 75 gigajoules is hardly extravagant if the people of countries like India and China, Haiti and Mali, are to lead tolerably comfortable lives while protecting their ecosystems and diversifying their economies. But if poor countries are to use that much energy, rich countries must bring down their own consumption. This is the magnitude of the challenge the world's overconsumers face, but which all humanity must together meet. In later chapters I will examine the responses that are possible and probable.

And there is another side to overconsumption, namely, depletion. Fossil fuels were created over the vast stretch of geological time out of the remains of prehistoric life. They are finite resources. It is one of the most telling commentaries on the nature of our voracious oil consumption that humanity is now burning every twelve months as much fossil fuel as nature took about one million years to produce. The planet still has enough known reserves of coal to last another two hundred years at present rates of consumption, but its proven oil and natural gas reserves are thought to have a much more limited life. The oil industry does not admit to this, and further reserves will no doubt be discovered and exploited as scarcity drives prices up and makes a gold mine of marginal reserves. Even so, it may be a close finish between warming ourselves to extinction through excessive fossil fuel consumption and exhausting the supplies of fossil fuel that now feed our appetite.

IN THE search for ways to counter global warming, much attention is being given to the importance of maintaining tropical rain forests. It needs to be remembered that much of the deforestation is driven by the consumption demands of the rich. Japan accounts for more than 53 percent of the world's tropical hardwood trade; wood is its biggest import after oil. The United States accounts for 15 percent, with demand expected to double by the end of the century. Europe as a whole accounts for 32 percent of the hardwood trade. But hardwoods are also being turned into more humble pulp, again to meet the consumption needs of the rich. The World Wide Fund for Nature's *Atlas of the Environment*, from which I have drawn information for earlier chapters, reports that a single Japanese company is transforming a rich rain forest in Papua New Guinea into packaging for cameras, calculators, and other electrical goods. For reasons already given, a ban on the hardwood trade is not the answer; in this, as in so many other areas of environmental stress, it is our market-driven consumption that lies at the heart of the problem.

But what of other resources besides timber from our forests? "Consumption Patterns: The Driving Force of Environmental Stress," a 1991 study for the UN Conference on Environment and Development made by the Indira Gandhi Institute of Development Research, documents the level of consumption in various countries over a wide range of products: food, raw materials, and industrial products. In cereals, for example, the annual consumption (both human and animal) is 716 kilos per head in industrialized countries and 246 kilos in others. The rich consume on average over three times as much as the poor, but the actual difference can be much larger (cereal consumption ranges from 800 kilos per head in Australia down to 130 kilos in Africa). A quarter of the world's people consume half of its cereal production, while the other three-quarters manage with the other half, some of which, livestock feed, ends up as meat products on the tables of the rich.

In milk and meat, both key sources of protein, the distribution is even more unequal. For milk, the average annual per capita consumption figures are 320 kilos in the rich countries and 39 kilos in the poor, with a quarter of the world's people having 70 percent of the milk. With meat it is much the same: 61 kilos in the rich countries, 11 kilos in the poor. In China, milk consumption is as low as 6 kilos per person, and in India (where cultural factors are relevant) meat consumption is 1 kilo per person per year.

"Consumption Patterns" also looks at the consumption of forest products (excluding firewood and wood used for charcoal), and found the shares for developed and developing countries in almost direct inverse proportion to their populations: 78 percent for the developed countries with 24 percent of the world's population, 22 percent for developing countries with 76 percent of that population. Per capita consumption of products such as plywood, particle wood, and veneer is 213 kilos in the rich countries and 19 kilos in the poor. Paper and paperboard made from wood pulp, and therefore requiring much more processing and energy input, are consumed at the rate of 148 kilos per person in the rich countries and 11 kilos per person in the poor, with industrial countries accounting for 81 percent of total use, and all the others for 19 percent.

In manufacturing, the study looked at industrial products required to fulfill the needs of food and housing and found consumption to be equally lopsided. With their larger populations and relatively less land, developing countries might be expected to use fertilizer in large amounts to meet food needs. In practice, their annual use of fertilizer works out to a mere 15 kilos per person, while in developed countries it amounts to 70 kilos. A quarter of the world's people use 60 percent of its fertilizer; the other three-quarters get by on 40 percent.

In the case of concrete, the basic material for housing, average consumption runs to 451 kilos per person in rich countries and 130 kilos in poor. Again, the differences between given regions can be larger. Africa's consumption of concrete is a meager 78 kilos per person, whereas in the former USSR it was as high as 485 kilos and in Europe is 477. World consumption of iron and steel is 80 percent for industrial countries and 20 percent for the rest. For a range of other metals and minerals, including copper and aluminum and some inorganic and organic chemicals, consumption is even more unbalanced, with 85 percent being taken up by industrial countries and just 15 percent by the others.

"Consumption Patterns" goes on to say that it would be tragic if in the name of environmental concern the economic growth of countries whose people consume so little should be disrupted. This point of view deserves to be considered seriously. The authors of the study do not, however, end on an uneasy note but rather on one of hope: "If we act well and wisely with charity, this is an opportunity to 'green' the earth. For earth's sake let us do that."

W H I L E the industrial countries' heavy use of fossil fuels pushes poor and rich alike toward an environmental abyss, consumption of other kinds adds momentum to the process. As we have seen, industrial activity tries both to create and to satisfy the appetite for food or metals or durable goods or automobiles or clothing or any of the innumerable products we have come to think of as necessities by the standards of the consumer society. The planet is struck twice—through resources that are directly consumed, and through those that are degraded or rendered unusable and end up as waste. It all goes back to consumption, and it needs to be added to the bill.

In recent years, air pollution leading to global warming and ozone depletion has received so much attention that it has obscured some of these other attacks on the environment. A few we have already looked at, like acid rain, ocean pollution from oil spills, and the disposal of sewage or hazardous waste. There are other less familiar forms of pollution that pose special dangers. UNEP has found, for example, that a wide range of pollutants has affected the Mediterranean. To the north are steelworks and chemical factories pouring effluents into the sea, while the whole coastal region, including parts of the south, is dotted with leatherworks, paper factories, and other polluters. Together, they put over 30,000 tons of toxic metals, including lead and mercury, into the Mediterranean each year, along with over 90 tons of pesticide residue and other pollutants. Mediterranean fish pack so much pollution that some are unfit for human consumption. The Mediterranean is a critical case because of geography; pollutants entering it do not have a larger ocean in which to wash away. Detailed study of other seas indicate that all industrial countries are dumping into them severe loads of toxic metal and pesticides.

Some of the industrial activity directed to meeting the needs of consumers in rich countries takes place in the Third World, conducted mainly by multinational entities operating offshore, as it were, and expecting to be less "hassled" by environmental regulators than in their home countries. Offshore also describes some of the resultant pollution. The Atlantic off West Africa now contains lead, cadmium, chromium, cyanide, fluoride, and a variety of other pollutants deriving from the production of aluminum, steel, and other metals mainly for use in OECD countries. Most of these pollutants enter the ocean in highly concentrated form, doing maximum damage. The picture is the same in the Indian and Pacific oceans, the Caribbean, and the South Atlantic.

Some of the pollution is caused by agricultural chemicals like DDT, once a salvation pesticide for contributing to the eradication (or so it was believed) of malaria, but now banned in many developed countries. Several such toxic chemicals are still aggressively promoted in poorer countries, often by local subsidiaries of multinationals based in the industrial world. The message of Rachel Carson's *Silent Spring* about the harm done by pesticides like DDT remains as compelling as in 1963; the setting is now wider.

I N D U S T R I A L I Z E D agriculture in OECD countries delivers some of the fiercest ecological blows. High agricultural productivity has fed industrial growth by supplying cheap food and also removing people from the land for employment in industry. The movement from farm to factory was at the heart of urbanization. But productivity cannot be measured only by the reduced human effort needed to produce food. It calls on other hands and other inputs, like water, fertilizer, pesticide, and fuel. The environmental effects of this amplified labor force are seen at their most stark in the use of fertilizer. UNEP estimates that in the twenty years between 1968 and 1988, world fertilizer use increased from 56 million to 139 million metric tons. In 1988, North America used 23 million metric tons. Europe used 32 million metric tons. The whole of Africa accounted for under 4 million metric tons.

The effectiveness of fertilizer in raising agricultural yields is beyond question. It has been a key to farming success in the industrial countries and in developing countries like India, where the green revolution has applied the methods of the North: new high-yield crop varieties, a large input of water, pesticide, large farms, and mechanization. But the very effectiveness of fertilizer encourages environmental overloading. Nitrates and phosphates destined for crops end up washed into rivers and seas. There they encourage biological productivity so that water weeds (one of the worst is the water hyacinth) and algae proliferate, using up oxygen needed by other plants and organisms. Nutrients also find their way into water courses or percolate into aquifers through the effluents of food factories like those processing meat products. One way or another, fertilizer residue is now causing serious damage to coastal waters of developed countries, for example in the Baltic and the North Sea off Scandinavia and Western Europe.

Like modern fertilizers, the pesticides used to kill weeds, fungi, and insects that harm crops can be highly effective. But often their victims are not only the ones targeted. Measured by the active ingredient that does the killing, over 2 million metric tons of pesticide a year is used worldwide. Of this, 585,000 metric tons is expended in Europe and 428,000 metric tons in Canada and the United States, while the whole of Africa uses only 67,000 metric tons, about as much as Australia. Pesticide has been detected far from the plants and insects it was meant to kill. Some pesticides, such as organic chloride types, were banned in industrial countries after being identified as having harmed fish and birds, both directly and by reducing their ability to have healthy young. The same contaminants have turned up in the breast milk and flesh of humans.

A really deplorable aspect of this matter is that not all pesticide use is directed at increasing the land's productivity. Some of it serves purely cosmetic purposes, such as lawn upkeep. The average West Indian has known over the centuries that the speckled banana is the tastiest there is. Consumer preference in Europe and America dictates, however, that bananas sold there must be unblemished, with no brown specks on their skin. So a massive amount of pesticide is showered on banana farms throughout the tropics. The result is more and more pesticide poison piled up in the tropical environment, and larger exports of pesticides from industrial countries.

B U T the impact on the environment of the drive to meet voracious consumption does not always take so obvious a form. Where the consumption of the rich is concerned, the whole world is their oyster, and their oyster is free for the taking. Nowhere is this better illustrated than in the massive "species subsidy" that the rich world has appropriated in recent centuries from the poor, subsidies of the kind that the pharmaceutical industry has drawn from tropical species, but subsidies too in the form of crop plants, including potatoes, beans, and corn, which are now staple foods for rich and poor alike.

In his profound and engrossing book *Seeds of Change*, Henry Hobhouse demonstrates how five products—sugar, tea, quinine, cotton, and potatoes—have determined the fate of millions of people from the rise of the Atlantic slave trade to the opening up of China, from the building of early colonial empires to the greening of America. The book is, as well, a history of how the biotic resources of the tropical world have been pressed, sometimes cruelly, into the service of the rich.

Today there are new revolutions in the making, prominent among them biotechnology. For centuries people all over the world used breeding methods to produce new plants and even, sometimes, new animals. These methods were slow and successful only when the animals or plants were closely related; and because they were slow crossbreeding did not exert undue pressure on the environment. Biotechnology shortcircuits old methods of crossbreeding by making it possible, at least in principle, for desirable genes to be transplanted between widely different species and even between plants and animals. This raises serious moral questions that will tax us in the years ahead.

One thing, however, is certain: Biotechnology cannot create the genes that it reshuffles according to the technologist's design.

The developing world's reserves of genetic material are essential for the biotechnology industry, which is dominated by multinational corporations. The Third World is aware of the issues at stake in what it sees as the further usurpation of its natural resources, and these issues will arise insistently for two reasons: The companies are aware of the huge potential for profit in these resources, and developing countries are determined not to be further exploited. Some tropical products like cocoa butter and coffee, for example, are priced not for their nutritional value but for their flavor, a property largely deriving from genetic content. There are already synthetic cocoa butters, but poor flavor limits their commercial success. In *Miracle or Menace? Biotechnology and the Third World,* Robert Walgate explains how Japanese, American, British, and Dutch firms are working to produce realistic artificial flavors like those of cocoa and coffee through isolating and engineering the genes that produce them. If they succeed, the economies of Malaysia, Brazil, and several west African countries for which cocoa and coffee are an important source of income will be seriously threatened. Another example is Thaumatin, a sweetener which is a thousand times as effective as sugar. It has already been patented for industrial use in the countries of the North. The people of Nigeria from whose land the plant that provided the original extract came will get little or nothing.

Our science and technology, our genius, must be harnessed to an ethic of equity if human society is to survive. At present, industrial countries, in their approach to intellectual property rights, show little appreciation of such an ethic. The firms that produce new animals or plants insist that they are artificial creations and should be patented like mechanical inventions. The genes that go into them, they say, are part of nature's gift to the planet and cannot be anyone's property. This is how it was of old, from the days of the quinqueremes of Nineveh. But genetic resources, after all, are like oil. While every part of the world has at least some genetic gold, most of it is concentrated in a few areas. Like the oil-rich states in the early stages of oil production, countries with genetic resources were unable to translate their native products into wealth for their own betterment. They were exploited by absent landlords. This pattern must not be repeated as we move into the new era of biotechnology.

T H E rich have already stripped their lands of any biological diversity they once had, and ruthlessly destroyed their animal life. Large animals like the bison were threatened with extinction when modern agriculture spread across the American Great Plains. They became victims of the consumption culture of the new people of the continent, having survived thousands of years alongside the first Americans. Indeed, in most of the industrialized world there are relatively few large wild animals left. The same is true of birds and plants. In *The Expendable Future: U.S. Politics and the Protection of Biological Diversity*, Richard Tobin has shown how in California, despite its extensive wild preserves, six hundred species of plants are in danger of extinction, and how Hawaii—a rare case of a developed-world island in the tropics—has suffered a higher rate of loss of distinctive bird and plant species than other areas in the world. Rich countries have been inordinately destructive of nature at home. They now turn to the rest of the world under the license of intellectual property rights. That, at any rate, is how it is perceived in the developing world, which is striving for a global view but finds itself thrown more and more into defensive national postures, guarding turf when it ought to be joining the industrialized world in acknowledging the planet as our country and its people our fellow countrymen.

The appetite of the rich for animals, sometimes to the point where the survival of entire species is threatened, is well illustrated by the example of whales, highly intelligent mammals with an ability to communicate with each other over large distances by means of a complex language. While they have long been hunted by some non-technological peoples like the Inuit of North America, the numbers these people want or need are too small to imperil the species. Whales are rather endangered by industrialized whale hunting, which is still carried out, in particular by Japan. That country has persisted in chasing down whales long after most of the world decided that it was both morally repugnant and unnecessary for the food it yielded. Whale oil, the product for which whales were first hunted, was pushed out of the market by petroleum, but the habit of consuming whale meat persists. It is considered exotic for humans and is even used as a component of pet food.

The 1991 meeting of the International Whaling Commission (IWC) decided to allow Japan alone to kill up to seven thousand Minke whales a year in the Antarctic, although in practice it is likely to kill far fewer. Still, whale meat turns up in restaurants with a high price tag. It is even possible that whaling will be resumed on a commercial scale in the North Atlantic, with threats by Iceland to quit the IWC unless it is allowed to kill greater numbers. In any event, commercial whaling is likely to be permitted once whale populations rise 54 percent above their levels before whaling began. The whaling nations think a threshold of 30 percent is enough.

One of the worst examples of pillaging the sea and its inhabitants is the use of high-technology drift-net fishing by deep-sea fleets. Even in waters as remote as those of the Falklands and South Pacific, fish stocks have dwindled because of overfishing; the chance of a proper diet for those living nearby is reduced as fish are removed for consumers in Europe, Japan, the United States, and the former Soviet Union. As well as catching fish, massive drift nets several kilometers long scoop up everything in their path. They are blamed, along with oil pollution—but probably with more justification—for a severe reduction in the numbers of large animals in the sea. In 1991, round-the-world yacht crews were issued forms to describe the dolphins, whales, flying fish, and other species they encountered. Some came back with sheets of paper as blank as the waters they had sailed, a radical change for the worse in just a few years.

The rich world's demand for the large animals and exotic plants no longer found within its own borders has given rise to a $5 billion a year trade. According to the World Conservation Union, that trade includes at least 40,000 primates, 1 million orchids, 4 million wild birds, 10 million reptile skins, 15 million fur pelts, and over 300 million tropical fish each year. The main demand comes from Europe, Japan, and North America, but the rich in a few developing countries add to it.

The demand for wild animals, for food, clothes, and other uses, has already made some species extinct, the bulk of these extinctions occurring, indeed, in prehistoric times. Several other species—various turtles, the great whales, and the larger land animals such as rhinoceroses and elephants—remain under threat, both from loss of habitat and wholesale killing. The threat to the African elephant comes from both causes. Long a prime trophy for hunters, the elephant was placed in acute danger primarily by the demand for ivory, the material of its tusks. Total numbers were halved between the 1970s and the late 1980s, and healthy elephant populations remained only in the forests of the Zaire basin and in some of the countries of southern Africa. A 1989 ban on the trade in ivory appears to have eased the immediate pressure, and in those southern African countries with large and growing elephant populations there is a call for a relaxation of the ban. Most of the countries with large elephant populations have severe economic problems and would benefit from the hard currency that elephant ivory and leather would bring. Intelligent, humanitarian, well-managed culling could have reconciled the needs of these countries with the interests of conservation. But it is clear that the unrestricted killing of elephants, in response to the demand for ivory, had gone so far that, as in the case of whales, there had to be a ban to save the remnant populations of the species over much of Africa. Tourism, which offers a less deadly way of appreciating the elephants, may eventually produce as much hard currency for countries with elephants as the sale of ivory would. Nevertheless, the pressures of growing human populations and their need for land to cultivate imply that the human species and the African elephant will remain on a collision course.

IN RECENT decades deep concern has been aroused by predictions that the consumption demands of the developed world would extend into two parts of the planet with no native human populations, the continent of Antarctica and the deep sea. Under the Antarctic Treaty, which came into force in 1961, countries agreed to ban nuclear and military activities in the region and to cooperate on scientific research. There are now thirty-nine treaty signatories, including developing nations like India, which carry out research and share in decisions about how to regulate activity in the area. Even science in the Antarctic is not completely clean; there have been oil and waste spills and other undesirable impacts, and controversy over the building of major facilities like runways. In recent years, greater environmental awareness and pressure from environmental groups have had a beneficial effect.

Concern for the protection of the environment and the conservation of unique Antarctic species has mounted dramatically between 1985 and 1990. This concern led to the agreement in 1991 of a new protocol to the Antarctic Treaty. Under this protocol, mineral exploration and exploitation is excluded for fifty years and tighter measures will be introduced to control logistic activities, the disposal of waste, the construction of installations, and the management of scientific research. At the moment the only commercial activities in the Antarctic region are the harvests from fisheries in the surrounding seas and tourism. Harvesting is governed by an international convention that demands the safeguarding of the ecosystem as a basic condition of activity, and tourism is itself subject to guidelines that are likely to be tightened under the newly agreed protocol. A comprehensive conservation strategy for Antarctica has been prepared by IUCN—the World Conservation Union—which is now cooperating with governments and the scientific community to review how particular areas of Antarctica might best be protected.

It is important that this protection remains. The fifty-year ban should be made permanent and pressure for that should be unrelenting. The Antarctic is a fragile region where environmental damage is slow to heal. Even though the bacteria in Antarctic waters are adapted to life in the cold, decomposition processes, including the decomposition of oil, are much less rapid than in warmer climates. The new measures, especially the moratorium on mineral development, are welcome, but they will succeed only if the commitment of the entire world community to safeguard the last of the world's great wilderness areas is reinforced.

The conservation of Antarctica needs to be a worldwide effort, not just the preserve of a minority of nations. If the present achievements can be built on and governance democratized, Antarctica could be a model for a new global consensus, and for the whole process of enlightened change. If that scenario fails and minerals are discovered in the area, the pressures for their exploitation will increase and human greed will once more imperil sustainable living on Earth. The recent agreements have provided a breathing space, not long-term certainty. What might appear as a virtuous decision perhaps owes much to the fact that many geological expeditions have so far revealed little of vital economic interest in the southernmost Antarctic, just some coal and iron ore but no oil, diamonds, or precious metals.

There have also been long-laid but so far unimplemented plans to mine the bed of the world's deep seas. Some areas of the ocean floor are known to be littered with what are often called manganese nodules, although they contain other metals as well. What is less well known is just what else goes on in these waters. Collecting nodules would require a sucking or scraping action that would disturb the whole sea floor. As in the Antarctic, any damage would take millennia to repair itself. In addition, exploiting the nodules would have a severe effect on developing countries dependent upon metals for their export earnings. Countries that might suffer include Cuba, the Dominican Republic, and Indonesia, which are leading producers of nickel, one of the main nodule metals, as well as Zaire, Zambia, Chile, and Peru, important producers of copper.

As with mining in the Antarctic, deep-sea mining has been the subject of long negotiations, in this case in the context of the Law of the Sea Convention. An arrangement by which profits would be channeled from seabed mining to world development was proposed; this would have treated seabed resources as global property to which the poor were given prior claim. But rich countries like Britain, the United States, and Germany would not go along with that idea. Low metal prices have cooled this dispute for the time being; mining companies see no way right now to make money by vacuuming the seafloor for metals. But the rich world's approach confirms that environment and equity, and the need to develop and respect principles governing shared resources of the global commons, are secondary to maintaining the consumption-fed flow of raw materials and money.

The attitude of the rich, technologically advanced countries to the Law of the Sea Convention does not inspire confidence in the prospects for global management of the resources of the planet for the good of all its people. The convention was the culmination of a nine-year process of international negotiation, the most ambitious attempt ever to provide for the international management of a part of the global commons. Its conclusion in 1982 with agreement on an integrated management regime for the oceans was a major step forward for the international community. One hundred and fifty-nine countries signed the convention.

Besides confirming the 12-mile territorial sea of coastal states, the convention establishes Exclusive Economic Zones of up to 200 miles; in these zones coastal states enjoy the right of management of natural resources, living and nonliving, in water, seabed, and its subsoil. But the convention's path-breaking achievement was to recognize that part of the seabed and its resources that lies beyond national jurisdiction—over 45 percent of the planet's surface—as international, the "common heritage of mankind." All mining activities in this area would be controlled by an international seabed authority. It is this aspect of the convention that has been opposed by a solid phalanx of powerful industrial countries.

In 1989, the UN secretary-general called for full recognition of the importance of the convention "for the progressive development of international environmental law and the formulation of more effective management strategies" and "as a valuable precedent for global agreements on other environmental issues and a fund of basic principles and obligations that could be applied equally well to such global issues as protection of the atmosphere and climate." Two years earlier, in the Brundtland Report, we had urged that "the most significant initial action that nations can take in the interests of the oceans' threatened life-support system is to ratify the Law of the Sea Convention."

As of October 1991, only fifty-one countries had ratified the convention, nine short of the sixty needed to make it official. No leading industrial country is among the fifty-one, and only Iceland and Yugoslavia from Europe. All the other ratifications are by African, Asian, and Latin American countries. The United States has specifically said that it is unlikely to ratify the convention, because it does not like the arrangements for international management of the common seabed. Even in respect of what should be treated as the common heritage of mankind, some rich countries assert the right of exploitation for their own benefit. Implicit in that assertion is the right to take without measure the planet's resources, to consume nature's bounty without let, or hindrance, or thought of sharing.

B Y F A R the most voracious of human appetites is that fed by military spending. Militarism is consumption of a special kind, with its own culture, its own accounting, and even its own governance. So unique and separate is this human activity that we tend to ignore it when reflecting on our daily lives and, in particular, when assessing the impact of humanity on the biosphere. And yet the whole complex of global military activity constitutes a more massive consumption of natural resources than any other single activity of our species. It is not a new phenomenon. When Horace wrote over two thousand years ago, "We are just statistics, born to consume resources," he would have had much in mind the militarization of the Roman Empire and the military culture that had been a feature of Greek civilization. That culture has changed; the emphasis has shifted from ironclad warriors on the battlefield to computerized warriors in command and control centers with nuclear explosives their ultimate resort. There are fewer military men today than military weapons, and the level of consumption has risen steeply.

Nearly fifty years ago we deceived ourselves into thinking that that level would come down, that we had learned the lesson that the pursuit of security through military arsenals placed human survival itself in jeopardy. That thought was to fade quickly; indeed, it was so subordinated to "rational" doctrines of deterrence as to be wholly ignored. At the height of the cold war, global militarization lost any such claim to rationality as it raced past levels that could be defended on grounds of deterrence. All the firepower expended in World War II, vastly destructive as it was, amounted to no more than 6 megatons of TNT. According to Ruth Sivard in *World Military and Social Expenditures, 1991,* the stockpiles of the six nuclear powers represent, despite recent reductions, an explosive force 1,600 times the total firepower released in World War II and the Korean and Vietnam wars. A single Trident submarine packs 24 megatons of destructive power, or four World War IIs. Two atomic bombs were dropped in 1945; despite all the negotiations on disarmament since then, the United States and the former Soviet Union together had 22,846 strategic nuclear warheads in 1990, according to data from the Stockholm International Peace Research Institute. With the START treaty in place, that number should come down to 19,500 by the year 2000. In addition to these strategic nuclear warheads and their remaining delivery systems (land-based intercontinental ballistic missiles, submarine-launched ballistic missiles, and long-range bombers), there remains a multitude of nonstrategic nuclear warheads and their delivery systems as well as a host of conventional weapons.

Now there are further developments. President Bush's dramatic announcement on October 4, 1991 of unilateral cuts beyond START, and the Soviet response, will bring down arsenals further. That is universally welcome. But the limitations cannot be ignored. *Time* magazine (October 7, 1991) summed up the initiative: "Bush's essential purpose is to accelerate the retirement of some of the Soviet Union's most advanced military programs while protecting key elements of the U.S.'s 'strategic modernization': the B-2 Stealth bomber, the Trident II submarine missile, and a scaled-back version of the Star

Wars antimissile defense." It was neither President Carter's dream about the "elimination of all nuclear weapons from Earth" nor even President Reagan's faith in a pure defense system that would render nuclear weapons "impotent and obsolete." Largely because of what remains intact—for example, continued funding for experimental weapon systems like the B-2 Stealth bomber, for the Strategic Defense Initiative, and for the modernization of existing systems—it is acknowledged that the Bush plan does not save money. The plan discouraged discussion of a "peace dividend" and did not cut into the military consumption culture.

What effect will the disintegration of the USSR have on these levels of American militarization, assuming it does produce substantial demilitarization in the republics of the new Commonwealth of Independent States? Certainly we must hope for an acceleration of reductions on both sides, but we need to be mindful of the factors working against it. The military-industrial complexes, particularly those in Western countries, can be expected to resist major reductions in resources for defense notwithstanding the disappearance of the old rationale for military budgets and nuclear arsenals. Already the prospect of such reductions has produced claims that a cutback in defense expenditure will severely disrupt economies and stoke unemployment. Major industrialized societies have been building prosperity on the consumption of resources for increasingly unusable weapons of destruction, to the point where keeping production going becomes a desirable, even compulsive, objective in itself. The military culture has spawned economic structures that in turn generate incentives, even imperatives, for further militarization. There is yet no reason to believe that overall militaristic consumption is about to be dramatically curtailed despite the claims of both necessity and opportunity.

In his timely and erudite book, *On a Hinge of History: The Mutual Vulnerability of South and North,* Ivan Head, reflecting that the age-old aim of civil government is "freedom and security," reminds us how in the nineteenth century the American poet James Russell Lowell warned against imbalance: "He who is firmly seated in authority soon learns to think security, and not progress, the highest lesson of state craft." In 1989, world military expenditure amounted to $950 billion. It had fallen a shade from the $1 trillion of 1988 but still averaged some $2.6 billion a day, or $1.8 million a minute. There is no larger consumer of natural resources nor of human skills, no greater threat to the world environment. Of all the world's scientists and technologists engaged in research and development, one in every four is working on weapons. Some scientists are, of course, trying to cauterize the danger that members of their profession have helped to create. Arthur C. Clarke, the science writer who first suggested geostationary and communications satellites, once proposed as a counter to Star Wars Peacesat: reconnaissance satellites controlled by an international monitoring agency to verify arms control agreements and warn of other visible threats to world peace. As he notes, "The real problem is not military hardware, but human software." Again it is a question of balance and excess. Future generations, if we allow them to live, may well wonder what so flawed our judgment that we should build a self-destruct mechanism into human civilization.

IN THE years I was growing up in Guyana it was natural for us to feel insulated from the arms race. If the Americans, Soviets, and Europeans chose to blow themselves up in a new round of tribal warfare, that would be their affair—sad, tragic, deplorable in every respect, but their affair nonetheless. Today we know better. People in poor countries are acutely aware that disarmament is not a matter of concern only to the nuclear powers.

In 1985, at a meeting in Mexico of the Six-Nation Peace Initiative, former President Nyerere of Tanzania expressed these common concerns of the Third World: "We have a right to be heard. As nations and people we exist. And whatever other rights our people lack, they have at least the right to continue to exist." At that same meeting, the novelist Gabriel Garcia Marquez gave vivid expression to the right of every human being to join the crusade for disarmament when he evoked a post–nuclear holocaust world of everlasting night, furious hurricanes, and polluted orange rain, a world "peopled" only by weeds and vermin. At Madrid in 1986, International Physicians for Prevention of Nuclear War, which brings together the medical professions of the United States and the former Soviet Union, reasserted that human life could cease on this planet in the wake of a major nuclear war. These fears will not disappear merely because we reduce the level of "overkill" in the post cold war era.

The Brundtland Report highlighted nuclear war as a threat before which "other threats to the environment pale into insignificance." It drew attention to the prospect of nuclear winter, authoritatively explored by some three hundred scientists from the United States, the former USSR, and thirty other countries working in collaboration across ideological divides. The report concluded that "a nuclear war cannot be won, and must never be fought"; that "in the aftermath, there would be no difference between so-called victor and vanquished."

But it is not only expenditure on nuclear weapons that drives military consumption. The diversion of seven hours of total military expenditure around the world would finance the eradication of malaria, which kills a million children a year. Five days of global military expenditure would finance the annual cost of a UN action plan against Third World desertification. Three days of global military spending would finance a UN action plan to save tropical forests over five years. With a 10 percent reduction in the combined annual military expenditure of the European Community, the United States, and Japan, the West could double the development assistance it gives to poor countries. "Caring for the Earth" estimates that reductions in world military spending by 5 percent in 1992, rising to 18 percent in 2001, would finance its plans to achieve global sustainability. There is no greater security need than the securing of sustainable living on Earth. We can meet it by diverting resources from "defense" spending. What are our real priorities: power in today's world, or a world for our children to inherit?

The Gulf war is the most recent example of the use of military weapons on a major scale. The money spent in one day on that war ($1.5 billion) could have financed a five-year global program to immunize children against six deadly diseases that now kill a million a year. The cost of one Apache helicopter could have provided eighty thousand hand pumps to Third World villages without access to safe water. One Patriot missile system ($123 million) could have provided housing for at least five thousand homeless families in the Third World; twenty-three Patriot missiles ($1 million each) cost the equivalent of one year's supply of clothing, seeds, and storage for two million Mozambicans.

Military spending has long been acknowledged to have a bearing on human development, because it preempts resources that could otherwise be invested in social and economic development. Its relevance to environment needs now to be equally acknowledged. To see that relevance purely in the direct impact of war on the environment is to focus too narrowly. It could lead us to regard war as the norm and devise new "rules of war" to protect the environment from the acts of warriors. What is really needed are rules of peace to protect the environment from the consumption of natural resources that the military culture ordains.

FIVE

✝

The Powerless Poor

> If a free society cannot save the many who are
> poor, it cannot save the few who are rich.
> — *John F. Kennedy*

IN THE years since President John F. Kennedy uttered those words
in his inaugural address, the rich of the world have grown richer and
the poor more numerous. And the gap between them has widened. The
task of saving the many who are poor is now both harder and more
insistent. Addressing the people, President Kennedy was reaching out
to new frontiers of hope. The poor of whom he spoke were America's
poor, the free society that of the United States. The president was on
good ground in his assertion; it was authenticated by a long and
consistent pattern of national histories.

Do national precedents have relevance for our wider world society,
and is that society a free one? To the first of these questions the words
of an earlier American president provide an eloquent answer. The
Four Freedoms speech of President Franklin Roosevelt on January 6,
1941 was not only about America and Americans. "In future days," he
said, "which we seek to make secure, we look forward to a world
founded upon four essential human freedoms": freedom of speech and
freedom to worship, freedom from fear and "freedom from want—
which, translated into world terms, means economic understandings
which will secure to every nation a healthy peacetime life for its
inhabitants—everywhere in the world." He went on to explain, "That
is no vision of a distant millennium. It is a definite basis for a kind of

world attainable in our time and generation. . . . The world order which we seek is the co-operation of free countries, working together in a friendly, civilized society."

Later we will discuss the prospects of making the world a more civilized society. Suffice it here to say that saving the many who are poor can no longer be a national goal only. It must be a world goal, along with making the global community a free society—which is something more than making it a community of free societies. With the momentous political changes of the last few years, the latter is within the world's grasp. Progress toward a free world society cannot, however, be taken for granted; indeed, there are many indications that we are as far away as ever from a democratic global state.

And, alas, President Roosevelt's vision of freedom from want worldwide has indeed proved to be a vision of another millennium, for as the second millennium draws to a close that freedom is not in sight for the great majority of people, the world's powerless poor. This failure to "secure to every nation a healthy . . . life for its inhabitants—everywhere in the world" has had far-reaching implications for the crisis of environment. It has brought together the issues of economy and ecology in ways that make it imperative for global society to integrate the issues of development and environment.

I H A V E addressed the proclivity of the rich for consumption that has placed unsustainable stress on Earth's life-support systems and brought us to our present confrontation with nature. As we have seen, as much as 70 percent of the world's consumption of fossil fuels, 90 percent of automobiles, 85 percent of chemical products, 85 percent of military expenditure, and almost 100 percent of space waste—to mention only a few—is attributable to the 25 percent of the world's people who are rich and technologically advanced. What of the other 75 percent of the human species? At the opposite end of the scale, not so much out of virtue as of necessity, they are underconsumers of the planet's natural resources. These are the people of the developing countries for most of whom the central, persistent reality of living is poverty. They are poor not just in relation to those who are rich, they are poor by any standard of human development save that of the spirit. For long, their poverty too had only a local impact on the biosphere; but that has changed and their condition of poverty has driven them to desperate ends. They have encroached on nature with far-reaching consequences. They have multiplied their numbers exponentially in the belief that having more children might be their salvation. The pathways they are pursuing will lead them not to safety but to desolation, and will add to the damage to the biosphere being inflicted by the rich. Obsessive overconsumption and the compulsions of undercon-sumption are both crimes against nature. The ways of the rich must be curbed by enlightenment and ethics—and fear of the consequences; the compulsions of the poor must be removed by the alleviation of poverty. Hence the insistence, essential and inescapable, that our problems in sustaining life on Earth are problems of environment and development, entwined and inseparable.

W H A T is poverty? In prosperous countries, in Europe, in North America, ordinary men and women certainly face genuine economic problems—business uncertainty, inflation, the fear and sometimes the fact of unemployment. There are poor in rich countries; but they rarely face the utter deprivation that is poverty in poor countries. In 1975, as president of the World Bank, Robert McNamara sought to convey the depth of this deprivation when describing in a speech to the bank's board of governors the then nearly one billion of the world's people subsisting in an environment of squalor, hunger, and hopelessness: "They are the absolute poor, living in situations so deprived as to be below any rational definition of poverty. Absolute poverty is a condition of life so limited by illiteracy, malnutrition, disease, high infant mortality and low life expectancy as to deny its victims the very potential of the genes with which they are born. In effect, it is life at the margin of existence."

In the Brandt Report issued early in 1980—the start of the "lost decade" for development—we spent much time on the problems of poverty, stressing the matter of survival:

> Many hundreds of millions of people in the poorer countries are preoccupied solely with survival and elementary needs. For them work is frequently not available or, when it is, pay is very low and conditions often barely tolerable. Homes are constructed of impermanent materials and have neither piped water nor sanitation. Electricity is a luxury. Health services are thinly spread and in rural areas only rarely within walking distance. Primary schools, where they exist, may be free and not too far away, but children are needed for work and cannot easily be spared for schooling. Permanent in-

security is the condition of the poor. There are no public systems of social security in the event of unemployment, sickness or death of a wage-earner in the family. Flood, drought or disease affecting people or livestock can destroy livelihoods without hope of compensation. . . . The combination of malnutrition, illiteracy, disease, high birth rates, underemployment and low income closes off the avenues of escape. And while other groups are increasingly vocal, the poor and illiterate are usually and conveniently silent. (p. 49)

A S   T H E   lost decade gave way to the 1990s, poverty was still the essential condition of the three-quarters of the world's population living in developing countries. Some 3.6 billion people live in the low-income and lower-middle-income developing countries. This does not mean that all the people in those seventy-nine countries are equally poor. In 1988, average incomes in these countries ranged from $100 per person per year in Mozambique to $2,160 in Brazil. In between, China and India—together accounting for more than half the people of the Third World—showed annual per capita incomes of $330 and $340 respectively. Bangladesh, Indonesia, Nigeria, and Pakistan, which with Brazil are the only other developing countries to have more than 100 million people each, similarly have very low average incomes of $170, $440, $290, and $350 per person respectively. What these figures mean is that even the better off are not well off, and the worse off are in dire distress. The corresponding figures of per capita income for France are $16,090, for Canada $16,960, and for Japan $21,020. There are pockets of wealth in poor countries, and some now have a significant middle class; but for a large proportion of the population, poverty is the norm, and for the poorest, life is unbelievably harsh. The absolute poor of whom Robert McNamara spoke in 1975 are with us still, only now there are more of them, and their number is growing still.

The World Bank has set a poverty threshold of $370 per person per year, roughly a dollar for daily consumption. In 1990 there were 1.2 billion persons below this poverty line in the developing world. But the bank has marked out an even more deprived category, those who are "extremely poor" with a consumption level of no more than seventy-five cents per day ($275 per head per year). There were some 630 million such people struggling to stay alive in 1990, 18 percent of all the people of the developing world. These numbers are rising; 1.2

billion will become 1.3 billion by the end of this decade and probably 1.5 billion by 2025. Asia's share is just over 40 percent, but Africa is fast overtaking that.

Meanwhile, the gap between the rich and the poor grows ever wider: 77 percent of the world's people earn 15 percent of total income. In the context of a nation, if 85 percent of its income went to only 23 percent of the population, we would not be surprised if that nation tottered on the brink of rebellion against an essentially inequitable and unsustainable distribution of wealth. We would understand a demand for fairer shares and support a call for reform of the most fundamental kind. What holds us back from applying these same values and judgments to world society? How can we tolerate so easily the perpetuation of so skewed a distribution of the product of human effort?

Every single indicator of human development throws up striking disparities. Whereas everybody has access to some form of health services in industrial countries, only two-thirds of the people in the Third World do. Maternal mortality in developing countries averaged 290 for every 100,000 live births in 1980–87, compared to just 24 in the industrial world. The average life span in poor countries is eleven years shorter than in the rich countries. Of every thousand children born in the developing countries, more than a hundred die before the age of five; the figure for the rich countries is less than twenty.

But it is not only the gap between rich and poor countries that is shameful. The disparities within some developing countries also have the capacity to shock. In Mexico, a very poor person can expect to live fifty-three years as opposed to seventy-three years for a wealthy person. In Chocó province on Colombia's Pacific coast, child mortality is 191 per 1,000 births, compared with 50 per 1,000 for the country as a whole. In some Indian villages, 90 percent of the Brahmins, the highest caste, are literate as opposed to 10 percent of the lowest castes.

In many countries the situation has been getting worse, not better. In Africa and Latin America, hundreds of millions of people became poorer in the 1980s, a time when average incomes dropped by 10 percent in most of Latin America and by as much as 20 percent in sub-Saharan Africa. During the 1980s, spending per person on health services was reduced in more than three-quarters of African and Latin American countries; spending per person on schools fell by about a quarter in the thirty-seven poorest nations.

A T T H E start of the 1990s the two principal international organizations concerned with development, the World Bank and the UN Development Program (UNDP), issued major reports on poverty. They are a rich mine of statistics, but the institutions have learned that statistics need the illumination of experience. The World Bank's "World Development Report, 1990" provided that illumination with vignettes of three poor families in Africa, Latin America, and Asia:

A poor subsistence farmer's household in Ghana: In Ghana's Savannah region a typical family of seven lives in three one-room huts made from mud bricks, with earthen floors. They have little furniture and no toilet, electricity, or running water. Water is obtained from a stream a fifteen-minute walk away. The family has few possessions, apart from three acres of unirrigated land and one cow, and virtually no savings.

A poor urban household in Peru: In a shantytown on the outskirts of Lima a shack made of scraps of wood, iron, and cardboard houses a family of six. Inside there is a bed, a table, a radio, and two benches. The kitchen consists of a small kerosene stove and some tins in one corner. There is no toilet or electricity. The shantytown is provided with some public services, but these tend to be intermittent. Garbage is collected twice a week. Water is delivered to those who have a cement tank, but this family has been unable to save enough for the cement. In the meantime, the mother and eldest daughter fill buckets at the public standpipe 500 yards away.

A poor landless labourer's household in Bangladesh: In a rural community in a drought-prone region of Bangladesh a landless labourer and his family attempt to get through another lean season. Their house consists of a packed mud floor and a straw roof held up by bamboo poles from which dry palm leaves are tied to serve as walls. Inside there is straw to sleep on and burlap bags for warmth. The labourer and his wife, three children, and niece do not own the land on which the shack is built. They are lucky, however, to have a kindly neighbour who has indefinitely lent them the plot and a little extra on which they are able to grow turmeric and ginger and have planted a jackfruit tree. (pp. 24–25)

Such is the cold reality of poverty worldwide as seen by international institutions inured to the horrors of deprivation. My own ancestors went to Guyana in the nineteenth century from India, escaping one bondage to enter another, moving from destitution in Bihar to indenture on the sugar plantations of Demerara. In his book, *India: A*

Wounded Civilization, the Trinidadian novelist V. S. Naipaul, whose ancestors also came from India, described the lineaments of poverty in Bihar a century later, where grinding need is still the lot of millions:

> In the village I went to, only one family out of four had land; only one child out of four went to school; only one man out of four had work. For a wage calculated to keep him only in food for the day he worked, the employed man, hardly exercising a skill, using the simplest tools and sometimes no tools at all, did the simplest agricultural labour. Child's work; and children, being cheaper than men, were preferred; so that, suicidally, in the midst of an overpopulation which no one recognized . . . children were a source of wealth, available for hire after their eighth year for, if times were good, fifteen rupees, a dollar fifty a month. Generation followed generation quickly here, men as easily replaceable as their huts of grass and mud and matting. . . . Cruelty no longer had a meaning: it was life itself. (p. 26)

F O R most of this century international poverty has been as national poverty was throughout most of the eighteenth century, a matter of peripheral concern to the rich. It touched the hearts of good people, but it was all too easily put off for reflection on Sunday. It did not intrude on workaday life; it did not seem to bear on the quality of that life or to have any relevance to sustained enrichment. For the rich, international poverty was another external issue. It did not affect the price of bread. It did not influence, yet, the price of oil. It did not threaten the value of currencies. It did not hurt.

It was possible, therefore, to indulge the pretense that things were not what they seemed, or that even if they were, they did not matter. It was possible to dismiss protest as rhetoric, to accommodate inequality and injustice as acts of God or nature, not of history and society, to come to terms with a world in which "the few are more than the many." In 1988, at the end of their Toronto summit, the leaders of the Group of Seven leading industrial countries actually described the 1980s with much self-congratulation as "the longest period of economic growth in postwar history." It was left to Professor Hans Singer of the Institute of Development Studies at Britain's University of Sussex to point out, in a letter to *The Times* of London, the contrast between their communiqué and the then recent Report of the UN World Food Council; this report had highlighted declining food production in all Third World regions in 1987 and a rise in the number of hungry people, with more children suffering from malnutrition than a decade earlier and over 14 million under the age of five dying needlessly from malnutrition and disease every year. So great remains the gap between perception and reality that the persistence of mass poverty and starvation is not even a matter for acknowledgment.

But, while such illusions are indulged, the pressures for change increase, just as they did in Europe when Victorians drew the curtains to shut out the misery that was pounding at the door. The eighteenth-century French philosopher Francois-Renë de Chateaubriand had this counsel to offer the privileged classes of his time: "Try to convince the poor man, once he has learned to read and ceased to believe, once he has become as well informed as yourself, try to convince him he must submit to every sort of privation, while his neighbour possesses a thousand times what he needs; in the last resort you would have to kill him." (p. 451) That eighteenth-century wisdom has a twentieth-century relevance to the environment. How do you convince the poor that they must join in saving the planet if you say nothing about saving themselves? To eliminate the poor was no option in the eighteenth century; nor is it today. It is poverty that we have to exterminate.

A JOURNEY through Earth's less productive, more fragile, and most disaster-prone locations would reveal that these are the places where the great majority of the poor subsist. In Latin America, the poor struggle to scratch a living out of the inhospitable heights of the Andes in Peru, Ecuador, Bolivia, and Guatemala, and in the arid northeast of Brazil. In Africa's Sudano-Sahel belt, from Senegal in the west to Somalia in the east, they inhabit water-scarce lands. In Bangladesh, those who manage to survive the annual floods and cyclones migrate perpetually in search of a tiny piece of land where they can live and farm until the next flood changes the course of rivers and leaves them homeless once more. In Nepal, they perch precariously on steep, eroding hills.

The ancient survival strategy of the poor was to migrate to more fertile areas when the land they occupied could yield no more in crops or pasture. But land degradation, partly caused by poverty, is closing that escape route. In Africa, over a tenth of rangeland north of the equator is degraded by water erosion, over a fifth by wind erosion.

Parts of Morocco, Tunisia, and Libya are losing productive soil from some 100,000 hectares of agricultural land every year. The rate of desertification is accelerating in parts of the Sahel, the Middle East, Pakistan, and northwest India.

Asia, the world's most densely populated continent, is home to six out of every ten human beings. It is already farmed intensively, and pressure on the land will increase in the next thirty years as Asia's population grows to 4.6 billion—as many people as there were in the entire world in 1985. A large part of Asia's soil, especially in wet tropical and subtropical zones, is not well endowed; many Asian regions are deficient in at least five of the thirteen nutrients crucial for agricultural production: nitrogen, phosphorus, potassium, sulphur, and zinc. To make matters worse, poor farmers are not able to replenish the nutrients their crops take out of the soil.

Without materials and practices to maintain soil quality, more and more land will become useless. Meanwhile, the global demand for food will be expanding by 3 to 4 percent a year as a result of rising population and income. The implications for the environment are direct and acute. The need for food among ever-growing numbers of poor is, for example, by far the main cause of deforestation in the tropics. Forty-five percent of all the forest cleared in the late 1970s was to make room to plant crops. The highest percentage, up to 70 percent, was in tropical Africa. Large numbers of peasants with neither income nor land who have no option but to cut down virgin forest to grow food are major agents of deforestation. Many of the illegal slash-and-burn cultivators in the Ivory Coast's Tai National Park, for example, are immigrants from drought-stricken Mali and Burkina Faso to the north. According to the preliminary results of an FAO assessment, tropical forests, which covered some 1.95 billion hectares or 54 percent of the world's forest area in 1980, may have been reduced by 200 million hectares by 1990.

Cutting down the forests to plant crops provides the poor with only short-term relief. The slash-and-burn cultivation of displaced farmers in Africa and southeast Asia is a technique ill-suited to fragile forest soils. The soil soon becomes so depleted that they are forced to move on and cut down even more trees. Soil on deforested hills swiftly erodes. With no tree cover water runs off, carrying topsoil onto land in low-lying areas and threatening agriculture there too. In arid and semi-arid areas, where wind rather than water is the main agent of erosion, forests that remain green when grasslands dry up can no longer save cattle from starvation once the trees are cut down. Nor can they provide food for people as in some parts of Africa, where as much as 70 percent of the animal protein comes from such forest game as birds and rodents, or firewood and charcoal, which account for a sixth of all the energy used in developing countries.

None know this better than the poor themselves. They know that when trees disappear a vital source of food, fodder, and fuel disappears too; that drought may become more frequent and severe, water more scarce. They act not out of ignorance or recklessness, but only in response to the compulsions of survival. Yet, combined with an absence of options, the environmental catastrophes inexorably precipitated by such actions only further impoverish the poor. It is a case of poverty leading to environmental damage leading to deeper poverty.

About 370 million people in the developing countries live in areas of low agricultural potential. Eighty percent of Latin America's poorest people, 60 percent of Asia's, and 50 percent of Africa's live in areas that are infertile or prone to erosion, floods, and other ecological scourges. Everywhere, larger and better-off farmers crowd the more fertile lands, forcing the poor to move to marginal areas—slopes that are too steep, soils that are too poor, places where it hardly ever rains, fragile lands that soon turn to dust. As populations grow and more peasants are displaced by modern agriculture and large infrastructure works like dams, the pressure on marginal areas, or on forestland unsuitable for sustainable cultivation, intensifies. With no capital to invest, using very basic tools, and in some cases even short of the human power needed to keep soil productive, the poor find themselves caught in a downward spiral of circumstance.

I N S O M E developing countries, one way to ameliorate rural poverty and safeguard the environment is to share land, water, and livestock more equitably. Today millions of peasants are reduced to scratching out a living as badly paid farm laborers or subsistence farmers while big landowners let substantial tracts of land lie idle. The most inequitable distribution of landownership is in Latin America. In Guatemala and neighboring El Salvador, for example, just 2 percent of landowners own 63 percent and 60 percent, respectively, of the agricultural land. No wonder both countries have been torn by civil war. It has aggravated environmental degradation: The military clear much of the remaining vegetation to deprive guerrillas of cover. If the hilly areas of El Salvador where the poor have sought refuge continue to lose their topsoil at the present alarming rates, nothing will be able to grow there in a decade or so.

"Food 2000," a 1987 report to the Brundtland Commission, noted that while each country has to devise its own formula for increasing access to productive agricultural resources, "redistribution of land is basic." Without it, government action to protect natural resources may end up making the distribution of income more lopsided and benefiting large farmers. FAO estimates that three-quarters of the world's rural households are smallholders or landless. Their number is expected to swell by another 50 million by the year 2000.

The British ecologist Norman Myers has estimated that clearance by landless peasants accounts for three-fifths of rain forest loss. In sub-Saharan Africa, small cattle owners are partly responsible for the deterioration of pasture and the spread of desert. With no tenure rights, pastoralists are being cornered in areas that are too small for their flocks to graze on sustainably. This is a major reason for the fact that, according to UNEP, desertification threatens 3.6 billion hectares, about one-fourth of the total land area of the world.

Property rights need not be individual. Over the centuries, people have shared the fruits of the land and the resources of nature. They have evolved sophisticated codes for maintaining the value of common resources. Though pastoralists are often blamed for taking advantage of common grazing lands by overstocking, in many cases they have a system of strict controls and penalties in place to ensure that the capacity of the land is not exceeded.

Regrettably, however, common property rights are being weakened almost everywhere, by rapid growth in population and by the action of landowners, bureaucrats, and the politically powerful. In sub-Saharan Africa the expansion of cash crops for export such as cocoa, oil palm, and coffee has led to new types of land tenure through which property owners benefit at the expense of the poor, who are denied access to land that formerly met their subsistence needs. Agrarian reform in reverse, namely, the nationalization of common land such as forest, has also loosened traditional restraints on the use of freely available resources, with dire consequences for the environment.

Landless people who clear forests and small farmers too poor to invest in soil conservation or more productive farming are only two elements in a complex web of factors. But rural poverty is now undeniably of global significance as a main source of environmental degradation, which in turn aggravates poverty. Where they can, the victims of this unremitting process flee to urban centers.

U R B A N drift offers little real comfort. It is the poor who suffer the brunt of mounting urban pollution. In many cities in the developing world, most of the people live in makeshift houses or run-down tenements. A WHO study calculated that 80 percent of urban dwellers in Malawi lived in substandard houses with inadequate or no services. Malawi is not exceptional. Sixty-two percent of urban dwellers in Burkina Faso, 59 percent in Lesotho, 80 percent in Maputo, 75 percent in South Yemen, 55 percent in São Paulo, 60 percent in Bangladesh—the list goes on and on—live in similarly appalling conditions.

With no piped water in their homes, no proper sewage or garbage disposal, the urban poor are in constant danger of being struck down by disease. Dangerous microorganisms thrive in household and human waste and infectious diseases spread rapidly in the cramped slums where the poor live. Diarrhea, dysentery, typhoid, and food poisoning are everyday risks. In addition, widespread malnutrition turns common childhood diseases such as measles into major killers. A child born in a squatter settlement is 40 to 50 times more likely to die before the age of five than one born at the same time in a rich country or to wealthy parents in the same country.

Most cities in Africa and many in Asia have no sewers at all, so human excrement and wastewater end up in rivers, streams, and canals that the poor in turn use for bathing and washing their clothes. Even where some sanitation exists, it does not necessarily ensure a healthy environment. In Dar es Salaam in Tanzania, for example, virtually all the 1.5 million people have pit latrines, but they regularly overflow and the government lacks the resources to empty more than a tiny proportion of them.

What basic services are available often go first to the richer residential, government, and commercial areas. Several studies have shown that where average water consumption in a city is in the range of 20 to 40 liters per person, the poor are likely to use less than half of that, which is well below the minimum required for good health. In Mexico

City, for example, 9 percent of consumers use 75 percent of the total water supply, and more than 2 million people get hardly any. When the urban poor have access to water it is often from a communal standpipe, so that they have to wait in queues and carry home heavy buckets or pots of water not once but several times a day. When there are no standpipes, the poor end up paying more to water vendors than the rich pay for having the water piped into their houses.

Many of the poor make their homes in environmentally hazardous areas. The slums in Rio de Janeiro, Guatemala City, and Caracas are perched on landslide-prone hillsides. Frequently the poor settle on polluted sites—around solid-waste dumps, next to open drains and sewers, or close to dangerous factories, as was tragically demonstrated by the chemical accident in Bhopal, India, in 1984. The poor are also found on land prone to flooding or inundation by high tides, as is the case in Bangkok, Bombay, Delhi, Quito, and Lagos. In Mexico City, one of the world's most heavily polluted cities, the poor southeast and northeast areas have the highest concentration of dust particles in the air. The poor do not choose these sites through ignorance; they are simply the cheapest ones available to them. Poverty makes them opt for environmental hazard; in doing so, they both enlarge the hazard and condemn themselves to being its victims.

R E C O G N I T I O N of the intolerably poor habitations of so many of the world's poor prompted the UN to mount a special effort to extend water and sanitation services. The 1980s were declared the International Drinking Water Supply and Sanitation Decade, but its achievements fell far short of its goals. At the end of the period, nearly 2 billion people, or 32 percent of urban residents and 58 percent of rural residents in the developing countries, had no access to a safe water supply, and 3.1 billion, or 62 percent of all urban dwellers plus 85 percent of those living in rural areas, had no sanitation. Garbage collection and disposal and pollution control get hardly any support. The amount that developing country governments have been spending to improve facilities in these fields is woefully inadequate. The poor simply do not have the political clout to claim a higher percentage of scarce resources.

Even if they did, it is clear that governments do not have the capacity to invest enough to clear the backlog and keep pace with expanding populations. An evaluation done in the 1980s of the needs of the

Brazilian city of São Paulo alone suggested that $50 billion would be required over fifteen years simply to maintain existing inadequate standards. Failing a dramatic improvement in the terms of trade or a large increase in foreign assistance, debt-ridden Brazil and other hard-up developing countries will find it impossible to make the large investments needed to provide services for all.

It is a sad but safe prediction that even more poor people will be living in unhealthy, even life-threatening, urban environments as the decade comes to a close. By the year 2000, there could be twenty-four cities of over 10 million people, and of these eighteen will be in developing countries. The growth of cities will be accompanied by the proliferation of poverty and intensification of environmental stress. The Greeks saw the city-state, the *polis*, as the ideal entity for the realization of citizenship. As Aristotle put it, "Men come together in cities in order to live; they remain together to live the good life." In poor countries, millions are now drawn to the cities in order to live; for most, the good life remains unattainable.

If the poor are not to become environmental casualties or culprits, their options must be enlarged beyond rural poverty and urban squalor. A major trap is the assumption that because the symbols of modern life—power plants, industries, cars—are associated with environmental stress, their absence spells elysium. In other words, if there is no economic growth, the natural world will be left in peace. The fact is that it is enormously difficult to protect the environment in rural or urban areas if national income is not growing, and virtually impossible to do so if national income is declining, as happened in so many countries in Africa and Latin America in the 1980s. Unless the vicious circle of poverty is interrupted, poor countries and poor people will be forced to continue to overexploit their land, their forests, and whatever other natural resources they have. Only if they move out of economic stagnation will they be able to invest in conserving their natural heritage, in cleaning up polluted waters and rivers, and in applying technologies that are friendly to the environment.

Unless the economies of developing countries grow faster than their populations, poverty will continue increasing and so will pressure on the environment. Yet only if poverty is curbed is population growth likely to decline and will the poor be enabled to earn livelihoods compatible with the sustainable use of resources. Poverty has been closely linked to population growth worldwide. One reinforces the other in impact on the environment. It is simply impossible to resolve environmental problems without attacking the causes that keep poor countries poor, poor people prolific, and both powerless.

N A T U R E ' S products still constitute much of what developing countries sell abroad to earn their way in the world. But in many instances the natural resources they need to export, sometimes mainly to keep up payments on foreign debt, are located in the midst of rich ecological zones. Despite the environmental damage that the exploitation of such resources may cause, hard-pressed countries find it difficult to forgo the income for nature's sake. Timber exports are an important source of foreign exchange for several tropical countries. Developing countries earn roughly $7 billion annually—about 9 percent of their agricultural export earnings—from forest products. Yet these nations are receiving contradictory signals: They are praised by international organizations such as the World Bank and the International Monetary Fund (IMF) for their export successes, and in the same breath they are required to be mindful of the environment if they are to qualify for further funding.

Chile's much-vaunted economic miracle was built on short-term expediency and long-term resource depletion. Its two largest new export products are seafood and wood products. It is now the largest exporter of fish meal in the world, the third largest exporter of salmon, and the sixth largest producer of seaweed. Earnings from sea products have gone from just $22 million in 1973 to $900 million in 1989. But catches are already dwindling and species such as cod and sardines have disappeared from certain areas because of overfishing. In the battle between long-term preservation of natural resources and short-term economic needs, the odds favor the latter. The intensification of exports paid political dividends for Chile's rulers for a while.

O U R times have indeed produced their contradictions. Another is the marked contrast between increased awareness of the importance of women's contribution to national economies and to human society in general and the deterioration in the economic position of millions of women in poor countries.

The decade of the 1980s saw significant economic and social setbacks in most developing countries, stopping and sometimes reversing the progress of previous decades. As we have seen, economic recession precipitated severe balance-of-payment problems and external indebtedness, and developing countries bore the brunt of the international adjustment process. The "stabilization" and "structural adjustment" programs they were obliged to follow as the price of IMF assistance were designed to restore current account balances within relatively short periods. Little attention was given to the social impact of economic adjustment. Much hardship was involved, of which women bore a disproportionate share as families suffered losses in income and faced rising costs and reduced public services.

It is women who have had to find extra work to supplement family income and to rearrange family budgets, switching to cheaper foods, economizing on fuel, and selling treasured possessions. It is women who have been most immediately affected by cuts in health and educational facilities resulting from reductions in government expenditure, and by the rising morbidity and mortality rates for children. Women have been in the frontline of the crisis in the developing world, bearing the greatest responsibility for adjusting their lives to ensure survival.

As secretary-general of the Commonwealth in 1989, I was involved in assembling an eminent group of experts, mainly female, from developed and developing countries to examine the impact on women of economic adjustment measures that poor countries had been forced to undertake to cope with the crisis. In their report, "Engendering Adjustment for the 1990s," the contributors quoted the following description of a woman's unending day in Mozambique, from Stephanie Urdang's *And Still They Danced:*

> The most vivid image of women in Mozambique is that of a woman in her machamba, or family plot, legs straight, her body forming a V as hour after hour she is bent over double, hoeing, sowing, weeding, day in and day out with a baby on her back and the only rest might be when the infant cries in hunger and the mother finds a place at the edge of the field to nurse her child. She can be in her field as early as 5:30 am, and she will work until midday when the sun, high in the sky and burning hot, is too harsh to work under. Men will help with seasonal tasks—clearing the land, for example. Ploughing the field, particularly if the plough is drawn by cattle, by tradition is strictly the man's domain. The image of women producers is repeated millions of times throughout the vast terrain of

sub-Saharan Africa, where women are responsible for some 80 percent of family production.

But when she returns home from the fields, the woman's work is only partially done. The food has to be processed—hours of pounding with a large pestle into a mortar, both fashioned from tree trunks, removing the husks from rice, pounding maize into flour for the staple porridge, grinding peanuts to a fine meal. The sound of pounding fills the air at all times of the day, a rhythmic thumping that is carried across the African veld. So is the smell of wood smoke from each family's cooking fire. The lighting of the fire comes only after hours of searching for fuel, often travelling long distances as the supplies nearer home are depleted. Water for cooking, for washing dishes, for ablutions, must also be collected. In some dry areas of Mozambique where water sources are few and far between, a journey of two hours in each direction is not uncommon and the return journey is made with a twenty-litre container of water carried on the head, so heavy that it takes two to lift it there. Laundry is often done at a river's edge or other water source, again a journey of greater or lesser distance. The house and living area must be swept and cleaned. Food must be cooked. Leaves must be gathered from wild plants to be used as supplements in cooking. And throughout the day, as a backdrop to all the other work, is the never-ending responsibility for child care. All these tasks are performed with little if any access to technology that could shorten the time involved and reduce physical strain. And all the time, unless a woman is infertile or past child-bearing age, she is virtually constantly pregnant or breast feeding. (pp. 59–60)

Having looked closely at all the evidence of the impact of the crisis on women, the Commonwealth group of experts expressed their conviction

that short-term stabilisation measures have too often been in conflict with long-term development goals, and have caused hardships severe enough to invalidate the process. It is only by recognising the economic necessity of protecting the social base, particularly as it affects women, and by incorporating these concerns into policy, that adjustment can achieve the desired results. In other words, adjustment policies which fail to incorporate women's concerns fully are not only unjust and cause unnecessary hardship but also imperil the effectiveness of the policies themselves. We must stress that our proposals will not be adequately implemented if they are seen and incorporated only as marginal additions to the present adjustment efforts. The problem of existing adjustment is not its omission of a few projects for women—but its failure to take adequate account of the time, roles, potential contribution and needs of half of each country's population. (p. 4)

The fate of women (and children) is intimately bound up with that of the environment. Whether the issue is firewood depletion, urban pollution, or population growth, the integration of environment and development will turn substantially on ending poverty in general and improving the lot of women in particular.

T H O U G H the prevalence of poverty is in many ways linked to imbalances in the world economic system, the primary responsibility for development and for environmental stewardship in poor countries rests with the countries themselves. The cause of development and therefore of environment can be assisted if developing countries change their spending priorities. It is outrageous that they have been devoting on average 5.5 percent of GNP (their total national income)—or around $480 million per day in 1987—to military expenditure. Of the countries for which figures are available for 1986, twenty-six, most of them in Asia, spent more public funds on the military than on health and education combined. As many as sixty-eight spent more on the military than on health care.

In a world without an effective system of collective security to protect countries against aggressors, and with predatory instincts among nations far from curbed, some expenditure on defense by developing countries is inevitable. But these are not the only reasons for current spending on the military. In an international climate heavily influenced by militarism, many Third World leaders have turned to armed might to create an aura of national progress and to prop up their regimes. Leading countries in the West and the East have been their suppliers, reaching across ideological divides to profit from the arms bazaar.

From 1980 to 1984 the value of conventional arms transferred in commercial or official trade totaled $69.7 billion. The United States held its lead as the world's chief arms exporter, supplying 39.7 percent of this total, but the Soviet Union was not far behind with 31.4 percent, while France, with 9.1 percent, was sprinting toward double figures. Attractive credit terms, often unavailable for food or medicine, are never in short supply for arms, and the United States and former Soviet Union have often provided arms as part of their aid. In the decade up to 1980, U.S. weapons were sold and transferred to 130 different countries on the authority of the Defense Department. This is to say nothing of the thriving illicit trade in arms. It is no wonder the world's terrorists have such an easy time getting hold of Kalashnikovs, Uzis, and M-16s.

Third World military spending has increased more than fivefold since 1960, rising much faster than the military budgets of industrial countries. It dropped from a peak of $173 billion in 1987 to $146 billion in 1989, but even at this level was more than 15 percent of the annual global military expenditure of $950 billion. The poor are finding resources for arms; but at what cost to poverty's victims? A significant part of the crippling debt of developing countries results from arms purchases. Saadet Deger and Somnath Sen, in their book *Military Expenditure: The Political Economy of International Security,* point out that while earlier estimates attributed roughly 20 percent of Third World debt until around 1980 to weapons imports, the World Bank estimated in 1989 that a full third of the debt of some major Third World countries was from arms purchases. While arms imports have fallen recently, partly owing to declining oil revenue and the debt crisis, arms production has continued to grow in the Third World. Over fifty developing countries now have indigenous arms industries. At present, the spread is of conventional arms technology, but developing countries will soon be demanding the next generation of conventional weapons systems now in the hands of industrialized countries. One result of the Gulf crisis will almost certainly be a new round of arms sales to developing countries that will have been thoroughly convinced of the need for state-of-the-art weapons.

The UNDP has proposed in its "Human Development Report, 1991" that developed countries earmark at least 25 percent of their peace dividend—the savings in arms budgets—for development assistance to poor countries. This would double aid in the 1990s to 0.7 percent of donor countries' GNP. As for developing countries themselves, UNDP says, a peace dividend should involve freezing military spending, promoting democratic regimes, settling regional disputes, and spending more on areas of human development like health and education. Freezing military expenditure could lead to savings of $15 billion a year in prospective increases, given that the trend from 1960 to 1987 had been for the arms expenditure of developing countries to rise an average of 7.5 percent a year. The coexistence of massive military spending with pervasive human need should be unacceptable to human civilization. It was a military man himself, General Dwight Eisenhower, who during his term as president of the United States observed in Washington, D.C. on April 16, 1953: "Every gun that is fired, every warship launched, every rocket fired signifies, in the final sense, a theft from those who hunger and are not fed, those who are cold and are not clothed. The world in arms is not spending money alone. It is spending the sweat of its laborers, the genius of its scientists, the hopes of its children."

The issue of military expenditure in poor countries was addressed in a forthright manner by a group of public figures from the Third World in 1990. The South Commission, under the chairmanship of the former president of Tanzania, Julius Nyerere, carried out a vigorous process of self-examination in considering the record of developing countries in the postwar period. Its conclusions on militarization constitute an unambiguous call to poor countries to abandon a path that can only lead to deepening poverty, and a call to other countries to desist from policies that make it easier for developing countries to buy arms than bread. The commission's report, "The Challenge to the South," included the following:

> The direct human cost of well over one hundred cases of international and civil conflict in the South since the end of the Second World War has been a horrific addition to the daily ravages of poverty and deprivation. By 1980 more than 10 million people had been killed in wars fought in the Third World; many millions more had been maimed or injured. . . . It remains an unfinished task of the countries of the South to work out effective mechanisms for settling international and internal conflicts through peaceful means. These mechanisms, together with the strengthening of democratic processes, can play an important role in curbing military expenditure.
>
> Militarization has perverse implications for development. The diversion of resources to pay for instruments of war and repression retards progress in many countries. Just as deleterious is the growth of a military culture which is contemptuous of democracy, popular participation, human rights, or the principle of government accountability. It breeds corruption, the abuse of power, and the consequent alienation of the people from the political system. These

disturbing symptoms can be seen in many countries of the South today. (p. 53)

There is a message here for rich and poor alike, and it bears ultimately on the environment.

E c o n o m i c growth fostered by a supportive international environment and guided by the right domestic policies is an important part of the answer to poverty alleviation. But it must be economic growth of a kind compatible with ecological health. As we have seen, many developed countries have not observed that precept, and developing countries are already experiencing what happens when development policies neglect the environment. The basic precept of combining economic growth with ecological health is universal in its application. Rich and poor may differ in circumstance but each in their own way, according to situation and capability, must make a living credo of this principle.

That is why, in the Brundtland Report, we developed the concept of sustainable development, which had been first advanced in the World Conservation Strategy in 1980. By sustainable development we meant that the world must meet its present needs in ways that do not diminish the ability of future generations to meet theirs; it must ensure that human progress is sustainable. We saw sustainable development as having two crucial components: the concept of need, in particular the basic needs of the world's poor, and the concept of environmental limits which, if breached, in particular by the world's rich, would affect the capacity of the natural world to sustain life today and tomorrow.

To expect only developing countries to follow a path of sustainable development would be to distort what the Brundtland Commission intended. "The goal," says the report, "is economic and social development ... defined in terms of sustainability in all countries— developed and developing." Those were measured words, seriously meant. This is an extremely important matter; that from the very beginning the commission urged sustainable development on all countries, rich and poor, cannot be emphasized too strongly.

At the end of 1990 in my inaugural remarks as President of the World Conservation Union, I felt obliged to emphasize this:

I want to say a few words about this concept of sustainable development—as one who had something to do with its evolution in the Brundtland Commission, and because of anxiety lest it become a code-word meaning different things to different people, all embracing it as a virtue, but only as a virtue that others must practice. 'Sustainable development', in the Commission's now classic sense of meeting the needs of the present without compromising the ability of future generations to meet their own needs, relates to all development; not just to 'development' in a specialised Third World context, but to the development of all countries, all peoples, indeed, to the development of our human society.

There were good reasons for my concern that sustainable development, which received much attention among thoughtful people in industrial countries, was being distorted in two ways in some quarters. First, it was regarded as a precept to be observed essentially by developing countries in pursuing economic development, something that had little to do with the rich world. And secondly, in the context of economic development, some felt environmental protection should be detached from the requirement that the essential needs of the world's poor should be met—a requirement the commission regarded as an overriding priority. There has also been a tendency in the same quarters to believe that environmental protection can be assured while neglecting certain critical development factors to which we drew attention in the Brundtland Report. These include income redistribution to ensure that countries are not forced to exhaust natural resources for short-term survival; the reduction of vulnerability, mainly again of the poor, to crises such as floods, droughts, and a collapse of agricultural prices; the universal provision of such basic attributes of sustainable living as health, education, water, and clean air; and the protection of the weakest members of society.

As a result, there is genuine concern in developing countries that failure to make the connection between economic and human development on the one hand and environmental protection on the other could encourage industrial countries to adumbrate policies for them that in the name of environment give scant attention to the basic needs of people and the critical importance of economic growth if those needs are to be satisfied. That would be a betrayal of the concept of sustainable development as the Brundtland Commission envisaged and advanced it.

A F R I C A N , Asian, and Latin American countries insist that environmental protection is part and parcel of development. The report of the Latin American and Caribbean Commission on Development and Environment, "Our Own Agenda," made the point directly: "There will be no sustainable development in Latin America and the Caribbean as long as almost half the population continues to live in abject poverty. Human development must be the keystone of our strategy if it is to be ecologically viable. This, together with the rational use of resources, must be the central focus of our strategy. Every other concern must be subordinated to it." (p. 47) That industrial countries are inclined to neglect Third World development for the sake of the environment has been a recurrent concern among developing country delegates to the meetings of the Preparatory Committee of the 1992 UN Conference on Environment and Development. While special negotiating groups were set up to discuss environmental themes such as forestry, soil conservation, and marine resources, the problems of poverty and development were lumped together with such matters as financial resources and the transfer of technology.

The document on poverty and the environment prepared by the secretariat for the UN conference in Rio de Janeiro clearly states that "an effective strategy to tackle problems of poverty, development and environment simultaneously in developing countries should begin with a focus not on resources or on production but on people." This means promoting sustainable livelihoods, which involves integrating antipoverty programs and rational management of resources. The objectives of such an integrated program give an idea of what is required. They include creating jobs for today and tomorrow; developing infrastructure, marketing, technology, and credit systems to widen the options of poor households; increasing the productivity of resources and ensuring that they are broadly distributed; rehabilitating degraded resources and introducing policies to prevent the unsustainable use of resources; and finally, opening up avenues for public participation, particularly by poor households, to ensure sustainable development.

The Latin American and Caribbean Commission has a further objective: to reform public spending and thereby give greater priority to basic services such as health, education, and social security. "Our Own Agenda" maintains that this is the best way of redistributing income in a democratic society. The report "Caring for the Earth," produced by the World Conservation Union (IUCN), UNEP, and the World Wide Fund for Nature (WWF) calls for the integration of development and conservation within each country and for a global alliance to make that integration effective, with poor countries being helped in their efforts to achieve sustainable development and environmental protection. Chapter 10 will identify some of the specific approaches these and other authoritative reports and studies have urged.

T H E great achievement of the sustainable development concept is that it broke with the old conservationist approach to natural resources and its tendency to place Earth's other species above people. Conservationists, many of them scientists in the tradition of Julian Huxley, rendered the world a great service in alerting us to the assault we were making on nature. Now they are helping to spread the broader message that unless we integrate environment and development, unless we care for Earth through a strategy for sustainable living, we will imperil the survival of all life. Ensuring that the children of our children have at their disposal as much of Earth's bounty as we do is a central task of today's conservationists.

We cannot save the freshness of the air or the purity of the water or the goodness of the earth, we cannot save the forests or the elephants or the whales, unless we save the people. We cannot ask endangered people to rescue the planet from the many threats it faces unless we link Earth's salvation to their own. Poverty threatens the survival of the poorest. To appeal to them to join in saving the planet is pointless unless we link it to their own survival. Simply to tell those at the margin of existence not to cut down the forest or not to have many children when they see both as necessary to their survival is to be not only insensitive to their predicament but also downright provocative. The poor need to share in the human commitment to change so that life on the planet can be sustainable for all. But to make an appeal for that commitment credible, the rest of the world must address not merely its own salvation but the relief of poverty as well. We must save the many who are poor because they are poor; it may well be the surest way of saving the few who are rich.

SIX

Population Pressures

And when one day our human kind becomes full
grown, it will not define itself as the sum total of
the whole world's inhabitants, but as the infinite
unity of their mutual needs.

— *Jean-Paul Sartre*

W H E N the world's nations assembled in Stockholm in 1972 for that
first international conference on the environment, there were about
3.8 billion people on Earth. When they reconvene at the Earth Summit
in Rio in 1992 there will be over 5.4 billion people on our small planet,
an increase of 1.6 billion, or 42 percent, in just twenty years. If the rate
of increase remains the same, in the thirty-three years between 1992
and 2025 world population will have increased by a further 3 billion—
as many people as the whole world had in 1960.

Time and again we have seen how the human species accelerated the
pace of its impact on the biosphere from the time of the industrial
revolution and then frenetically from the middle of this century on—
as if, already traveling too fast, we suddenly spun out of control. Of no
issue is this more true than population.

It took from the first appearance of *Homo sapiens* on Earth over 4
million years for the human population to reach 1 billion. For a long
time, our numbers grew slowly. When Christ was born, world population is believed to have been about 300 million. It took from then until
the middle of the eighteenth century for human numbers to reach 800

million. World population was doubling about every 1,500 years. Had we held to this rate of increase it would not have been until the fourth millennium, about the year 3250, that world population reached 1.6 billion. But by 1800 the rate of increase had begun to quicken, and in 1900 world population reached 1.7 billion. It had taken a mere 150, not 1,500, years to double.

That was the period of the industrial revolution at its most vigorous. It was also a time when medical science was making great contributions to the quality, and particularly the length, of human life. Mortality rates were falling; people were living longer; more children were surviving the early years of life. The rest of the world was eventually to benefit in varying measure from these advances, and by 1950 world population reached 2.5 billion. It had doubled this time in less than a hundred years. Led by a surge in population in the industrializing West, human numbers were increasing exponentially. A base was being laid for the massive increases in population that were to dominate Earth's landscape in our time and beyond.

Between 1950 and 1987, a mere thirty-seven years, human numbers doubled again to reach 5 billion; in 1991, we were at 5.4 billion; by the year 2000 we will reach 6.25 billion. The decade will in effect add a new India, the world's second most populous country, to the global population. In the first millennium world population hardly grew; it was stable at around 300 million. In the second millennium it will have grown by about 6,000 million (6 billion). This gives rise to mounting concern about Earth's capacity to sustain such numbers, to say nothing of the further doubling that could lie ahead if we do not put a brake on human fecundity.

The implications of these figures are staggering. It has been calculated by Robert Repetto, for example, that if world population grows continuously at its present rate of 1.67 percent a year, Earth's land area, excluding Antarctica, would be packed solid with people by 2667. If Antarctica were made habitable, it would provide standing room for seven more years of growth. Erich Harth, an American physicist, has similarly pointed out in *Dawn of a Millennium* that if we held to the present growth rate there would be 30 trillion of us by the year 2500. "If all this humanity were spread evenly over the entire land mass of the earth, there would be one human for every 20 square feet of ground," he comments. (p. 144)

Questions about Earth's capacity to accommodate rising numbers were slow in forming, and the issue is still not everywhere acknowledged to be as foreboding as it is. In 1766 the English novelist and poet Oliver Goldsmith published *The Vicar of Wakefield,* in the first chapter of which a vicar, Charles Primrose, declaimed: "I was ever of opinion, that the honest man who married and brought up a large family, did more service than he who continued single and only talked of population." (p. 9) This would not have been an unpopular opinion among Britain's upper classes. Labor was going to be needed for the new centers of industrial production, and any surplus could be siphoned off abroad as colonists or convicts or simply impoverished masses. They would go to the new settlements, which would become markets for the industries at home.

But not everyone remained complacent. The clergyman-economist Thomas Malthus, born the year *The Vicar of Wakefield* was issued, published *The Principle of Population* in 1798. "Population," he asserted, "when unchecked, increases in a geometrical ratio. Subsistence increases in an arithmetical ratio." (p. 4) This doom-laden juxtaposition was out of tune with the optimism and confidence generated by the industrial revolution, but more disquieting was the conclusion attributed to Malthus (whether rightly or not) that war, famine, and disease were necessary checks on population growth. Not surprisingly, such seeming lack of charity was to leave a scar on the very concept of population control that has lasted to this day. As population increase in the twentieth century came to be more a phenomenon of the poor world than of the rich, Malthusian views on how population growth could be curbed acquired frightening overtones.

Malthus was wrong in believing that the world's population would rapidly outstrip global food supply. Since his time advances in agricultural technology—in seeds, plants, fertilizers, pesticides, and irrigation techniques, for example—have greatly improved the capacity of the human race to feed itself, despite its growing numbers. But food supply is not the only issue. The current rate of population increase aggravates the pressure we are exerting in a variety of ways on the environment, carrying it to levels that could endanger human survival.

D E C L I N I N G death rates in the industrializing countries of the nineteenth century caused population to rise, and within a few generations economic modernization, growing prosperity, and improving living standards led to a fall in birth rates as well. Population growth was checked not by war, famine, or disease; these abominations in fact were curtailed. There were wars still, ferocious ones, and epidemics and other forms of desolation, but they were increasingly departures from the norm, particularly famine and disease, and particularly in the countries that achieved effective economic development. In the more secure, healthier circumstances created by economic and scientific progress, families grew smaller. In *The Population Explosion*, Paul and Anne Ehrlich explain this simple but profound change as "the result of individual couples perceiving that more of their offspring were surviving and that large numbers of children were an economic burden in industrializing societies, and therefore limiting their families." (p. 56)

While experts still debate the precise causes of this demographic transition, as it came to be called, what the Ehrlichs point to is a fundamental condition for the moderation of population growth worldwide—the creation of an economic and social climate in which people reach the conclusion that industrializing Europeans reached in the late nineteenth and early twentieth centuries. Without that climate and that conclusion, not all the birth control facilities in the world would hold human numbers in balance with Earth's resources.

At the time in human history that population growth was slow, it was slow everywhere. Between 1750 and 1850 growth rates in the then-industrializing countries of Europe, North America, and Japan averaged 0.6 percent a year; in Africa, Asia, and Latin America growth was even slower at 0.4 percent. In the next century each group increased its rate, the industrialized nations to 0.9 percent, the developing countries to 0.6 percent. That is where growth rates stood in 1950, when there was a dramatic change.

Between 1950 and 1970 not only did population growth accelerate but the developing countries overtook the developed in the pace of growth. As a result of this reversal, the population of the developing countries has been increasing steadily in proportion to global population. By the end of this century, of the 6.25 billion people on Earth as many as 4.95 billion—78.4 percent—will live in the developing countries. In the present decade, annual population growth is expected to average 0.5 percent in the rich countries and 2.1 percent in the poor. Accompanying the rise in the developing countries' share of world population came a fall in their share of production, from 44 percent in 1880 to 17 percent in 1950. The developing countries' share of production recovered to 21 percent by 1980, but their share of population was 75 percent. Widening poverty and high growth rates went hand in hand, aggravating problems of hunger, disease, malnutrition, and illiteracy. Overcoming these evils requires an economic climate that supports real, broad-based, sustainable development. As the next chapter demonstrates, this climate has not been a feature of the last few decades. Its absence has impeded development and contributed to high rates of population growth, with deleterious consequences for the environment everywhere.

T H E impact we make on the biosphere is sometimes expressed mathematically by economists and ecologists and now ecological economists as I = PAT, I being impact, P population, A affluence (consumption), and T technology (environmentally bad technology). There may be other ways of measuring our environmental impact, but that question aside, the environmental debate is often conducted without acknowledging equations of any kind. Analysts usually isolate population as a factor, giving a distorted picture of the environmental impact of human numbers.

There was a time when Western populations were rising and it was fashionable to believe that population growth and an improved standard of living went hand in hand. Goldsmith's vicar would no doubt have thought so. Today that view is less frequently advanced in the West. Kenneth Boulding's comment, quoted by the Ehrlichs in *The Population Explosion*, that "anyone who believes exponential growth can go on forever in a finite world is either a madman or an economist" (p. 267) would be the more widely held notion, not only in the West, and even some economists would agree. Today, inevitably, concern over population increase focuses on the developing world, since it is there that growth is exponential. That attention is legitimate, but it is also necessary to recognize that people are by no means equal in their impact on the environment; hence A and T in the I = PAT equation.

Take, for example, the impact on the biosphere of energy consumption in two different countries. According to calculations made by the Indira Gandhi Institute of Development Research for the Earth Summit, the average person in the United States is responsible for adding to the atmosphere 27 times as much carbon dioxide as the average Indian. In impact on the environment through carbon dioxide emissions, the 33 million Americans who live in the states of California and Florida would therefore cause more stress than all of India's 850 million people. In many respects, overconsumption burdens the environment more than overpopulation does. That is certainly how it must feel to the planet.

In this sense, injunctions to bring the environmental stress caused by their populations under control have relevance to both the United States and India, even though the ways of addressing that end are different, namely, through reduced consumption in the United States and poverty alleviation in India. Population cannot be taken as an isolated factor in determining environmental stress; population numbers alone do not tell the whole story.

Y E T , when all this is acknowledged, moderating the growth of population remains absolutely vital for the health of the planet. The more people there are, the greater the consumption and the greater the impact on the environment. While the kind of technologies they use and the aggregate amount they consume determine the per capita impact of a country, population determines the number of people consuming resources and using technologies. As Dr. Nafis Sadik, who heads the UN Population Fund (UNFPA), says in "State of the World Population, 1991," population is the multiplier that fixes the total impact. What then is the prospect?

The UN's earlier forecasts that world population would reach a stable level at around 10.2 billion before the end of the next century have recently been revised up, as progress in reducing birth rates has been slower than anticipated in several key countries. The medium-level projection of UN demographers now is that world population will go on rising until it levels off at around 11.6 billion (more than double today's global total) about the middle of the twenty-second century, having reached 11.2 billion by 2100. Only much faster progress in reducing fertility could lead to a stable world population earlier. Though the rate of world population growth has slowed to 1.7 percent a year, it is still high enough to bring about a doubling of population in forty years. If growth continues at the present rate without any slowing down, world population could exceed 14 billion in the next century; this is the high projection of the UN. Over the next twenty years, of every 10,000 births over 9,000 will be in the poor countries. Population will grow and, unless we correct our course, poverty and environmental stress will grow with it. Clearly there is need for urgent action on all fronts to moderate population growth, and we must be mindful of the fact that lower fertility (that is, a reduction in the number of children a mother has in her lifetime) takes a generation or two to translate into a reduced growth rate.

As part of a major international effort over the last few decades, support for family planning in developing countries has grown, reinforcing the effect of economic and social development. This has helped to reduce the rate of population growth in the developing countries as a whole to 2.1 percent a year from a peak of just over 2.5 percent a year between 1960 and 1965. But reducing fertility to replacement level, that is, the level necessary to stabilize the population, will require intensified global effort. Ironically, some years ago the United States, the largest source of assistance for population activities, withdrew support from international family planning agencies, notably UNFPA, on the grounds that they supported the right of women to have abortions, even though they did not finance abortion programs directly.

A population time bomb may not be ticking away as it once seemed, or it may just be ticking more slowly. What is certain is that we are still a long way from stabilizing the world's population. Fertility rates have been falling in many developing countries, including China, India, Indonesia, and Brazil, which together account for well over half of the population of the developing world. A significant part of the decline in the global rate of growth was due to China's one-child policy. China has over 20 percent of the world's population and almost 30 percent of the population of developing countries; what that country does with regard to population will influence world trends. But its stringent policy on population growth, however significant its impact on global growth rates, was pursued through governmental diktat and met with such resistance by rural families that strict enforcement was for a time relaxed. The 1990 census showed an upturn in the birth rate, and the state is now pursuing its one-child policy with renewed vigor but questionable success, particularly within the poorest sector of China's population.

While there have been impressive advances overall, it is now proving difficult to achieve further reductions in fertility in countries that have already lowered it substantially. India, the Philippines, Morocco, Tunisia, Trinidad and Tobago, Costa Rica, and Colombia all shaved around one point (0.1 percent) off their birth rate every year in the decade ending in 1975 but only managed one-tenth to one-third of a point each year in the following decade. The worldwide decline in fertility in the 1980s was considerably smaller than in the 1970s. UNFPA traces this trend to the economic troubles of the lost decade of the 1980s, which forced many developing countries to curtail government spending on education, health, and family planning services. An additional reason is that the proportion of women in their reproductive years has increased since 1970, leading to an increase in the number of births.

But there is a further reality. In conditions of chronic poverty, it is easier to persuade parents to reduce the number of children per family from six to four than to bring it down further to two; short of a coercive policy of the kind adopted in China, the second stage requires significant economic and social progress in which women also share. Historically, the population of countries has shot up when improvements in the standard of living and health care enable people to live longer but remain insufficient to create the economic and social security that induces them to have fewer children. Only when further economic progress brings that security, and when women are educated and their status in society improved, do couples start preferring smaller families. This is what has happened without exception in every industrialized country. We have to change people's circumstances if we are to change their desire to have large families.

T H E experience of Latin America shows the connection between economic circumstances and the number of children couples have. Fertility declined in Latin America from six children per woman on average in the early 1960s to slightly over three in 1990. Paulo Paiva, a director of the Centro de Desenvolvimento e Planjamento Regional in Belo Horizonte, Brazil, explains that large families were an asset in the early part of the century when the economy was based on the export of staple foods. In the coffee plantations in Brazil, for example, the whole family was hired. With food and employment for all family members assured, there was no incentive to have smaller families. In the 1960s the economy shifted to consumer industries. The population was growing fast, mortality having declined in the 1950s with better health services. Migration to the cities intensified. The new industries had the workers they needed, and because there were many job seekers wages were low. Meanwhile, in the Brazilian countryside family labor contracts gave way to individual contracts and a wage, though the lucky ones could also be sharecroppers. As capitalism entered the rural scene in the largest countries and private farms were mechanized, peasant families faced unemployment and an uncertain future. Children became a cost rather than an asset. Fertility went down.

Fertility declined in urban areas too, perhaps faster than in the countryside. In fact, the most urbanized countries—Uruguay, Argentina, Chile, and Venezuela—experienced the sharpest drops in fertility. What was first a middle-class phenomenon has now reached low-income families. Economic modernization, more women with education and employment, family planning services—all these contributed to the trend toward smaller families. Progress on the development front was helping to lower population growth rates.

If the experience of Latin America demonstrates that development reinforced by the provision of family planning services helps to lower birth rates, Africa represents the other side of the coin. In Africa, where social and economic change has been slower, birth rates are the world's highest; they are unlikely to decline substantially before the turn of the century. Overall, Africa is a sparsely populated continent, with about a quarter of the world's land area for only 12 percent of its population. But while a fourth of the African countries have a million or fewer people each, Egypt and Nigeria together have nearly 150 million, or about a quarter of the continent's population. There are also wide swings in population growth. Birth rates are high in west and east Africa, lower in central Africa, where 14 to 32 percent of the women are childless due to diseases that induce infertility. Two islands, Mauritius and Seychelles, have seen their population growth rates fall to very low levels: 1.2 percent and 1 percent respectively between 1985 and 1990; all the other countries have rates of 2 percent or more. The average for the continent was 3 percent between 1985 and 1990, compared with 1.7 percent for the world as a whole.

Most of the world's poorest countries are in Africa, where economic decline has been so sharp that in 1987 per capita GNP in the sub-Saharan region was well below the GNP of 1970. Most people in the forty-two countries that make up sub-Saharan Africa are subsistence farmers. Illiteracy is rife and infant mortality high. With more and more men leaving rural areas to look for work in the cities or abroad, women have been taking on the primary responsibility for farming. About 70 percent of the Congo's farms, for example, are managed by women; in Ghana there are more women farmers than men. As soil fertility declines, firewood gets scarcer, and water sources recede because of deforestation, the life of these women becomes progressively harsher. This has important implications for the number of children they bear. Traditional agriculture in Africa is labor intensive. Women subsistence farmers cannot cope with the work on their own. Nor can they afford to employ help or better techniques. The temptation to see children, who should really be in school, as a way to increase production often proves too strong. By the time they are seven or eight years old, even if they are not working in the fields or tending livestock, children can help their families by collecting water and firewood, looking after younger children, and freeing older family members for work outside the home.

High infant and child mortality resulting from poor nutrition and health care is a further potent inducement to have many children. Women tend to have more children to make sure at least one son survives to maintain them in old age. In India, it has been calculated, a couple must have an average of 6.3 children to be 95 percent certain that just one son will survive until the father is sixty-five years old. African women often have no assets and do not inherit land, so their sons are their only long-term security. This trend of producing too many children rather than too few applies particularly to the poor, whose mortality rates are highest.

As many as ninety-four infants under the age of one year die in Africa for every thousand that are born, twice as many deaths as in Latin America and ten times the average in Western Europe and North America. About half the total deaths in Africa are infants and children. In Angola, Ethiopia, Guinea, Malawi, Mali, Mozambique, and Sierra Leone, only 75 percent of children make it to the age of five. Where environmental degradation makes water and firewood scarcer, it has a direct impact on infant and child mortality and therefore on the number of children a mother has. Breastfeeding, a natural way of preventing births, abruptly ceases if a baby dies, making it possible for another to follow soon. The short period between births, moreover, is not good for the health of either mother or baby.

There are other causes for the high fertility rate among African women. They gain status primarily through motherhood. Polygamy and the custom of marrying older men, neither ideal for reproduction, also increase a woman's social and economic dependence on sons. A prevalent system of common property tends as well to encourage large families. Often the amount of land a community allots to a family depends on its ability to clear and cultivate land. A larger family stands to receive a larger piece of land, hence children are seen as an economic asset.

The African experience seems to confirm that family planning is more likely to be realized as a country makes social and economic progress. Some would argue that the social and economic climate conducive to a preference for fewer children simply does not exist in Africa. It needs to be noted that for a variety of reasons, including underdevelopment, access to family planning services is very limited through large parts of Africa. UNFPA draws encouragement from the increase in contraceptive use and declining trends in fertility in countries where family planning services have been made more available; it points out that the less developed the country, the more intensive the program efforts must be.

T H E countries of the world are at different stages of demographic transition. While most have begun the movement from many to few births, a disappointingly large number still have fertility rates averaging over six children per woman. They include many of the poorest countries in the world. At the other end of the spectrum are the industrialized countries; with very few exceptions, their rate of fertility has dropped below the replacement level of 2.1 births per mother and their rate of population growth has fallen below 1 percent a year. A few are recording a zero (Italy, Belgium) or negative (Germany, Hungary) growth rate. The environmental problem presented by these countries stems not from a rise in population but from overconsumption and a reluctance to adopt environmentally friendly and sustainable technologies.

A few developing countries have joined industrialized countries in the below-replacement-level fertility league. They are NICs (newly industrializing countries) (Hong Kong, Singapore, South Korea) and islands (Cuba, Mauritius, Puerto Rico) and mostly small countries. But Thailand and China, the country with the most people in the world, are not far behind, having brought their fertility rate down to 2.2 births, just above the level required to achieve zero growth in population.

In another category we can place countries that have brought their fertility rate down to around or below 3. Some countries in the Caribbean (Guyana, Jamaica, Trinidad and Tobago) and in Latin America (Argentina, Chile, Costa Rica, Colombia, and Uruguay) have fertility rates of between 2.3 and 3. Brazil and Mexico, the region's two largest states, are close to reaching a fertility rate of 3, as is Indonesia. The island of Sri Lanka has brought its fertility rate down to 2.5. The populations of these countries will nonetheless continue to grow rapidly for some time; they still have a large proportion of women of childbearing age and therefore exhibit what is called demographic momentum: the brakes will take some time to act. Brazil, for example, which had lowered its fertility rate to 3.2 by 1990, is still set to add to its 1990 population of 150 million almost another 100 million by 2025. Indonesia, with 184 million people in 1990 and its fertility rate down to 3.1, is similarly expected to have another 100 million people by 2025.

India, right behind China in world population, may be classed with such countries as the Philippines, Malaysia, Egypt, and Morocco, which have brought down their rate of fertility to between 3.5 and 4.5; their rate of population growth has fallen to between 2.1 and 2.4 percent. They have not reached safety yet, but there has been movement toward it.

Fertility averages a high rate of 6 in Africa, with most countries in the sub-Saharan region reporting rates higher than the average. By the end of the 1990s, Africa will have 900 million people compared with under 650 million at the start. Population will continue expanding at 3 percent, the highest regional growth rate the world has seen, and the UN projection is of a figure of 1.6 billion by 2025. The pressures on some countries will be daunting. Nigeria, Africa's most populated country with 108.5 million people in 1990, is set to double its population in the next twenty years. Even assuming steadily declining birth rates, Nigeria could have some 500 million people toward the end of the twenty-first century. This is as many as all of Africa had in 1982. There would then be over ten people for every hectare of arable land in Nigeria. Modern France has only three people per hectare.

UNFPA sees some signs of hope, however. Even in some high-fertility countries of south Asia and Africa, women are starting to have fewer children than in the early 1960s. Fertility rates have come down in north Africa and in some countries in the rest of the continent, including Ghana, Botswana, Mauritius, Senegal, Zambia, and Zimbabwe. They have even fallen slightly in Kenya, whose president, Daniel arap Moi, once lamented that he was described as the leader of one of the world's fastest-breeding countries. Yet, even after some family planning success in Kenya, the average Kenyan woman has 6.8 children and population growth is a steady 3.7 percent a year.

Another favorable sign is that cultural and religious barriers have proved more yielding than was earlier feared. The Vatican's strongly registered antipathy to contraceptives has not prevented Italy from moving to zero population growth. Several other predominantly Roman Catholic countries have moved toward common acceptance of family planning. In Latin America, progress toward lower fertility has been slower, but this is more likely to reflect levels of economic development than the influence of religious dogma. Strong family planning programs have been mounted in the region, several with government backing. In the Islamic world too, specifically Indonesia and Tunisia, the performance of family planning programs offers encouraging evidence that reproductive behavior can be influenced despite traditional resistance.

E X P E R T S have attempted to find out whether expanding human populations are harbingers of their own, and the planet's, fate by applying the concept of carrying capacity, first used by biologists to calculate the maximum number of animals that can survive in a given habitat. In 1984 an FAO/UNFPA study on carrying capacity, the most comprehensive study so far, calculated on the basis of intermediate levels of agricultural technology that the 117 countries surveyed could together support around 25 billion people, or four times the population projected for 2000. That exercise, however, is essentially a theoretical one. It assumes that every square meter of land would be used to grow what is required for a barely sufficient, mainly vegetarian, diet, and takes no account of the transport and storage of foodstuffs. Huge migrations of farm laborers would be needed to bring the yet unexploited lands under cultivation; much of this land is infertile and unsuitable for intensive use.

Moving from the global perspective to focus on individual countries, the study found that even with an intermediate level of agricultural technology, thirty-six countries, mostly in Africa, Asia, and Central America, would be unable to feed all their people by the turn of the century. If they had to depend on subsistence agriculture, sixty-four countries would be in a critical situation. Most of these countries have little unused arable land and are already burdened with ecological problems. Four countries, Cape Verde, Mauritius, Rwanda, and

Western Sahara, would be incapable of feeding their people even if they used the best farming practices. And this takes no account of the possible impact of climate change on tropical agriculture.

Attempting to match a country's food-growing potential with the numbers of mouths it must feed is at best, however, a poor indicator of impending hunger. Growing enough food locally is no assurance that everyone will get enough to eat. Malnourishment is widespread in India and the Philippines, for example, though both have exported grain in recent years. The problem is not lack of food, but that many people are too poor to afford it. Correspondingly, a country that can afford to satisfy all its wants by imports need never have a deficit of food.

But it is not merely a matter of imports. Food yields per person are still critical to the millions of subsistence farmers who eat what they grow and only what they grow. It is they who are suffering most from degraded soils, disappearing forests, erratic rains, and water shortages. In Africa a string of causes, including population growth, government policies that favor cities over rural areas, general economic decline, and drought, slashed food production per person by a fifth between 1970 and 1985. At 3 percent a year, the growth of population was double the rise in farm output. According to the FAO, more than 500 million Africans are on the verge of life-threatening hunger. Four-fifths of emergency food aid from the World Food Program in 1989–90 went to sub-Saharan Africa.

Africa may be a sparsely populated continent, but the families trying to scratch a living from minuscule plots of land under the constant threat of drought would not know it. Most of the world's underutilized land is in the humid tropics. Much of it, however, is at present unusable—some inaccessible, some covered with rain forests supported by fragile soil, some unsuitable for habitation because of animal and human disease. Africans are crowded in the cool, dry tropics and sub-tropics. Unequal distribution of arable land compounds the problem.

One result is that cultivable land in areas of high population is being subdivided to such an extent that it discourages the traditional practice of allowing the land to lie fallow from time to time so that it can regain its fertility. Shifting cultivation and pastoralism made sense when people were few and land was abundant. But the surge in population that began in the 1950s, when mortality rates went down sharply while birth rates remained high, has upset the balance between people and the environment. Things would be different if farmers earned enough, and knew enough, to get the most out of the soil without depleting it. But now any growth in the number of people making a living from marginal soil accelerates environmental degradation. As Erik Eckholm points out in *Down to Earth,* agricultural experts estimated that, in the devastated landscape of the Mossi Plateau in Upper Volta in the late 1970s, at most thirty people per square kilometer could be fed with today's best technology without damaging the soil irreparably; moreover, there was enough firewood at the most for twenty-five people per square kilometer. But population density was already more than fifty people per square kilometer in many parts of the plateau, and more than a hundred in some areas.

I N   A L L three developing continents, particularly Latin America, population growth is clearly leading to the loss of forestland. The increasing demand for food leads, inevitably, to more land being put to the plow. Countries with high population growth rates tend to increase the amount of cultivated land faster than those with less population pressure. Soon these countries will run out of land. In Latin America, increasing the farmed area accounted for two-thirds of the growth in output between 1950 and 1975, but less than half after 1975, since few areas with good soil were left. In sub-Saharan Africa, the amount of cultivated land rose by a fifth in eight countries between 1965 and 1985. These countries now find it difficult to push the agricultural frontier farther because water is short.

When farm plots can be divided no further, the youngest members of the family who do not migrate to cities move into forested areas or agriculturally marginal highlands and start growing food there. In the Himalayas of Nepal, environmental disruption has accelerated in the last three decades of rapid population growth. This pattern of land shortage leading to environmental degradation is repeated in Africa— the devastation in Ethiopia is an example—and in Latin America.

In most cases, the impact of population growth on tropical deforestation and soil erosion is aggravated by other factors. In the region of Mount Kenya, high population density was reinforced by government road construction and private appropriation of land in accelerating deforestation and soil erosion. In Peru, settlers moving from the crowded highlands to the eastern slopes of the Andes caused environmental havoc because of inadequate technical guidance and assistance from the government. The connection between population growth and soil erosion in areas where land is inequitably distributed has been shown in several countries, including the Philippines and Pakistan in Asia and El Salvador, Guatemala, and Bolivia in Latin America.

The increasing demand for fuel wood as population expands is another important factor in deforestation. In Latin America, firewood collection to meet the needs of growing numbers is the second biggest cause of deforestation after land clearance for agriculture, and far ahead of the destruction wrought by loggers. In sub-Saharan Africa the demand for fuel wood is rising at about the rate of population growth. In *The Greening of Africa,* Paul Harrison claims that if African birth rates were in line with the lower levels prevailing in south Asia, Africa's demand for fuel wood forty years from now would be about a third lower than it is likely to be. (p. 209)

UNFPA said in its 1990 report that population growth may have been responsible for as much as 80 percent of the forestland cleared between 1971 and 1986 to make room for agriculture, cattle ranching, houses, roads, and industries. It is estimated that in that period nearly 60 million hectares of forest were converted to farmland and a similar amount of forest was put to nonagricultural uses. This is equivalent to the loss of 1,200 square meters of forest for each person added to the population.

When the land becomes too barren or too limited to accommodate growing numbers, migration may offer a way out of rural destitution, as it did to the hungry of Ireland after the notorious famine of 1846–48. It is instructive to recall that disaster of the mid-nineteenth century, about which David Grigg, quoted in *Poverty and Population* has observed, "In 1840 there were few Englishmen who doubted that Ireland's miseries were due to excessive population growth, but there were few Irishmen who did not blame Ireland's woes on England's economic policies." In their crucial differences, the assertions of Irish victims and British rulers in explaining the famine echo some of those advanced today by developing and developed countries. In sub-Saharan Africa poverty is driving many to migrate to urban areas and to neighboring countries. In Latin America, there has been so much migration that most of its people already live in urban areas.

B Y T H E end of the decade, for the first time in human history, a majority of the world's population in both rich and poor countries will live in urban areas. In the industrial countries, and also in Latin

America, almost four out of every five people will live in a city. Contrast this with the situation in mid-century, when the urban population was 30 percent of world population, and at the start of the century, when it was a mere 15 percent. The increase in the number of city dwellers has been staggering: from 730 million in 1950 to 2 billion today and perhaps 3 billion by the year 2000. Three-quarters of this increase is expected to have been in the developing world, with its urban population climbing rapidly from 300 million in 1950 to over 2 billion by 2000, an increase of nearly sevenfold in fifty years.

It is in the megacities, the giant metropolitan areas, that the most dramatic changes are occurring. There were ten cities of over 5 million people in 1950: six in developed countries, three in China, and one in Latin America. By the year 2000, according to UN estimates, there are expected to be forty-four cities of over 5 million; of these only eleven will be in developed countries. And we shall increasingly have to think of supercities, ones that dwarf even the megacities of today. By the year 2000, there will be six cities of over 15 million people: Mexico City, São Paulo, Tokyo/Yokohama, New York, Calcutta, and Bombay. Today Mexico City, which had around 3 million people in 1950, has 19 million—equal to the combined populations of London and Paris. By the end of the century it is expected to have 25 million, almost as many as the whole of Canada has today. If attempts to control its expansion fail, Mexico City may end up with 35 million in the year 2000.

In many developing countries, cities have grown beyond anything imagined a generation ago. In just over eight years from now the developing world as a whole will have to increase the capacity of its cities by a half. In Africa the capacity of cities will need to double. To maintain even existing standards of sanitation, water supply, housing, transportation, employment opportunities, and law and order will be a formidable challenge to many countries already facing great economic difficulty and uncertainty, with resources diminishing relative to needs and rising expectations.

These cities of the developing world might follow the pattern of cities in developed countries, with their growth slowing down after a period of rapid expansion. Certainly, the UN expects the urban growth rate in developing countries to drop from 3.7 percent between 1970 and 1975 to 2.3 percent between 2020 and 2025; but urban growth will still present difficult social and economic problems. Moreover, unlike urbanization in the developed countries, which was coupled with fast industrial expansion, urbanization in the developing countries is out-pacing industrial development and resulting in shantytowns, over-crowding, bad housing, inadequate water and sewage facilities, and armies of unemployed and underemployed people, some of whom can only survive through crime. Poverty and underdevelopment cause mi-gration from rural areas and the appalling living conditions of the urban poor, but population growth intensifies the impact in both cases.

T H E challenge of urban growth can be measured by the often abys-mal conditions that already persist. A survey in the 1980s found that in Lagos, Nigeria, three out of four families lived in single-room dwell-ings, almost 80 percent shared kitchen facilities with other families, and only 13 percent had running water. A recent study of Indian cities found that only one in fifteen had any sewage system. Barely a tenth of Manila's 9 million people are served by sewers. In many sprawling Third World cities, Jakarta, Bangkok, and Santiago, for example, sewage and toxic waste contaminate the limited drinking water. Con-gestion and unregulated industrial activity generate air pollution that seriously reduces life expectancy. In Calcutta, 60 percent of the popu-lation suffer from respiratory diseases related to pollution. Law and order often break down; the much-publicized drug barons of Rio, who exercise complete sway over its large shantytowns, are typical of many megacities—and not only in the developing world—where violence, drunkenness, drug addiction, and now AIDS are rampant.

The rapid emergence of big cities in developing countries is not difficult to understand in the context of widespread poverty, hunger, and economic crisis. Food is usually available in the cities, but not in remote villages when crops fail. Cities provide a certain amount of security for refugees, from both war and the environmental degradation—deforestation, erosion, and desertification—that has drained the agricultural potential of many rural areas. Regular work may be rarely available, but there is usually some menial task to perform in the unregulated economic underground, the "informal sector," and there are enough success stories to encourage newcomers. Urban life offers some real benefits, not just the mirage of bright lights, and city squalor is often offset by other attributes. Health facilities and schools may be inadequate, but some basic facilities are at least within reach. Cities generally have higher levels of literacy and education, lower infant mortality, and better standards of nutrition. Those who throng in hope to the cities may be adding to a set of unmanageable problems, but individually they may be making a rational decision.

There is now broad recognition that urban bias needs to be reversed and priority given to the countryside, especially to small-scale peasant farming. But difficulties abound. Governments that sought to shift the internal "terms of trade" in favor of farmers by raising food prices have faced urban food riots in a number of countries: Tunisia, Sudan, Zambia, the Philippines, Morocco, Jamaica, Egypt. Many governments walk a tightrope between sound economic policy and political survival. In a command economy like China's tight controls can be used to reverse urban bias, but most societies will rightly reject the denial of individual freedom implicit in that approach. Better policies would exert some restraint on the expansion of cities, but given the combined pressures of poverty and population growth, it is unrealistic to expect that the process can be reversed. These pressures must be relieved.

D E V E L O P I N G countries are not alone in contending with urban growth. The cities of the industrial world also face immense challenges: the complexities of municipal management, the financing of public services, housing, poverty, and the control of crime. In some cases, whether a city is governable at all has come into question. Physical and economic well-being are not the only measure of the quality of city life. In the cities of rich countries many millions are trapped in rundown housing or soulless tower blocks. And there are few cities in the world that can match the alienation, despair, and violence of those in South Africa, where the perversion of apartheid rather than lack of resources condemned millions to decades of degradation.

The American writer Raymond Chandler in *The Long Goodbye* described Los Angeles—although it could have been New York, or Tokyo, or London, or Paris—as "a city no worse than others, a city rich and vigorous and full of pride; a city lost and beaten and full of emptiness." That dualism—schizophrenia, almost—all cities express in their being. They are cities that contain fine buildings and parks, impressive urban landscapes, sophisticated systems of transport, communication, and planning. They are repositories of the most up-to-date technology, of leadership and the most forward-looking ideas. They have financial acumen and embody worldly success. But they also stand for mindless materialism, a lack of morality and basic values, for alienation of the individual in the maze of what T. S. Eliot called in "The Wasteland" the "unreal city." There are street children and vagrants with no home but the pavement, drug addiction, squalor, violence, and impersonality.

The city is continuously evolving, for example when the middle class fled city centers to suburban fringes, leaving behind insulated pockets of the rich amid urban squalor and the masses. The cities of the future can be a vast resource of creative energy and economic wealth. They can also be settings for anarchic violence and terrorism, epidemics and organized crime whose consequences could extend far beyond national boundaries. The population explosion is indeed an apt term.

A MAJOR question that has yet to be answered satisfactorily is whether people in developing countries are in fact having more children than they want because they do not know about, or do not have access to, contraceptives. Surveys completed in 1986 show that women use modern contraception far less in Africa than in Asia and Latin America. For example, contraceptives are used by only 4 percent of the women of reproductive age in Burundi, Togo, Uganda, Mali, and Senegal, compared with 18 percent in Bangladesh, 65 percent in Thailand, and 45 percent in Mexico. Surveys also show that in most African countries 70 percent or more women know about modern contraceptives, and in a few countries, Kenya and Zimbabwe for example, contraceptive use is high. Are Africans having large families because they want them, as Thomas Goliber concluded in his 1989 study "Africa's Expanding Problem"? He found that ideal family size among Africans ranged from 5.3 to 8.8 children, and that for most countries ideal family size was actually higher than, or about the same as, the fertility rate.

Would family planning services therefore make any difference? Certainly they would make it easier for many women who want to limit their families to do so, and they would make birth control safer. But there is evidence that women in the developing countries do limit the number of children they have even if they do not use modern contraceptives. In the absence of contraceptives, they resort to abstinence, prolonged breastfeeding, and abortion to control the size of their families. What this suggests is that when couples are sufficiently motivated to limit the number of children they have, they find ways to do so. And people are generally motivated when social and economic conditions improve to the point where they are able to determine the

size of their families without fear for the survival of their children or
for their own well-being. Family planning experts would contest the
claim that child survival is a precondition for the success of their
efforts, citing experience in countries as varied as England and Colombia, but there is no disagreement on the point that reductions in infant
mortality encourage families to plan for smaller families.

Sri Lanka and Indonesia are countries where fertility has declined
though per capita incomes are still low. It is significant that in Sri
Lanka, government policies favoring investment in health and education led to a decline in mortality rates as well as improvements in
literacy and educational standards among both men and women. There
has been movement in the same direction in Indonesia. The south
Indian state of Kerala provides another example where, despite a low
per capita GNP, sociocultural factors improving health care and
women's status have helped to bring about a marked decline in fertility.
Family planning agencies also point approvingly to Bangladesh, where
a significant increase in contraceptive use has been secured against a
backdrop of severe deprivation and high rates of infant mortality.

The general lesson from attempts to influence reproductive patterns is that both development—especially social development—
and effective family planning services are required if fertility is to be
brought down rapidly. Reducing poverty, improving the standard of
health and education, raising the status of women and increasing their
opportunities: these are the conditions that can increase the impact of
available contraceptive services. In other words, availability is important, but it is not sufficient for lowering growth rates. Zimbabwe,
which has the highest rate of modern contraceptive use in sub-Saharan
Africa, has combined its child-spacing campaign with free health care,
expansion of hospital and health facilities, and programs of immuniza-
tion, diarrhea control, and nutrition. Despite the higher use of contraceptives, birth rates have not fallen as much as expected. Large families
are still welcome.

A W O R L D Bank study exploring the population, environment, and
agriculture nexus in sub-Saharan Africa recommends that the emphasis in population policy should be on strengthening the desire for
smaller families rather than on the supply of family planning services
and contraceptive methods. That female literacy and education are
closely linked to fertility is illustrated by the contrasting experiences of

Pakistan and Thailand. Pakistan, with a low level of female literacy, continues to have a high fertility rate (5.9 births per woman) and low contraceptive use despite a long-standing family planning program. Thailand, where a high percentage of women are literate, has brought its fertility rate down to 2.2. Improvement in the status of women is greatly facilitated by economic development but does not always depend on it. In Tunisia, for example, President Habib Bourguiba's personal leadership of the campaign for women's rights is seen as having contributed to the success of population policy. Fertility in Tunisia dropped from 7 births per woman in the 1960s to 4.4 in 1988.

It is important to extend this trend throughout Africa in continuation of the drive to reduce fertility on that continent. The World Bank study explains Africa's particular dilemma:

> Environmental integrity and resource conservation are critical for sustainable long-term growth of agriculture and of the economy. But this will be very hard to achieve if present rates of population growth persist. Population growth is unlikely to come down unless agriculture, and the economies dependent on agriculture, grow more vigorously. Agricultural growth will be increasingly constrained by rapid population growth. (p. 18)

A concerted attack on poverty and underdevelopment remains, therefore, the most secure way forward for our increasingly crowded and environmentally threatened planet. The situation is now so critical that we cannot merely wait for economic prosperity to influence reproductive behavior. By then it will almost certainly be too late.

Development and family planning are not alternative paths for reducing population growth. Family planning should be seen as part of the development process itself, and a part that does not have to wait for the fulfillment of the process in all respects. Development takes time. It advances more purposefully and more quickly in some countries than in others. Poverty alleviation is more effective in some regions of a country than in others. Some aspects of development, like improvements in education, health services, and the status of women, can come faster than other elements of development, like industrialization and agricultural diversification and land reform.

Family planning services must be on hand to respond to these diverse developmental changes that encourage families to turn to such services. Their very existence, and official and community support for them, encourages families to make use of them. So the success of family planning facilities must not be seen as contingent on overall economic development. Without development, the provision of family planning services is not enough to bring the growth rate down to acceptable levels quickly; but it does make a contribution at all stages.

In 1990, about half the couples in low-income countries, some 381 million, regularly used some method of family planning. By the end of the century, that number must be increased by at least an additional 186 million couples, an increase of almost 60 percent, if the UN population projection of 6.25 billion people for the year 2000 is not to be exceeded. Surveys in these poor countries show that 50 to 80 percent of married women actually wish to space or limit their children, but not all are able to do so. It has been estimated that if all the women who said they wanted no more children were able to stop bearing, the number of births would be reduced by 38 percent in Africa, 33 percent in Asia, and 35 percent in Latin America.

The case for increasing national and international financial provision for family planning services should not require intensive advocacy, yet it does. In the developing countries, some $4.5 billion a year is spent on family planning services, of which as much as $3.5 billion comes from these countries themselves and only $0.7 billion from OECD countries, representing a mere 1.3 percent of their development assistance. UNFPA has called for the rich-country contribution to be increased to $4.5 billion by the year 2000 so that global expenditure on family planning activities can be doubled to $9 billion. This suggestion is beginning to receive support internationally. The report "Caring for the Earth" has lent considerable weight to the call. Part of the increase in external support should come in the form of contributions to UNFPA itself, from which, as indicated earlier, the United States has withdrawn support.

It is both fallacious and unfair for the rich to imply, as they all too often do, that the poor are making little effort to limit their numbers. Birth rates have actually fallen two to seven times faster in today's low-income countries with effective family planning programs than they did in Europe and North America during a similar transition from high to low fertility. The developing countries must maintain, and indeed intensify, their efforts, but these must be assisted much more by the industrial countries, both directly and in the wider context of development. Rich nations share with the poor a real interest in ensuring that human numbers do not exceed Earth's carrying capacity.

T H E pressures of population on the environment are widely manifest. Even when proper allowance is made for distortion, excessive population growth remains one of the greatest pressures we have placed on our planet's resources, one of the self-destruct mechanisms we have built into our future prospects. As the experience of India in the time of Sanjay Gandhi's vigorous efforts to bring down the birth rate shows, and as China's recent experience also demonstrates, policies of compulsion cannot be relied on to ensure success in reducing rates of growth.

The best chance we have lies in creating a socio-economic climate in which couples will make the decision for themselves that small families are best. Confidence about livelihoods, economic and social security—all that is encompassed in genuine economic development—is a central element of that climate.

In the last resort, the rich are no more isolated from the environmental stress caused by poverty and overpopulation than the poor are from the environmental stress caused by affluence and excessive consumption. Rich and poor are locked in an environmental freefall; they must cling to each other if they hope to pull the release cord in time and parachute to safety. That time is surely now. As the overall population picture changes, it grows more threatening. By 2025 poor countries will provide 84 percent of world population, up from 68 percent in 1960. Of all the babies born in 1990, 93 percent were born in developing countries. This is a remarkable change in the world's demographic balance. It is not free of implications for rich countries.

Gradually, and largely through their own efforts, poor people are acquiring more education and a wider range of skills, and they are traveling more easily in a world shrunk by the revolution in communications and transportation. But their economic opportunities do not match their rising skills; they constituted 77 percent of the world's people in 1990 but earned only 15 percent of the world's income. They will respond as people have done from time immemorial when entrapped by poverty and lack of opportunity: They will strive to better themselves. Without economic opportunity at home, they will travel toward economic opportunity abroad, opportunity that beckons them insistently through media images of affluent lifestyles. As of 1990 the industrial countries already had 14 million economic refugees from poor countries, and the ranks are inevitably swelling. Not surprisingly, UNDP concluded in its "Human Development Report, 1991," "The pressures for international migration are building rapidly, and the next few decades could well see unprecedented movements across international borders—movements that could exceed the migrations from Europe that settled the USA, Canada and Australia." (p. 80)

The quest for human betterment, which once found fulfilment in the occupation of a whole continent and the founding of a great nation, remains just as noble as it always was and just as persistent, as the phenomenon of twentieth-century "boat people" reminds us. The process of migration will be different, perhaps less formal and orderly, and host countries almost certainly less welcoming, but the driving force will be the same—the escape from poverty, injustice, and despair. The promise of succor may be withheld, but the claim upon it is no less just or urgent—unless there is some other form of relief from the desperation that validates it.

How can matters not get worse if we tolerate poverty and double the numbers of the poor? Is this the best we can do with all the affluence we have acquired and all the science and technology we have mastered? Or have we lost both our wisdom and our compassion in the process? If we were wise and caring we would recognize our species, as Jean-Paul Sartre urged in the quotation from his preface to *The Wretched of the Earth*, with which this chapter began, not as "the sum total of the whole world's inhabitants" but as "the infinite unity of their mutual needs." It is by enlightened response to mutual need that we will most effectively keep human numbers balanced against Earth's life-sustaining capacity.

SEVEN

⚶

A Feudal World

> *Tien xia wei gong:* What is under Heaven is
> for all.   — *Sun Yat-Sen*

N E S T L I N G in the Purple Mountains overlooking Nanjin in eastern China is the Sun Yat-Sen Memorial on whose pinnacle are immor-
talized the words above. Sun Yat-Sen took them from one of the
ancient books of China to provide the guiding principle for the revolutionary movement that liberated his country from its feudal past. That
past was not peculiar to China; it has been a part of the history of most
countries, East and West, North and South. The words above speak
for all the world, and though they are ignored by it, they are especially
relevant to our global society.

Feudalism as a system of economic, social, and political organization was a system that held people in permanent subordination. Narrowly construed, it justified itself on the ground of contract: the service
of the serf in return for the protection of the lord and master. In essence
it was a system that divided society into strong and weak, powerful
and powerless, haves and have-nots, those who made the rules and
gave the orders and others whose role was to defer and obey. To the
great credit of our species, the history of human society has been one of
movement away from feudalism to systems less unequal and unjust,
systems in which Earth's bounty and the fruits of human toil are
shared more fairly, societies that more closely respect the precept that
"what is under Heaven is for all." But the movement away from

feudalism stopped at national frontiers; the concept of sharing, even of fairness, generally evolved within states, not between them. Human society, the world of people, remained beyond the reach of that civilizing precept. What is under Heaven has not been for all on Earth.

IN ADDRESSING the role of the international economy in securing our common future, the Brundtland Report made the basic point that "the pursuit of sustainability requires major changes in international economic relations." It elaborated in "Our Common Future" as follows:

> Two conditions must be satisfied before international economic exchanges can become beneficial for all involved. The sustainability of ecosystems on which the global economy depends must be guaranteed. And the economic partners must be satisfied that the basis of exchange is equitable; relationships that are unequal and based on dominance of one kind or another are not a sound and durable basis for interdependence. For many developing countries, neither condition is met. (p. 17)

In the Brundtland Commission's view, environmental issues were making it more essential that the world community strengthen international cooperation in advancing development in the Third World as poverty was a major threat to the environment. The commission also emphasized that economic interdependence among nations was being reinforced by ecological interdependence, and that issues of ecology and economy were becoming entwined at national, regional, and above all international levels. People and countries, rich and poor alike, were as dependent on each other in the environmental context as they were in an increasingly globalized economic context; and economic and ecological issues were affecting each other. Environmental compulsions were relevant to and making more urgent the dialogue through which poor countries had long sought to engage the rich to establish more favorable global conditions for development.

These efforts have so far made little headway. But the need to improve development dialogue—the North-South dialogue, as it became known—is now reinforced by the crisis of environment. Global warming, ozone depletion, the loss of forests, the threat to genetic diversity—all these signal that North and South, rich and poor, need each other. Correspondingly, success in advancing development in poor countries will be of critical significance for the pursuit of sustainability. The Brundtland Commission focused on environment and development; so will the Earth Summit in 1992.

T H E overwhelming majority of today's developing countries were once colonies of one or another of the European powers—Britain, France, Spain, Portugal, the Netherlands, Belgium. Apart from those in Latin America, most developing countries regained their independence only after World War II. Newly come to nationhood, they soon found that the economic disparities that had existed between themselves and their former colonizers not only persisted into the new era but were widening. It did not take them long to see that the global economic system that governed trading, financial, and other economic relations needed to be adapted so that their interests would also be taken into account.

The system, a hangover from the days of empire, evolved to suit the needs of the European countries that had once dominated world trade. Some revision of it was undertaken as the war was coming to an end, but the interests of poor countries were largely ignored at the international conference at Bretton Woods, New Hampshire, in 1944. There it was agreed to set up the World Bank and the IMF as the key institutions of the new system. The leading industrial countries of the West were the main participants. Most of today's developing countries were still colonies and powerless to influence the decisions shaping the world they would inherit. Some of the more farseeing ideas proposed at the time, which could have strengthened the position of developing countries, were rejected.

The World Bank and the IMF did go some way in responding to the interests of emerging developing countries, but they could not make up for the deficiencies in the world economic system. To developing countries, it seemed to have built-in features that hobbled their efforts at economic progress. In contending that the struggle against poverty should be considered a global responsibility, they had the support of many people of goodwill in the rich countries. The Pearson Commission's report of the 1960s, "Partners in Development," expressed that goodwill and also acknowledged the existence of mutual interests. But conviction about the imperfection of global arrangements grew only as developing countries experienced continuing frustration in trying to speed up development. Progress was incommensurate with effort. Frustration led the poor countries in the early 1970s to call collectively and vigorously for changes in the basic relationship between themselves and rich countries to make the relationship more supportive of Third World progress.

The discussions resulting from this call, the North-South dialogue, received some impetus from OPEC's initial success in raising the price of oil. Developing countries were encouraged by OPEC's use of collective strength. Industrial countries, for their part, were concerned that OPEC members, then seemingly in a strong position, would make common cause with other developing countries in seeking concessions from them. The North-South dialogue reached its high point in the mid-1970s with consensus between rich and poor countries in the UN General Assembly in 1974 and at the UN Conference on Trade and Development in 1976. But momentum soon flagged, and the developing countries' achievements in those years turned out to have little more than "declaratory value," as the South Commission concluded in its report, "The Challenge to the South," in 1990.

What happened was that the apparent willingness of the industrial countries to make limited concessions dissolved as OPEC's effectiveness ebbed. They had been influenced less by considerations of justice and equity (or even by the prospect of long-term business opportunities if the South developed) than by their assessment of OPEC's power. With a few exceptions, notably the Scandinavian countries, industrial powers tended to see the demands of the poor as a tedious aggravation. For the rest of the decade their approach was to let developing countries weary themselves in inconclusive dialogue. The innovative suggestions about reform of the global economy, far from perfect though they were, came mainly from poor nations, while the rich offered lectures on the technical imperfections of these ideas, their counterproductive effects, and their unacceptability to parliaments and congresses. Sometimes the rich just said no. Occasionally, as with the proposal to set up a common fund to bring some stability to the prices of commodities exported by poor countries, the rich adopted a somewhat less inhospitable approach, but only after the original design had been so transformed and its scope so whittled down as to render it largely ineffectual. Developing countries cannot ignore this experience as they begin in the 1990s, with an agenda drawn up largely by rich nations, a new round of "dialogue" on environment and development issues.

Though industrial countries tend to resist changes suggested by developing countries, they have always found it possible to take quick action when they felt the need to protect their own interests. America's Marshall Plan for the postwar reconstruction of European economies was established by virtually unilateral action. The International Energy Agency was set up in 1974 within months of a perceived energy crisis. Much more recently, with the collapse of communism in Eastern Europe and its implications for OECD countries, it took only months to create the European Bank of Reconstruction and Development, for the European Community to provide some $7 billion in credit to the then Soviet Union, and for the United States to provide a further $1 billion to buy food. All this was a worthy and welcome response to need. By contrast, when the Brandt Commission proposed a world development fund in 1983 to serve some of the same purposes in relation to developing countries, the proposal could not find a sponsor among the governments of the wealthy countries.

At another level international financial institutions, the IMF in particular, have moved swiftly to assist a developing country when a particular Western interest called for such assistance, as in the IMF's program of support for Turkey, important in a NATO context, or for El Salvador, perceived as important to U.S. interests. Moreover, the industrial countries have not hesitated to use the facilities of these institutions themselves, though the countries tend to oppose proposals to strengthen them. Take the case of special drawing rights (SDRs), the IMF's reserve asset. The United States drew down 1.1 billion SDRs from the IMF in 1978–79 to support the dollar in foreign exchange markets, and EEC countries drew down 1.5 billion SDRs for currency support between 1973 and 1977. Yet the United States has led the resistance to the call by developing countries for a link between the issue of SDRs and development needs so that they, the poor countries, would be beneficiaries.

D E V E L O P I N G countries were not wholly blameless for the failure of the North-South dialogue. They were too strident in making their case for fairer international arrangements. They had excessive faith in their bargaining power and mistakenly believed they could prevail through confrontation. They also offered hostages to fortune with some of their tactics. On the matter of fair prices for commodities, they put too much emphasis on a single strategy, calling for a common fund to finance price stabilization schemes. On the other hand, at successive meetings of the UNCTAD, they made the mistake of pressing to put too many issues on the agenda. And all too often they were inadequately prepared and lacked effective technical support for complex negotiations. Consequently, they tended to lose by default. The poor did not do themselves justice.

In a talk I gave some years ago at a meeting in Cartagena, Colombia, I underlined this failure by alluding to an important event in Latin American history. The first major document of Simon Bolivar, the liberator of Latin America, was the Memorandum of Cartagena, which he wrote in 1812 after his first defeat. In it he identified the external causes for his defeat and also examined his own conduct and that of his fellow revolutionaries: "We had philosophers for leaders, philanthropy for legislation, dialectics for tactics, and sophists for soldiers." In calling for similar self-examination by developing countries, I remarked that perhaps they too would find that for the Third World generally there had been too much philosophy, too much dialectic, too much sophistry, and perhaps too much philanthropy. Above all, I warned against mistaking voting power in the UN for the power to make decisions, and against pressing for resolutions that flatter only to deceive. Since then, the South Commission has been able to undertake the task of self-examination with the frankness of Bolivar. That is not to say that either questioned the goal; it was the strategy that was critically examined.

In pressing for reform of the international economy, developing countries have been looking for a global system that would be less obstructive to their efforts to make progress and overcome poverty. The many millions of poor people in these countries are, of course, unaware of the international factors that bear on their poverty and, therefore, on the pressure they unwittingly place on the environment as they struggle to live from day to day. But their conditions of life are linked in a multitude of ways, invisibly but surely, to such factors as the prices their crops fetch on world markets, the trade barriers rich countries impose on the exports of the poor, interest and exchange rates in the money markets of London, the budget deficits of the United States, the European Community's farm subsidies, the resources available to the World Bank, and the decisions of the Group of Seven at their annual summit. For the greater part, the poor and poverty seem invisible to those who control these factors. What tends to be visible, often magnified, are policy failures and other weaknesses within developing countries. These are perhaps neither more frequent nor more venal than in rich countries, but they blacken the image of developing countries and hamper their efforts to obtain fairer international arrangements. Enlightened opinion within poor countries is alive to the danger this poses to their collective interests. As the South Commission report concluded:

> In the final analysis, the South's plea for justice, equity, and democracy in the global society cannot be dissociated from its pursuit of these goals within its own societies. Commitment to democratic values, respect for fundamental rights—particularly the right to dissent —fair treatment for minorities, concern for the poor and underprivileged, probity in public life, willingness to settle disputes without recourse to war—all these cannot but influence world opinion and increase the South's chances of securing a new world order. (p. 287)

D E V E L O P I N G countries have made some progress in improving the conditions of their people over recent decades, despite the many impediments thrown up by the global system, by inherited disadvantages, and in some cases by bad government. There have been remarkable strides in advancing literacy, reducing mortality rates, and developing scientific and entrepreneurial resources. Some nations, particularly the NICs of east and southeast Asia, have made sustained economic advances. But poverty remains the lot of far too many people on our planet. After strenuous efforts to achieve economic progress, the developing countries (excluding a handful of high-income countries) have seen their average annual per capita income rise (in 1989 dollars) from $447 in 1965 to $800 in 1988–89. The corresponding movement for OECD members has been from $10,390 to $19,090.

In addressing the issue of the disparities between rich and poor in the world, the Brandt Report commented: "The extent to which the international system will be made more equitable is essentially a matter for political decision. We are looking for a world based less on power and status, more on justice and contract; less discretionary, more governed by fair and open rules." (p. 65) Those last words are specially apposite. In one sense, the difference between the eighteenth and nineteenth centuries on the one hand and the twentieth on the other is that we now have not so many separate feudal societies but a global society that bears some of the attributes of a feudal state. The trouble is that we have lived for so long in separate communities that we find it hard to recognize the respects in which we have become one world and to admit the need to act as its members. Over the millennia our separatism fed on differences of tribe and race, of language and religion, on divisions of class and on human aggrandizement and on the lust for power; and eventually it came to be institutionalized in the nation-state and sustained by the concept of sovereignty. It might almost be said that disunity, indeed antipathy, was the natural human condition. And yet, over the centuries, we have been moving away from this primitive instinct, our loyalties evolving from family to clan to tribe to nation to region—always toward steadily larger groups, each stage marking an advance from a narrower vision and a smaller world.

I N   T H E   closing years of the 1960s, Lester Pearson, former prime minister of Canada and a great internationalist, was asked by then President of the World Bank Robert McNamara to head a team that would look at the record of twenty years of postwar cooperation for development. "Partners in Development" was the title of the ensuing report. I quote below from its opening pages, which set the scene for the report's conclusions:

> The widening gap between the developed and developing countries has become a central issue of our time. . . . In some of the rich countries the feasibility of development, even its very purpose is in question. The climate surrounding foreign aid programs is heavy with disillusion and distrust. . . . The acceleration of population growth is straining against the absorptive capacity of many societies and nullifying much of the development effort. . . . Unemployment and underemployment have reached critical proportions in many developing countries and will probably grow worse in the 1970s. . . . The foreign indebtedness of the developing countries has risen rapidly. . . . The need for export growth was underestimated, agricultural development was usually neglected. . . . (But while) stagnation prevailed in many countries, the rapid growth in others effectively demonstrated that underdevelopment can be overcome. . . . (pp. 3, 4)

That is where we were at the end of the 1960s. That is where we were at the end of the 1980s, and could be still at the end of the century. Over the decades, not much has changed. The rich have conceded little to the claims of the poor. Their interlocutors may regard that as unqualified success. In the eyes of the poor, however, the global economic system remains inhospitable and unfair. What is under Heaven is not yet for all.

The deficiencies of the world economic system in relation to developing countries were thrown in high relief in the 1980s, the lost decade, as we have seen. The early years of the decade were admittedly marked by worldwide recession, which hurt rich countries as well as poor. But the former were soon to recover and to enjoy the longest uninterrupted postwar period of growth. Not so the developing countries, many of which are still struggling to overcome the hardships into which recession had plunged them.

For developing countries, the 1980s were a decade in which the prices of many of the commodities that are their principal exports fell to the lowest levels since the Great Depression of the 1930s; world interest rates were at unprecedentedly high levels; the problem of external debt assumed staggering proportions as interest rates soared, incoming capital diminished, and debt service preempted an exceedingly high proportion of export earnings; and protectionist barriers in industrial countries against exports from developing countries multiplied. The effects of these calamities were seen in drastic reductions in both development and consumption expenditure, in retrenchment and growing unemployment, and in reduced support for vital services like health and education. For the people of most developing nations, it meant a lower standard of living, widening poverty, and increased deprivation and suffering. For the environment, the consequence was increasing degradation.

Three areas of economic relations between rich and poor countries—trade, debt, and aid—illustrate just how fundamentally these relations bear on the prospects for development, how entwined they are with environmental issues, and how essential it is that global conditions for development be improved if we are to keep the environment safe and sound.

INTERNATIONAL trade is a major engine of growth. It is certainly held in the Third World to be the most effective engine of growth for developing countries—if there is an open trading environment in which countries can benefit from the comparative advantages they possess. But that is not the environment developing countries have encountered during their debut into the world marketplace. They have had to face wide-ranging restrictions on exports to industrial countries. The General Agreement on Tariffs and Trade (GATT) was designed to be a global bulwark of trade liberalization and non-discrimination, but protection and discrimination continue. Nothing better illustrates this than the Multifiber Arrangement (MFA) concluded in 1973 under GATT expressly to slow the growth of exports of textiles and clothing—made from cotton, wool, and synthetic fibers—to Western markets from "low cost" suppliers. Japan had earlier been the leading such supplier and main target; but developing countries, for whom the manufacture of textiles and garments can be crucially important at the earliest stages of industrialization, soon came to be the MFA's principal victims. Some of the world's poorest nations, like Bangladesh, which had an average per capita income of only $170 in 1988, have suffered from the application of MFA quotas by wealthy countries, including the United States and Canada. Some of the world's smallest countries (the Maldives, Nepal, and Jamaica, for example) have also come up against the protectionist policies of industrial countries in the textiles and garments sector.

Other quantitative (nontariff) barriers against the exports of developing countries were to follow, bearing such euphemistic labels as "orderly marketing arrangements" and "voluntary export restrictions." For poor countries it was virtually Hobson's choice: They had to accept "self-imposed" export restraints or face even more severe protectionist measures imposed unilaterally by industrialized countries. These measures typically do not require approval by parliaments or by GATT as tariff restrictions do; indeed, they are frequently not even in the public domain. The impediments to developing countries as they try to trade their way out of poverty now make up a long list. It was reported in September 1991 that the GATT secretariat had counted 284 discriminatory export-restraint arrangements imposed by industrial countries. In 1991, a group of experts who made a study for Commonwealth countries on the impact of global economic and political change on the development process commented as follows in their report, "Change for the Better":

While only about a third of the 250 or so discriminatory export restraint arrangements in place at the end of the 1980s were explicitly targeted against developing countries, they do fall disproportionately hard on these countries. The products involved include consumer goods such as shoes, cutlery, cars, televisions and radios; intermediate goods such as certain types of steel, chemicals and transistors; and some producer goods such as ships.... All the major Western European and North American importing countries have invoked them, finding this politically easier, if economically much less appropriate, than adjusting to changes in competitive advantage.... The irony is that the exemplar for such measures had been negotiated some 30 years earlier under GATT's own auspices: the biggest "orderly" marketing arrangement of them all, the Multi-fiber Arrangement which regulates (and restricts) exports of developing countries' textiles and clothing. (p. 100)

The principles of an open economy driven by market forces are supposed to favor producers whose efficiency and lower costs give them a comparative advantage over competing producers. This advantage the developing countries have in a wide range of labor-intensive manufactures, the first fruits of the industrial process. But no measure of comparative advantage will enable them to surmount the barriers industrial countries put up in the form of quantitative restrictions, as these apply irrespective of price. Ironically, such barriers are also expensive for the countries that erect them, because while they are intended to protect low-productivity jobs in local industries, they lead to much higher costs for consumers. The consequences for developing countries are not limited, however, to slowing economic progress. As restrictions block exports of labor-intensive manufactures, developing countries are thrown back on their traditional role in the world economy as exporters of primary products, for which they must raid their natural resources. It is the environment that pays the ultimate price.

The rich countries use an array of measures that make it difficult for poor countries to move beyond the export of raw materials. They do this to protect their own processing industries, even those at the earliest stage of the transformation of raw materials into manufactured products—the industrial space that at the very least developing countries could expect to be left free for them. Industrial countries, for example, invariably charge import duties on a graduated scale so that the more processed the imported product, the higher the rate of duty. Timber is an example. Raw logs may be imported duty free into industrial countries, but sawn timber is slapped with a tariff of 5 percent, furniture 15 percent. The impact of these rates is greater than the nominal figures convey, as the higher tariffs are levied on the value added in processing or manufacture.

This system of tariff escalation leads developing countries to try and earn more foreign exchange by exporting a greater tonnage of logs rather than by adding more value to each ton by sawing the logs and manufacturing the timber products. Tariff escalation affects many exports besides timber, including cotton, jute, leather, rubber, paper, iron, and tobacco. The effect of tariff escalation is also pronounced on farm products. Import duties levied by industrial countries on prepared vegetables are more than twice those charged on fresh vegetables. Similarly, prepared fruit faces double the tariff of fresh fruit.

Not only is the system unfair to development, it is pernicious in its impact on the environment. The net effect of tariff escalation is to oblige developing countries to export a high proportion of raw or unprocessed materials. More than 90 percent of developing countries' exports of sugar and cocoa, for instance, is shipped without processing; so is more than 70 percent of their meat, fish, and vegetable exports. As in the case of logs, the exporting countries find that to increase their earnings they must export more of the raw product; in most cases this means using more land and water and adding more fertilizer and pesticide, all at the expense of the environment.

The trade policies of industrial countries operate in other ways to diminish the trading opportunities for developing countries. In agriculture, an area of particular export potential for poor countries, industrial nations heavily protect their domestic producers, effectively closing their markets to Third World exporters who are thereby prevented from benefiting from the comparative advantage they would have in many farm products. Even worse, industrial countries dump surplus agricultural products on world markets, depressing prices and impeding agricultural production elsewhere.

The European Community's Common Agricultural Policy (CAP) is the most flagrant example of large-scale agricultural protectionism, and it deserves to be condemned on many grounds, not least because of its consequences for the environment. Farmers are induced by heavy subsidies to maximize production with intensive use of fertilizers and other such inputs. Such protectionism is contrary to the espoused principles of a free market economy, inimical to the efforts of poor countries to lift themselves out of poverty, and a major (perhaps fatal) impediment to a liberal world trading system. Few winners emerge from protectionism. It imposes heavy burdens on consumers and tax-payers in the industrial countries themselves. Agricultural support in OECD countries has been priced at over $140 billion a year, money that could certainly be better used in developing and introducing environmentally friendly farming methods. This amounts to £700 annually for each family in Britain, three and a half times the average annual income of a person in India. Protection for the textile and clothing industries under the Multifiber Arrangement is estimated to cost each U.S. household over $500 a year, which is four times the annual income of an average Ethiopian.

Protectionism is estimated to cost the developing countries as much as $100 billion a year in lost earnings from agricultural products, and a further $50 billion from textiles and garments. These are severe losses to bear; they represent income that could have been used to combat desertification, replace firewood with less destructive sources of energy, or provide water and sanitation for the millions who lack such basic necessities. Compared with what is received in development aid from industrial countries, a total of $54 billion in 1990, the losses are inexcusable. Protectionism prevents the developing world from bene-fiting fully from the growth of international trade. Between 1968 and 1988 the share of developing countries, excluding oil-exporting ones, in world trade shrank from 15.2 percent to 12.9 percent. By the end of the 1980s, exports from Africa were over a fifth below the level at the end of the 1970s. The reduction of imports, made unavoidable by the drop in export earnings, was equally severe and its impact devastating.

F O R many developing countries, especially the poorest, the export of primary commodities—agricultural products like sugar and rubber and minerals like bauxite and copper—is still the economic mainstay. Some have two or three commodities. Tanzania grows coffee, cotton, and sisal (a fiber), and Papua New Guinea produces copper, coffee, and timber. There are several countries that are dependent on just one commodity: a few of the Caribbean islands on bananas, Zambia on copper, and Uganda on coffee. In all these countries, economic vigor is closely linked to the income from sales of commodities and therefore to the prices they fetch in world markets. Prices are peculiarly prone to fluctuation, but there has been a general tendency for prices of com-modities exported by developing countries to move down—unlike those of manufactured products, like trucks or turbines, which move steadily up. In the 1980s commodity prices dropped sharply and stayed depressed for years. Though they picked up somewhat in 1988, the World Bank reckoned that by 1989 average prices other than for oil were down a third from what they had been when the decade started. What would have happened in rich countries had that been their experience with exports in the last decade?

The effect of low prices is generally to drive countries to produce and export more so that earnings may be maintained. The result is additional pressure on the environment, not to mention the risk of pushing prices further down. Oversupply sometimes weakens commodity markets, with developing countries offering more on the market than demand warrants. But in several farm products, as indicated earlier, prices have been forced down because of industrial countries' agricultural subsidies. For certain other commodities, slacker demand is the result of competition from manmade manufactures in industrial countries or of the introduction by these countries of industrial processes requiring less use of a particular commodity. One way or the other, commodity producers in poor countries are victims of forces and trends beyond their control.

International commodity markets and trade barriers seem far removed from the fact that the soil and the water, agriculture's very foundation, are being destroyed. Yet as the FAO, whose role is to promote efforts to increase food production, underlines in its report "Sustainable Development and Natural Resource Management":

> Creating a truly effective and integrated international effort to promote sustainable development . . . implies, above all, a recognition that the environmental problems of developing countries ultimately are woven into international markets, trade patterns and capital flows. As a consequence, reform of these structural relations is also needed: sustainable agriculture requires investment which developing nations, and especially the poor, cannot afford. (p. 35)

Developing countries are lectured insistently about the virtues of the free market and the benevolence of market forces. But their experience is of an international marketplace that is not always free. In recent years, industrial countries have come face to face with the contradictions in the Uruguay Round of Multilateral Trade Negotiations under the auspices of GATT. These negotiations, intended to extend the area of liberal trade, have foundered on a reef of irreconcilable differences among industrial countries themselves, essentially between the United

States and Europe, on the liberalization of trade in agriculture. The talks may have been refloated and some agreement reached by the time this book appears, but the developing countries' interests are not likely to be significantly advanced in the process.

T H E debt problem, which has engulfed a large number of developing countries for over a decade, is another striking example of the way global economic arrangements can impede the progress of the Third World. It also illustrates the inadequacy of international machinery for dealing with problems that have a critical effect on these countries. The 1980 Brandt Report drew attention to the serious implications of growing debt, an offshoot of the Western response to the energy "crisis" of the 1970s during which banks saw an opportunity to profit from recycling the surplus funds of OPEC countries to other developing countries. In 1983 the Brandt Commission reconvened specifically to address the question of debt and to alert the world community to the magnitude of the crisis. In a second report, "Common Crisis, North-South: Cooperation for World Recovery," the commission called on Western governments to give loan waivers to the poorest countries and to reschedule other debts, while providing adequate resources through the support of lenders.

What followed were years of limp responses, always reluctant, always limited, always late. It took almost a decade for industrial countries to recognize the need for debt relief or reduction on a large scale, and so far relief has been provided mainly in terms of the official debt (government-to-government debt) of least-developed or low-income countries and, for special political reasons, to Poland and Egypt. To date only six other countries have been offered some relief on their commercial debt, that is, debt owed to Western banks, through arrangements under the Brady plan, named after the U.S. treasury secretary. The progress of that plan has been slow, and resources have not been adequate to affect the debt burden in significant ways in many developing countries.

In 1980, the total foreign debt of developing countries was $640 billion. By 1990 it had more than doubled to $1.3 trillion, which amounted to about 45 percent of their total annual income (GNP). In several countries debt was a much higher percentage of the national income: 140 percent in Egypt and Zaire and 400 percent in Mozambique in 1989. In 1990 the debt of severely indebted low-income countries was estimated to be 120 percent of their combined annual income and 446 percent of their annual exports; corresponding figures for the seventeen severely indebted middle-income countries were 59 percent and 283 percent.

It is debt service payments, swollen by high interest rates, that made external debt a major problem in the last decade. In 1990 the 111 developing countries reporting their debt to the World Bank paid $66 billion in interest and $75 billion in repayments of capital, a total debt service of $141 billion. As debt service went up with interest rates, and as Western banks sharply reduced the flow of fresh loan funds, debt-related transactions, which had up to then resulted in a net transfer of resources to the developing countries, started to produce a net transfer in the reverse direction—from poor to rich countries—after 1983. Between 1984 and 1990, the 111 developing countries covered in World Bank data transferred a total of $247 billion to creditor nations, an average of over $35 billion a year from poor to rich. The situation can be likened to that of a poor family in bondage to a rich money-lender, eking out an existence without hope of end.

Even when all financial flows (private investment and government grants in addition to commercial and official loans) are taken into account, the net transfer of resources for ninety-three developing countries covered in UN data was consistently in the direction of the developed countries from 1983 until 1989, with transfers averaging over $13 billion a year. If the gold standard had been in place and gold bullion used in payment, this would have meant an annual transfer from the poor countries of 1,120 tons of gold bullion—enough gold to fill eight rooms, each 10 feet wide, 12 feet long, and 8 feet high. In 1990, for the first time in eight years, there was a positive transfer to developing countries of $1.7 billion; but this was a small fraction of the $41.9 billion transferred to developing countries in 1980.

Among the great men chronicled by the Greek philosopher and biographer Plutarch in his *Parallel Lives* was Solon, the Athenian statesman and poet of the sixth century B.C. His constitutional reforms laid the foundations for Athenian democracy; his economic reforms included the abolition of serfdom and debt-incurred slavery. Plutarch had this to say of him:

> Peculiar to Solon was his remission of debts, and by this means especially he confirmed the liberties of the citizens. For equality under the laws is of no avail if the poor are robbed of it by their

debts. Nay, in the very places where they are supposed to exercise their liberties most, there they are most in subjection to the rich, since in the courts of justice, the offices of state, and in public debates, they are under their orders and do them service. And what is of greater moment here, though sedition always follows an abolition of debts, in this case alone, by employing opportunely, as it were, a dangerous but powerful medicine, Solon actually put an end to the sedition that was already rife, for his own virtue and high repute prevailed over the ill-repute and odium of the measure. (p. 17)

The world of lenders would do well to reflect on not only the justice but also the wisdom of Solon.

One does not, however, have to go back to the Athens of Solon to find precedents for the relief of sovereign debt, or debt owed by governments. There is a substantial record in the financial history of industrial countries themselves of nonpayment of debt and of its acceptance by creditor governments in the interest of restoring stricken economies and giving the world economy a better chance to prosper. In the eighteenth century that list included Denmark, Holland, and czarist Russia, each defaulting once, and Austria, Spain, Greece, Portugal, and some preunification German states doing so repeatedly. Defaulting too were some American states: Maryland, Pennsylvania, Louisiana, and Mississippi.

A comprehensive solution to the debt problem has eluded the political reach of the rich world, though it has been well within its economic grasp. Debtor countries remain helpless victims of the policies of creditor nations. With the United States running huge deficits, global interest rates remained at unprecedentedly high levels for many years in the 1980s. According to the World Bank, real interest rates in the 1980s were on average nearly six times higher than in the period from 1974 to 1979, when developing countries contracted most of their loans. Each additional 1 percent of interest rate adds another $6 billion a year to the debt service—the payment of interest and repayment of capital—of the Third World. In large parts of the developing world, debt service absorbs so much of the country's income that no development is now possible without a significant reduction in external debt.

In many cases debt service takes up more than one-fourth of the earnings from exports. In 1990, the Ivory Coast saw debt service claim 62 percent of its export income. Argentina had a debt-service ratio of 45 percent despite some rescheduling of debts to lighten its burden.

For countries in economic crisis, the burden has been an insurmountable obstacle to attempts at reviving economic growth and improving the living standards of citizens. Its impact on poverty has had pervasive implications for the state of the environment. This connection finds a reflection in some of the debt-relief measures now being pursued in the form of "debt for nature" swaps. Countries are in effect relieved of some of their debt by repaying it at a discount in their local currency; the payment is then used to finance environmental conservation measures. But conservation is not sustainable without development.

Some of the implications for the environment are more direct. Debt has not only eroded the capacity of developing countries to care for the environment, it has led some countries to countenance continuing damage to the environment. Lester Brown and his colleagues at the Worldwatch Institute in Washington have clearly set out how financial difficulties aggravated by the debt crisis affect the behavior of poor countries toward the environment. They made the following contribution to an important World Bank environment working paper (No. 46—not an official position paper of the bank):

> Lack of capital has made it nearly impossible for developing countries to invest adequately in forest protection, soil conservation, irrigation improvements, more energy-efficient technologies, or pollution control devices. Even worse, growing debts have compelled them to sell off natural resources, often their only source of foreign currency. Like a consumer forced to hock the family heirlooms to pay credit card bills, developing countries are plundering forests, decimating fisheries, and depleting water supplies—regardless of the long-term consequences. Unfortunately, no global pawnbroker is holding on to this inheritance until the world can afford to buy it back. (p. 80)

How is a poor country, its basic development crippled by a debt burden it can never shed, to muster either the will or the means to help to save the planet?

Those questions are all too pertinent to my country today as Guyana struggles with an IMF economic recovery program, a high per capita debt, and a swing to a free market economy with an emphasis on privatization and foreign investment, particularly in natural resource development. It is a combination widely welcomed, at home and abroad, but it is clearly not without an ecological price in areas like forest development and mining. On those issues of the price to the environment, the international community so far offers little constructive assistance.

A N D what is true of debt is true as well of aid. Aid, or official development assistance, is at its best directed to the relief of poverty and the promotion of real development. There is no question that a sense of moral obligation of the kind implicit in Roosevelt's articulation of the fourth freedom, freedom from want, has underpinned the aid efforts of industrial countries over the last fifty years. It clearly continues to motivate those countries that provide high levels of aid in relation to their income. The ethical ʹdimension has been, and is, immensely important.

But there is another aspect to aid, one the Brandt Commission was at pains to underscore, namely the mutual interest of rich and poor in facilitating economic progress in developing countries. There are sound economic reasons why the industrial world should help the Third World become less poor. Before the onset of the economic crisis of the 1980s, developing countries accounted for one-fifth of global production, a share comparable to that of the European Community. Their role as markets for exports was also significant; they were then buying about a quarter of the goods exported by developed countries. They provided a market for nearly 40 percent of U.S. exports and for 50 percent of Japan's. Sustained development of poor nations can only enlarge their demand for the exports of the rich.

The significance of the developing countries to the global economy was amply confirmed by the crisis of the 1980s, which caused them to reduce their imports sharply. As the report of the South Commission pointed out in 1990, if the ability of developing countries to import in the period from 1984 to 1987 had been at the same proportionate level as in the period from 1981 to 1983, their purchases from industrial countries would have been $300 billion more than they were. What the rich countries lost in potential exports in those four years exceeded in value an entire year's global exports from the United States.

The poor countries as a group are therefore not insignificant to the health of rich economies and of the world economy in general. Aid that injects economic vigor into a developing country serves the interest of both donor and recipient. But even more directly—a fact of which the general Western public is not aware—a large proportion of "aid" is tied to the purchase of goods and services from the aid-giving country, thereby creating business and markets for Western firms and technical experts. In 1988 the proportion of bilateral aid that was tied—returned to the donor country as payments for purchases—was 58 percent for Australia, 60 percent for West Germany, 76 percent for Canada, 82 percent for the United States, and 90 percent for Britain. The tying of aid prevents the receiving country from buying from the cheapest source through worldwide procurement, and some critics have complained that aid-tying has the effect of increasing the costs to developing countries by 25 to 30 percent. Aid not only blesses, it directly serves both giver and receiver.

Contrary as well to popular thought, aid funds are carefully monitored by donor governments and agencies and are not simply handed out to developing-country governments. Not all aid projects have hit the target of development, but that is not a fault of the recipients only. It is part of the difficult process of evolving effective responses to human need in an international environment often unsupportive of those efforts. Third World governments and development aid agencies, both bilateral and multilateral, have worked hard at improving the effectiveness of aid, and they have succeeded in many respects. The greatest handicap to effectiveness remains an inadequate amount of aid.

The trends in global development aid have been on the whole far from favorable. More than two decades ago, in 1968, the UN established a target of 0.7 percent of a donor country's national income (GNP) for official development assistance to poor countries. A few countries—Denmark, the Netherlands, Norway, and Sweden—have achieved and in some cases exceeded this level of aid for several years. They have done so without damaging their own economies and, to the credit of their people, without losing public support for such policies. Their performance places a question mark over the economic and political difficulties often cited by leading industrial countries when rationalizing their failure to reach internationally accepted targets. Several of them have, in fact, regressed, giving a smaller proportion of their income in aid as they become more prosperous. These include the United States, whose aid amounted to 0.32 percent of the GNP in 1970 and 0.21 percent in 1990, and the United Kingdom, down to 0.27 percent in 1990 from 0.42 percent in 1970. Aid from the industrial countries as a group has slipped from 0.37 percent in 1980–82 to 0.35 percent in 1990, less than half the UN target, despite big additional contributions by Japan, now the largest donor. Two oil-exporting developing countries, Kuwait and Saudi Arabia, have also for many years provided more than 0.7 percent of their GNP in development aid.

For the poorest and most vulnerable countries, development assistance will continue for some time to be an important, even a major, source of foreign capital, as they have limited ability to attract and service private capital as loans or investment funds. In these countries, and also in the larger group of more advanced developing countries, development assistance has the further value of acting as an instrument for the transfer of knowledge, expertise, and technology. In many situations, too, aid serves humanitarian purposes. International financial institutions like the World Bank have an important role in assisting development. But when rich countries keep a tight rein on concessional resources, the capacity of these institutions is diminished, as agencies like the International Development Association (IDA), the World Bank arm that lends on easy terms to the poorest countries, are financed from the aid budgets of industrial countries. It is one of the sadder aspects of the recent record of international action on development that these institutions have not received from the industrial countries that control their policies and practices the level of financial support that would enable them to make a worthier contribution to development.

The two main multilateral institutions, the World Bank and the IMF, have over the last several years themselves become net recipients of resources from developing countries. These institutions have a specific responsibility to assist developing countries that distinguishes them from private banks, whose operations are governed by commercial considerations. That they should also contribute to the transfer of funds out of developing countries at a time when these nations are hard-pressed for resources is therefore most disturbing. Over the five years up to fiscal year 1991, the World Bank has been receiving an average of $3 billion a year net from developing countries on its loan transactions. At the IMF the net flow has been consistently negative—that is, flowing from developing countries to the Fund—since 1985. Over the six years from 1985 to 1990, the IMF took in a total of $30 billion net from developing countries whose external debt had forced them to seek its support. This drain of $5 billion a year from the Third World contrasts with a net flow to them of $5 billion a year in 1983 and 1984, immediately before the flow went into reverse.

Now there are fears that most of the energies, if not necessarily the resources, of these institutions will be directed toward lifting up the economies of Eastern Europe. The desperate need of developing countries risks being downplayed once again.

To obtain World Bank and IMF loans, borrowers have to agree to an economic reform package that typically includes trade and financial liberalization, streamlining the public sector, privatization of public enterprises, removal of subsidies in such fields as agriculture, forestry, and energy, and elimination of price controls. These structural adjustment policies are severe austerity programs. Poor countries have borne so much of the burden of increased prices and reduced government spending that some are now being offered special programs to alleviate the effects of structural adjustment.

By changing relative prices and introducing taxes and other measures, adjustment programs can have an impact on the environment. But only a handful of them address environmental considerations. It is imperative for structural adjustment programs to focus on their effect on poverty and the environment—their social and ecological costs. Equally important is the recognition, which is taking far too long to influence practice, that one prescription will not do for every country, that sustainable growth, including ecologically sound management of natural resources, requires policies specific to each country.

A s D E V E L O P M E N T goes, so goes the environment. Care for the environment requires substantial financial allocations to help developing countries to play their part in achieving sustainable development worldwide. It is obvious that these allocations should not be taken out of the already inadequate resources now set aside for development. Sustainable development, which is development guided by environmental considerations, requires greatly enlarged flows of aid. If developed and developing countries are to jointly contribute to saving our endangered Earth, the countries whose industrial success and prosperity have been bought at the price of massive environmental degradation must contribute out of that prosperity to the salvation of themselves and the rest of the world's people.

In 1990 a modest and exploratory mechanism, the Global Environmental Facility (GEF), was established through cooperation among three UN agencies: the World Bank, UNEP, and UNDP. The GEF is designed to provide concessional funding, low- or no-interest loans, for programs in four areas: protection of the ozone layer, reduction of greenhouse gases, protection of international water resources, and protection of biodiversity. There are clearly other areas that a full-fledged environmental facility should cover, particularly some of special importance to poor countries like land degradation. If the GEF is not to finance action on such problems, there must be adequate provision for them under established programs of bilateral and multilateral aid. The concern is that "green aid" will not be additional but rather be taken from the already shrinking pool of development aid.

The GEF is an important beginning; its potential should be harnessed in an effective way. First, it needs substantial additional resources to expand its services. Second, its policies should be so framed that its capacity to help developing countries to protect the environment is not vitiated by unrealistically stringent conditions imposed on the countries that seek its support. Rich countries, which protest against the imposition of even modest burdens in the interest of environmental relief—witness the aversion of the American public to higher, albeit modest, gasoline taxes—should at least be sensitive to the inability of poor countries to adopt much more radical measures.

The integration of development and environment—achieving a better life for hundreds of millions of poor while safeguarding the environment—is the major issue confronting human society. As we approach the threshold of the twenty-first century, that perception is clear to many; the global constituency of concerned people is now substantial. They include scientists, economists, ecologists, demographers, and geographers whose professional interests have brought them close to the issues raised by human degradation of the environment. Their ranks are swelled by large numbers of ordinary people who are concerned not just about the quality of life for themselves but the kind of world their children and grandchildren will inherit. Together, this global constituency is producing a powerful consensus for action.

I M P R O V I N G the prospects for progress in poorer countries is an essential element of the response to both languishing development and an endangered environment. As Indira Gandhi asserted in a speech at the Stockholm Conference on June 14, 1972, "The environment cannot be improved in conditions of poverty"; development itself must be part of the response.

For the industrialized countries the need for development is not the

issue. For them, the challenge is to make their development quali-
tatively better—to make it sustainable. Without sustainability their
development is threatened. For the developing countries, however, the
challenge is twofold: It is both to develop and to develop sustainably.
With the development compulsion to produce at any cost to the environment, sustainability becomes an impossible mandate. But without
sustainability, development will in the long run fail. Maintaining snail-
paced development alongside rampant poverty is a sure prescription
for further endangering the planet and the common future of its
people. It is therefore the basic challenge of development that must be
addressed, and while the developing countries must rely primarily on
themselves in meeting this challenge, their prospects of success are
closely tied to the role of the international economy and relations
between themselves and industrialized countries.

There is another question that cannot be left unanswered. If the
development of the quarter of the world's people who are now rich has
brought us all so close to the limits of sustainable living on Earth, how
is the development of the three-quarters who are poor to be accommo-
dated? Our answer in the Brundtland Report was that the rich must
improve the quality of their development and so relieve the stress they
now place on the planet, while the poor must develop on a basis of
growth that respects the Earth's capacity to sustain life.

There really is no other way. The poor must be helped to grow out of
their poverty quickly or their wretchedness will overwhelm the planet.
Our global society must become less feudal. It must reform its trading
arrangements and economic relationships so that developing countries
can make faster progress. As their economies become stronger and
their people more prosperous they will be able to take better care of the
environment—improve their sanitation and water, prevent degradation of the land, curb pollution, protect forestland, reduce population
pressure, use technologies that are friendlier to the environment.

The rich for their part must be less aggressive toward the planet, or it
will strike back with vengeance. The planet will always have the last
word; in the final resort, it will secure the sustainability of the biosphere at the expense of the agent who threatens it. Following the
instinct of self-preservation, the planet will recognize no distinction
between rich and poor. If we do not adjust our relationships to respect
the precept that "what is under Heaven is for all," we might find that
there is nothing under Heaven left.

PART FOUR

Responses

EIGHT

卜

Ethics of Survival

Not till we are lost, in other words not till we
have lost the world, do we begin to find ourselves
and realize where we are and the infinite extent of
our relations.
— *Henry David Thoreau*

UP TILL now I have laid out the varied ways in which the human
species has been unwittingly, unevenly, and with quickening intensity
unraveling the fabric of Earth's surface, its biosphere, and its envelop-
ing atmosphere. In the process we have not only imperiled existence
everywhere but committed generations just born and to come to an
increasingly problematic and uncertain future. Our generation, as
custodians of the present and trustees of the future, must take responsibility for our acts and for their impact on Earth. Aware now of the
magnitude of our wrongdoing and its consequences, we must change
the ways we encounter nature.

Some factors are unchanging. We have only one Earth. Our science
may increase its bounty and our husbandry make its resources go
further, but its capacity to support life cannot be indefinitely extended.
On the eve of India's independence Mahatma Gandhi was asked if,
after independence, India would attain British standards of living. His
reply was prescient: "It took Britain half the resources of this planet to
achieve its prosperity. How many planets will a country like India
require?" If life on Earth is to be sustained we shall have to care for the
planet, and share it, better than we have done. That is the essence of an

enlightened response. But it will not come merely by our wishing it. We are as we are; and it is being as we are that has brought us to this pass.

Enlightenment precedes change. That should give us hope, since it is our cerebral gift most of all that sets us apart from other species. The same capacities that have borne the human race to great peaks of achievement have allowed it to adapt in the face of threats. Change must be driven by reason, but it has to be guided by ethics as well. There is an ethical dimension to our predicament; there must be an ethical dimension to our response to it. Unless there is, the response will not be worthy of our highest potential as a species. We will not be true to ourselves, and we will be false to the generations that follow us. We are now at the point that the great American writer and naturalist Henry David Thoreau envisaged when he wrote in *On Man and Nature*, that we must "begin to find ourselves and realize where we are and the infinite extent of our relations," or we will indeed lose ourselves and the world.

O N   S E V E R A L occasions in this book I have referred to *Only One Earth* in acknowledgment of Barbara Ward's immense contribution to the ecological awakening of the 1970s. She would have been the first to emphasize, however, the great role that her coauthor René Dubos played in moving their generation to an awareness of man's disharmonies with nature. As our generation develops responses to its present predicament, Dubos's insistence on the ethics of human survival—on an ethical foundation for those responses—carries across the years to offer us both practical and moral counsel.

In 1976 the Carey Arboretum of the New York Botanical Garden had completed construction in upstate New York of a privately financed solar-heated building, the largest in the northeastern United States. The director of the garden was Dr. Howard Irwin. One afternoon in January 1976, Dubos and Irwin sat talking in the Botanical Garden's magnificent public conservatory in the Bronx. Their thoughts were on that arboretum upstate. It was the pride of the director and much admired by Dubos because it held out hope for a solution to the world's energy predicament. That was fifteen years ago, and Dubos was to pass on not long after; but that afternoon he reflected with his friend on the human condition, which had occupied so much of his life's work as microbiologist, pathologist, writer, and one of the premier scientific humanists of this century.

In a splendid oxymoron, Dubos described himself as a despairing optimist. He was deeply worried about nuclear war as the ultimate cataclysm, about overpopulation as an incessant tide that could swamp all human achievement, and about environmental deterioration, especially the desecration of nature. He was keenly troubled by the destruction of tropical forests; he saw it as leading inexorably to the loss of a biotic treasury that was little understood yet whose diversity and dynamics were vital to the stability of all natural systems. He was also greatly worried about the excessive use of energy, which, rather than a shortage of energy, he recognized as the real energy problem, especially in industrial countries. Talking about their preoccupation with oil and access to it, he summed up his anxiety in these words: "I have no doubt that the energy problem will be solved; but that is the problem, we will solve it." Hence the significance to him of solar heating.

Dubos had several other worries: the social evolution of Earth's neighbors, the people of rich and poor countries; the rudderless nihilism of the young in so many urban societies; the masses of dispirited people leading purposeless lives of unemployment, drunk on images of material satisfaction spawned by television screens; and the growing ranks of hundreds of millions the world over leading abbreviated, harassed lives, increasingly cut off from cultural sustenance, focused almost entirely on surviving from one meager meal to the next.

Dubos was not to know how all this would get worse in the 1980s. Meanwhile, he remained sustained by his faith in the human capacity for change, especially social change, assisted by "humanistic technologies"—faith he saw as resting on our accepting that we are a part of nature and on our consciously working with the forces that govern it. That afternoon in New York, in a setting that conjured up the great heritage of nature, René Dubos put the challenge to Irwin succinctly: "We must seek our way home . . . we can manage the Earth so as to create environments that are ecologically stable, economically profitable, aesthetically rewarding and favorable to the continued evolution of civilization. We need only muster the will."

It is an ironic footnote to these reflections that only a few years later the reduced cost of oil, and the consequential disappearance of solar technology maintenance firms in the United States, led to the dismantling of the entire solar installation—of which Dubos had talked with such hope as a symbol of the way forward—at the arboretum. It returned to conventional oil heating. The turn of events would have strained Dubos's optimism that much more, but assuredly not broken it.

T H E desire for an ethical dimension to human conduct is of course not new, nor is it the preserve of minds not tuned to political realities.

> Over the centuries scores of great men have laid down a mosaic of ethical concepts treating with almost every aspect of human life. Yet, strangely enough . . . millions of persons the world over appear to be groping for new ethical guidelines as if they had never before been traced, or as if the old ones were no longer relevant. . . . Men everywhere are now living under a new shadow of fear as the horrendous and universal implications of nuclear holocaust become more apparent. . . . It is no wonder that this is the anxious age and that we want an ethic—an ethic for survival.

Those were the words of another American, born a few generations later than Thoreau, the great statesman of the postwar period, Adlai Stevenson. He spoke them at the inauguration of a foundation in his name in New York in May 1961, when he was U.S. ambassador to the UN. Today, the new shadow of fear is cast far less by the possibility of a nuclear holocaust than by the prospect of environmental disaster; but the shadow is as menacing in 1992 as it was in 1961. How much has changed, how much remains the same! For many, the age is just as anxious, the need for an ethic for survival just as desperate.

As Adlai Stevenson acknowledged, the search for ethical guidelines for human endeavor is age-old. But it is the premise of this chapter that never before in human history has the need for these guidelines been as great as it is now. The all-encompassing nature of the danger that faces us is beginning to be widely acknowledged; and in a strange reversal of the human predicament, the threat comes not from hostile forces of nature ranged against the human race, but from the power human genius has vouchsafed us over nature itself. The threat to human survival comes now from ourselves. When we speak of survival today, we no longer mean as in past ages survival of family, of tribe, of race, of culture, or even of civilization. We mean, comprehensively, saving the human race from itself.

The ethical dimension of this predicament is inescapable. It was given poignant expression in September 1990 by the Dalai Lama, the spiritual and political leader of the Tibetan Buddhists. He was attending the Conference on Religion and the Environment at Middlebury College in Vermont, one of a growing number of such gatherings in recent years to bring together adherents of different faiths to talk about issues normally regarded as the domain of scientists or politicians: pollution, deforestation, depletion of the ozone shield, overpopulation. The Dalai Lama's warning in a speech on September 16, 1990, in Vermont was sounded with special clarity: "Mother planet is showing us the red warning light; she is telling us to take care of our house the planet!"

A similar message was earlier signalled from a quite different quarter. The same year, Vaclav Havel, just released from imprisonment for upholding freedom in communist Czechoslovakia, delivered a moving address to the U.S. Congress on February 21, 1990 in Washington. Among the many important things he said was this:

> Without a global revolution in the sphere of human consciousness, nothing will change for the better in our being as humans, and the catastrophe toward which our world is headed . . . will be unavoidable. . . . We are still incapable of understanding that the only genuine backbone of all our actions—if they are to be moral—is responsibility: responsibility to something higher than my family, my country, my firm, my success, responsibility to the order of being where all our actions are indelibly recorded and where, and only where, they will be properly judged.

As we contemplate our responsibility to the planet, including our responsibility to ourselves, we must recognize that it is only such a revolution in human consciousness that will provide the ethical impetus for change, and only change that will set right our relationship with nature and secure our common future.

THERE are many sources of resistance to a revolution through which we would acknowledge responsibility to something higher than ourselves or our country. At each stage in our evolution, the impulse to mark out and possess turf has been as irresistible to us as to several other species. It was perhaps inevitable, therefore, that we evolved into a world of states separated by frontiers, and perhaps equally inevitable that the virtuous attributes we developed in the process of our evolution, like loyalty and solidarity, came to be expressed mainly in relation to our separate national communities. The great Cuban nationalist of the nineteenth century, José Marti, proclaimed *"para nosotros la patria es America Latina"* ("Our country is Latin America"), and many Europeans today have a vision of a single European home; but regionalism of that kind is about as far as our allegiance reaches.

Otherness nourishes the dark side of humanity: insularity, intolerance, greed, prejudice, bigotry, and above all a desire for dominance, not only over nature but also over each other. Race, religion, ideology, all have fed the urge for power and superiority. Hence those pages of world history that chronicle man's inhumanity to man, a catalogue of genocide and subjugation, of exploitation and dispossession, of human bondage and degradation, abysmal wrongs justified, sometimes glorified, in the name of "us" and "them." Human relations have been dominated by division marked not only by national frontiers on the ground but also by barricades of otherness in our minds. Even now, this dark side tends to overwhelm our more civilized instincts. The predilection for otherness endures, frustrating progress along enlightened pathways. Our social and political structures and values have not adjusted to the globalization that has made boundaries increasingly irrelevant, or to the threats to our existence whose amplitude demands a global response.

Historians will record, for example, that in the last decade of the twentieth century the leaders of the world's people met at an Earth Summit in Rio de Janeiro for an emergency discussion on humanity's future. They will also record that the leaders met behind flags that were a constant reminder of the narrow domestic walls that kept them apart and of the constituencies within those walls whose short-term interests they felt obliged to serve. The old instinct to secure survival by protecting turf persists, and it is strongest among those who believe they have the most to protect. A central need is to ensure that such instincts, more appropriate to another time in human evolution, do not undermine our capacity to secure a common future under the single banner of one Earth. Some people, in all countries, already rally to that banner, proclaiming allegiance to the wider human community—and repudiating the claims of otherness.

But we are not all so emancipated from the tenacious evil of otherness. One of its worst manifestations was slavery. Yet, it is an instructive one, for all forms of enslavement of one human being by another begin in the mind, in the perverted judgment that those enslaved are not fellow members of the human race. For slavery to be formulated by law and institutionalized into a system, it was necessary to perpetuate a measure of dehumanization—often gross, sometimes subtle. Slavery relied on an assumption of superiority by the enslaver; "the other," perceived as not only different but also inherently inferior, is the one enslaved. Otherness is not merely a matter of race or color; to the Romans, all those outside the Empire were barbarians. Feudal society had its serfs and bondsmen. The West Indian and American plantations were worked in their earliest, pre-slavery decades by indentured poor whites or white criminals. The ruling groups within some African tribes sold their own serfs into the plantation slave trade, together with captives—the spoils of war—from other tribes. An equally overweening arrogance marked those who presided over later empires, claiming to be bringing the virtues of "civilization" to "lesser breeds without the Law."

Otherness has many accomplices. Extreme nationalism is one: the division of the world into we and they, our side and the others—a ritual patriotism that blocks dispassionate judgment and hardens division. In the end it thwarts internationalism, and we enter the danger zone in which our global village threatens to turn into a global jungle. The ferocity of ethnic tensions and conflicts in central and Eastern Europe as old structures crumble and old enmities erupt tells a grim tale of otherness in these end-years of the twentieth century. What a terrible price otherness has exacted from the people of Yugoslavia.

In responding to the crisis of the environment, nothing would be more calamitous than for us to be influenced by considerations of otherness—the very opposite of the values necessary to create a global alliance for sustainable living. Without those values, without a sense of human identity transcending national loyalties, without an acknowledgment of others on the planet as fellow countrymen and women, without a conception of the world as one human community, we are unlikely to summon up the will to act together to save ourselves. Without the ethics of survival to guide us, we are likely, when faced with disaster too close to be ignored, to try to save ourselves and leave others to their fate. In so doing, we would be overlooking the fact that their fate is ours too. We are bound together by a common destiny. We would be missing the crucial truth that we cannot save ourselves alone. An ethic of solidarity—moral underpinnings for joint action to save our endangered human family—cannot develop or subsist within a culture that allows otherness its head.

Yet as we reach toward new concepts of belonging we must temper our vision with realism, lest our reach too far exceed our grasp. We must not abandon that vision out of past habits of thinking or myopia or inertia, nor should we pursue it in ways that are too far removed from practical realities. Bankers and businessmen may have reached the limits of geography in daily transactions that skirt the world, but the nation-state continues as the essential unit for the organization of human society and the conduct of its affairs and seems destined long to remain so. Recognizing the planet as our country does not call for an end to nation-states; it is not premised on the replacement of national by global government; it does not mean we have to abandon human variety any more than national identity means smothering cultural heritages. That is why *Only One Earth* spoke of each of us having two countries, "our own and Planet Earth."

Dual citizenship will in fact enrich and stabilize us as we grope toward a wider perspective of Earth as the home of many nations and peoples. Nor, strangely, is it at odds with what is happening in the world of the 1990s as some nations fall apart and others come together. In the wake of communist collapse in the Soviet bloc, old nationalisms are not merely asserting themselves in separatism; there are also examples like the Baltic states, and the new Commonwealth of Independent States evolving out of a dismembered USSR, where the vision of a new identity leaves space for new national or regional reconfigurations. A single European home may in the end have many more rooms than its architects blueprinted, but it may be a stronger mansion for that. So with our country the planet.

R E L I G I O N has been a source of conflict for ages past and there are parts of the world where it still divides people from their neighbors. But that is not the spirit of the most creative tendencies of our time. The ecumenical movement is a timely response to humanity's need for communication, for understanding, and for sharing, and it is relevant to the crisis of environment and development. In the language of the Independent Commission on International Humanitarian Issues's report "Winning the Human Race," the holy texts of many religions, not to mention legal traditions, philosophies, and custom "abound in moral injunctions that imply an ethic of human solidarity.... For centuries, the great religious texts have taught the essential oneness of the human race." (p. 9) What scriptures have not always taught is that nature is the loom on which is woven life's seamless fabric of which humanity is a significant, but not unduly dominant, part.

In his autobiography, Albert Schweitzer remarked that the great fault of ethical systems, especially in the West, was that they dealt only with the relations of person to person. In *Sustaining Earth,* David Gosling explained this deficiency in Christian thought by reference to the ideas of the eighteenth-century German philosopher Immanuel Kant:

> Kant believed nature to be a collection of irrational forces which needed to be subdued and kept in check by human effort. "Man" was a rational and spiritual being whose holiness was associated with his moral personality, and part of his moral duty was to subdue nature. Thus the world of morality, with its inherent possibility of holiness, was sharply distinguished from the world of nature. (p. 99)

Though the Jewish scriptures are often held up as reflecting an environmentally sensitive approach, Gosling recalled that "the majestic cedars of Lebanon, praised for their strength and longevity in the Psalms, were soon cut down to fuel innumerable wars and to provide wood for the restoration which followed them" (p. 9), a mixture of the ethical and the expedient that has been a common feature of human conduct throughout the ages.

In Asian traditions nature is commonly infused with religious significance. Buddhism and Hinduism consider it wrong to cause injury to any living creature; strict adherents of Jainism go to great lengths to avoid harming even the smallest insect. In the West, too, though there is no religious foundation for this, the treatment of dogs, cats, and horses sometimes verges on the sacred. The tradition of St. Francis of Assisi is evident today in organizations for the prevention of cruelty to animals, for the protection of wildlife, and for the exclusion of animals from research experiments. The spread of vegetarianism is largely motivated by ethics.

As they come together the world's religions are also moving away from a view of nature as an appendage to humanity, whose moral duty it is to subdue the environment, as Kant would have had it, to one that recognizes humanity as an integral part of nature. The same year that the Dalai Lama spoke at the Conference on Religion and the Environment in Vermont, the North American Conference on Religion and Ecology was also held. So, too, was a global environmental forum of parliamentary and religious leaders in Moscow. All this signals movement away from individualism to interdependence, and it strengthens the process of change in man's relations with nature and man's relations with man.

It is a movement well captured by Anglican Archbishop Robert Runcie, now Lord Runcie, in his address to the Conference on Christian Faith and Ecology jointly sponsored by the World Wildlife Fund and the British Council of Churches and held at Canterbury Cathedral in 1989. The conference brought together representatives of seven world religions—Bahaism, Buddhism, Christianity, Hinduism, Islam, Judaism, and Sikhism—but as David Gosling recalled in *Sustaining Earth*, Dr. Runcie spoke of convictions whose provenance went beyond particular faiths:

> The conviction that nature does not exist simply and solely for the benefit of humankind . . . is becoming increasingly widespread and articulate. Because it finds its true source at such deep levels of the human spirit, it must, I think, be called a religious conviction. But it is not a conviction unique to any one religion in particular, and it is shared by some who would profess no religion at all. (p. 103)

Before the meeting in Canterbury, an interfaith ceremony at Assisi marking the twenty-fifth anniversary of the World Wildlife Fund had emphasized the important links between religious faith and a holistic view of Earth. Much similar ecumenical activity has taken place since. A new crossfaith network has developed in support of conservation that can only help the wider effort to establish an ethical basis for sustainable living.

T H E teaching that all life is sacred commands increasing respect among those both inside and outside the framework of established religion. Where, however, does one stop? The Erewhonians satirized by Samuel Butler eschewed all food of animal origin and also living plants, holding that plants have rights. They had to subsist on cabbages certified as having died a natural death. As Marston Bates asked in *The Forest and the Sea*, "Monkeys, deer, cows, rats, quail, songbirds, lizards, fish, insects, molluscs, vegetables—where do you draw the line between what can be properly killed and eaten, and what not?" (p. 256) There is no easy answer, but that does not mean that the search for it is over.

It will help if we recognize that in this century we have drifted into a position of ethical relativism that more often than not leaves us without absolutes of good and bad, of right and wrong. Things tend to be deemed good or right according to context, depending on the values of a particular society. Yet as we become aware that this is one world, that how we live in one place can affect everyone and everything everywhere, now and in the future, ineluctably we must seek some universal basis of right conduct, a standard applicable to and acceptable by all the people of the world.

In recent times science has undermined dogma and revelation, which had been the traditional trappings of active minds seeking answers to inexplicable mysteries. Science now provides for many the basis for a sort of faith, the humanism René Dubos exemplified that could perhaps meet the need for an articulated code of ethical conduct. But our scientists and philosophers and humanists have not yet succeeded in explaining ethical humanism in a way that reaches any significant number of people. When someone does finally emerge to provide us with a rationale for universal ethical conduct, it must, as Albert Schweitzer insisted, go beyond the realm of conduct between humans and deal with human conduct toward nature.

The image of the noble savage was never a wholly valid one. Early humans were as ignoble in some respects as we are; we are as savage in some respects as they were. Yet the world's indigenous peoples have much to teach us, particularly in their evolved respect for nature, their caring for Earth, and their intuitive understanding of the value of sustainable living. From such respect, caring, and understanding have come knowledge, skills, and virtues that in our arrogance we either ignore or disparage. We would do well to be more humble and learn from our fellow humans who have lived in greater harmony with nature.

THE Commission on Humanitarian Issues, chaired by Crown Prince Hassan of Jordan and Sadruddin Aga Khan, was one of five international commissions in the 1980s. The others were the South Commission, which issued its report in 1990, the Brandt Commission, the Brundtland Commission, all referred to in earlier chapters, and the Palme Commission on Disarmament and Security Issues. Each was an effort to find a new worldwide vision and a new way in an area crucial to human survival. Each functioned as a kind of international think tank, independently of governments and burdened neither by orthodoxy nor by short-term national interests. Together, they brought home the reality that we are all one people facing common crises, needing common security, sharing a common future.

What the overall experience of the commissions' search for responses to pressing world problems confirmed for me, as a member of all of them, is the interconnectedness of those problems. Development, security, environment, humanitarian issues—these cannot be treated effectively in isolation. Our response to them must be unified by ethics. Ethics alone can provide the essential foundation on which to build responsive programs and structures. Without ethics we build in vain; or we do not build at all. The work of all the commissions recognized the importance of that foundation.

For all the reasons stated in earlier chapters, we could well be entering a time more favorable to the erection of an ethical foundation. On June 5, 1991, one year before the opening of the Earth Summit in Rio de Janeiro, a "passing of the torch" ceremony was held in Stockholm to commemorate the spirit of the conference held there in 1972. Maurice Strong was the secretary-general of that conference and he will have a similar role at the Earth Summit in Rio in 1992. His passion and conviction and indefatigable drive to turn the world toward sustainable living have formed a bridge of hope over that span of twenty years. As Sweden's then prime minister, Ingvar Carlsson, passed the torch symbolizing "a more secure, sustainable and promising future" for the world to President Fernando Collor of Brazil, Maurice Strong spoke on June 5, 1991 in Stockholm about ethical compulsions:

> People and nations have always been willing to accord highest priority to their own security and to providing the resources necessary to protect it. The world community now faces together greater risks to our common security through our impacts on the environment than from traditional military conflicts with each other. And out of the moral, ethical and spiritual values which provide the ultimate basis for the motivations of people and nations, we must now forge a new "Earth ethic" which will inspire all peoples and nations to join in a new global partnership of North, South, East and West to ensure the integrity of the Earth as a secure, equitable and hospitable home for present and future generations.

F U T U R E generations must be at the forefront of our attention as we consider the challenge to human survival. The concept of sustainable development crystallizes our obligations when it speaks of meeting the needs of the present without compromising the ability of future generations to meet their own needs. In a very real sense, we do borrow the present from the future. Perhaps earlier civilizations understood this concept better. When the leaders of the Iroquois nation in North America met in their Council to take important decisions, they began with this commitment: In our every deliberation we must consider the impact of our decisions on the next seven generations. As we come to the end of the second millennium, is there a national council on any of our continents today that is guided by consideration of the impact of its decisions on even the next generation?

The most inviolable of human rights is the right to life—not only for us or our generation but for the innocent, unborn generations of the future. We have already so depreciated our stock of the ecological capital that we cannot deliver the planet to our heirs in pristine condition. That is the magnitude of our offense. We can plead that for most of the time it was wrongdoing unwittingly wrought, unperverted by malice; we were bettering ourselves without intending to harm either ourselves or future generations. But even that plea will not hold any longer; we now know the consequences of our conduct for ourselves, and for those who will inherit our fractured civilization. Some of those heirs are already with us. They know what we are doing to their planet, and they are calling on us to stop. When the report of the Commission on Environment and Development was launched in London on April 27, 1987, one of the young people invited to receive it from Mrs. Brundtland was Jenny Damayanti of Indonesia. She made this plea: "Please, Presidents, Prime Ministers and Generals, listen to the poor, to the voice of the hungry people who are forced to destroy the environment. Listen to the silent death of dying forests, lakes, rivers, and the seas, the dying soil of the earth, poisoned and trampled by human greed, poverty and inequality. We, the young, hear them loud and clear!" That plea will grow more insistent, and more angry, if we fail to show a change of heart, if we fail to adopt an ethic of survival that acknowledges our obligations to our children and the need to give them a chance to do better than we have done.

It is here that real hope lies. If future generations have an opportunity to do better there are signs that they will avail themselves of it. The Council of Europe's 1988 public campaign on North-South Interdependence and Solidarity had as its theme "One World is enough for

all of us," from the song by Sting and Ziggy Marley. This new generation understands better than mine that the world is more than an
assortment of sovereign states and separate peoples; that there is a
human society not divided by national boundaries; that each of us
does belong to two countries, our own and planet Earth.

In his 1985 Wiles Lectures, *Nations and Nationalism since 1780*,
the British historian Eric Hobsbawm envisioned the way future historians will write the history of the late twentieth and early twenty-first
centuries:

> . . . it will inevitably have to be written as the history of a world
> which can no longer be contained within the limits of "nations" and
> "nation-states" as these used to be defined, either politically, or
> economically, or culturally, or even linguistically. It will see "nation-
> states" and "nations" or ethnic/linguistic groups primarily as re-
> treating before, resisting, adapting to, being absorbed or dislocated
> by, the new supranational restructuring of the globe. Nations and
> nationalism will be present in this history, but in subordinate, and
> often rather minor roles. . . . It is not impossible that nationalism
> will decline with the decline of the nation-state, without which
> English or Irish or Jewish, or a combination of all these, is only one
> way in which people describe their identity among the many others
> which they use for this purpose, as occasion demands. It would be
> absurd to claim that this day is already near. However, I hope it can
> at least be envisaged. (p. 182)

As an Earth ethic becomes a more central part of global culture, being
compatriots in our country the planet must come to be among those
many ways in which people perceive and describe their identity.

N O T H I N G highlights the need for an ethic of survival as much as its
absence. What must naturalists think when they watch roaring bull-
dozers and snarling chainsaws level acres of tropical forest in just a few
hours? They must wish that somehow they could have led people on a
tour through these seemingly ordinary acres and opened their eyes to
the hidden threads of mutual dependency among the thousands of
species of birds and animals and trees and vines and insects living
there. Yet, to those doing the felling and clearing, the idea of a tour
would be absurd, an obstruction of progress. To them, the forest is an
enemy to be fought and destroyed, a resource to be exploited; beauty

lies in the buildings and fields and orchards that replace it. This was and remains the attitude of settlers the world over, from medieval Europe to seventeenth-century coastal North America, then to the banks of the Congo and now of the upper Amazon. What we wouldn't give for samples of those lost forests! But the idea of saving a part of the wilderness has always been foreign to pioneers. How can people be helped to profit from the mistakes of others? How do we inculcate ecological truth?

Some truths we ignore at our own peril. To paraphrase the biologists Louis and Margery Milne, modern knowledge of the environment reveals that, in the game of life, the final play is not ours to make. The trump card takes its power from one simple fact: Whereas *Homo sapiens* possesses the greatest cultural organization of all species, green plants have all the chlorophyll. The photosynthesis they so quietly carry on is so vital to human sustenance that it is the clinching capability in any confrontation between man and the environment. And that is why, in relation to anything in the world of nature, we cannot simply ask, "What good is it?" Such questions, too often on our lips, are really a vestige of the Middle Ages, when everything had to have a purpose in relation to man. They are a vestige of the days before Copernicus removed the Earth from the center of the solar system, before Newton explained how the stars appeared to move, before Darwin put the human species in proper relation to the rest of the living world. Faced with the enormities of astronomical space and geological time, with the immense diversity of living things still only partly discerned and studied, how can one ask of a particular kind of plant, for example, "What good is it?"

The world remains a mosaic of ways of living. In parts of it, as on the chilly banks of the canals of Magellanes, in the sere-baked Kalahari sands or within the damp sylvan depths of uppermost Amazonia, hunting man still lives in balance with the natural world, cropping animals and plants at well below their sustainable yields. Elsewhere, here and there, the kind of pastoralism and agriculture used by our early forebears endures. But throughout so much of the world, prime forest has given way to squalid, impoverished settlements, damaging to inhabitants and environment alike. Some countries have made great advances toward high agricultural productivity, though often along with misguided planning and misapplied technology.

The present world situation is one of disequilibrium in too many areas. Runaway growth in human populations and in human demands for non-renewable natural resources continues and the generation of pollution soars. Yet we have the basic means to control both, while at the same time alleviating poverty. No technological breakthrough is required. The very technology that has created pollution has provided means for its abatement. We can regulate births rather than depend on premature death to regulate population. We can cut back in the rates at which we use precious resources. The basic question is whether mankind will move to stability—to sustainability—smoothly and deliberately, or whether overshoot, resource depletion and massive death will bring about stability.

On this finite planet, there is no doubt that stabilization will ultimately ensue. In the days of primitive man, limitations were imposed from without, by physical environmental factors. Among other species, it is not uncommon for the young and weak to be sacrificed when there are threats to survival. The only course open to us is to change our behavior. No other species has accomplished such a change; but no other species has even approximated the accomplishments of mankind, for the simple reason that no other species has the human mind. There is no basic reason to defer the change to sustainability. We need to embrace it voluntarily and as a direct consequence of our improved understanding of ourselves and of our world.

If an ethical basis is to be established for our custody of the environment, if Vaclav Havel's revolution in the sphere of human consciousness is to come about, if we are to take care of this planet the way we do our homes, as the Dalai Lama urges us, then the people of all countries and the leaders who represent them must begin to see the world with new eyes. In 1971 Barbara Ward, in a paper to the Pontifical Commission on Justice and Peace, underlined this need in memorable words:

> The most important change that people can make is to change their way of looking at the world. We can change studies, jobs, neighborhoods, even countries and continents and still remain much as we always were. But change our fundamental angle of vision and everything changes—our priorities, our values, our judgments, our pursuits. Again and again, in the history of religion, this total upheaval in the imagination has marked the beginning of a new life. St. Paul struck blind on the road to Damascus, St. Augustine converted to

Christianity by his mother's prayers, St. Francis stripping off his rich clothes in Assisi—all experienced a turning of the heart, a "metanoia," by which men see with new eyes and understand with new minds and turn their energies to new ways of living.

We have to begin by seeing each other on the planet, our fellow human beings, not as aliens from other countries but as fellow citizens of one world. We will find it easier then to see Earth as our community and all people as our neighbors. It will be possible for us to live by neighborhood values in our wider, yet much smaller, world. One of those values is the duty of care.

In the process of civilizing our societies we have come to recognize the duty we owe our neighbors, the responsibility to behave in a reasonable manner toward those likely to be affected by our actions. The duty of care is embedded in most systems of law. But in some systems, as in the common law, which applies to most of the English-speaking world, its full realization came only in this century. Recalling how it did may be instructive, both for its relevance to life within nations and its potential application to life in the global society.

The duty of care as it is expressed in common law derives from a famous decision of Britain's highest court delivered in 1932. The litigation that gave rise to it had a humble beginning, a snail in an opaque bottle of ginger beer. What the court adumbrated was an extension of the rule of law to relations between individuals. This was a giant step; it confirmed that we all have a duty to our neighbor, the duty to act in a reasonable way to avoid injury to him or her. In the court's judgment, our neighbor is anyone we ought reasonably to think may be affected by our actions. And reasonable behavior is what ordinary people understand to be reasonable, like not selling an opaque bottle of ginger beer contaminated by the remains of a snail. In a general sense, such behavior had always been unreasonable. After that decision of the court it was unlawful as well, and that has made all the difference.

Today the concepts of neighbor and neighborliness are being enlarged and refined in our interdependent world, but they have yet to be brought under the rule of law. What global interdependence means is that we all need each other in some measure: for prosperity, for subsistence, for survival. Our planet offers no sanctuaries. There are no shelters that insulate anyone, anywhere, from disease, from the effects of poverty, from military holocaust, from environmental collapse. The concept of national jurisdiction is increasingly the preserve of lawyers alone. Planet Earth has become a global neighborhood. The duty of care we owe is to all the world's people; they are our neighbors now.

The notion of what is reasonable conduct toward those who are our global neighbors is beginning to be understood by ordinary people the world over. We must accordingly develop new precepts of rights and duties that are as relevant to global society as those formulated in an earlier era were to nation-states. The global imperatives of the environmental crisis dramatize this need, whether the problem is greenhouse warming, ozone depletion, or deforestation. But our response is being barred by the fences of nationalism. We built those fences in the name of freedom. In the context of survival, they can make us prisoners.

W H A T was significant in the evolution of the common law's duty of care was the conversion of a moral obligation into a legal one. As we develop an ethic of living together worldwide, we shall have increasingly to convert neighborhood values into legal obligations. The Brandt Commission's report called for a world "less discretionary, more governed by fair and open rules." That is the pathway from a feudal world toward one in which there are fairer opportunities for all countries and all people. A joint compact is what we must have to sustain human life on Earth. If it is to endure, that compact must be fair and equitable in every sense; it must include the acceptance of a larger share of responsibility by those who have most harmed the planet and prospered in so doing. But the compact will not be enough if we do not give it the authority of enforceable law. If we are to bring about enlightened change, we have to lay the foundation in ethics and build on it the structures of law. The world society toward which we are moving must be governed by the rule of international law, under which all are equal, countries and people alike, large and small, rich and poor. Equality is the mark of a civilized society; it can be no different in a civilized world.

At a lecture some years ago in London, the German philosopher C. F. Von Weizsacker cited certain views of Immanuel Kant on relations among states (more enlightened than his views on nature): "Kant says that the civilized state has been achieved within our nations, but that between nations the natural state still prevails. The civilized state means the rule of law. . . . . Kant continues that there will be no end to the sufferings and tragedies of history until the civilized state, the rule of law, is also established between nations." (pp. 9–10) We do not have to endorse Kant's idea of the natural state to accept the conclusion Von Weizsacker reached, namely, that the rule of enforceable law is a minimal condition for both a functioning world economy and the preservation of peace. To the threatened goals of human society we must add today the goal of sustainable living. The custody of the environment equally requires the rule of enforceable law.

A few years before Weizsacker's lecture the Brandt Commission in its report "North-South: A Program for Survival" reached a not dissimilar conclusion. At one point in our report we spoke of the ethical dimension of the "new world order": "All the lessons of reform within national societies confirm the gains for all in a process of change that makes the world a less unequal and a more just and habitable place. The great moral imperatives that underpin such lessons are as valid internationally as they were and are nationally." (p. 77) Not just the "sufferings and tragedies of history" but human survival itself now makes it imperative that we invest global society with the attributes of a civilized state. This mandate has an inescapable ethical dimension; we must find the right and just way to behave toward each other and toward nature—to behave consistently, not occasionally, universally, not selectively, and not as a matter of discretion or goodwill but as one of obligation.

T H A T is why it is so important to strive for formulations of international goals and commitments, of the rights and duties of states, of the responsibilities of corporations and of people. Declarations toward this end are easily dismissed by cynics, or by those who do not agree with their substance, as pious platitudes or empty rhetoric. They could be both, but need not be either. They have their place in establishing an ethical framework for global action, in laying down principles to guide human conduct. They are the necessary foundation for the more specific rules to which such conduct must conform.

The UN's adoption of the Universal Declaration of Human Rights was not a wasted effort. The declaration laid the foundation for the International Covenants on Civil and Political Rights and on Economic, Social, and Cultural Rights. None of the rights these documents proclaim are universally respected, but by inspiring constitutional guarantees of human rights and regional human rights conventions and commissions they have significantly advanced the protection of human rights.

A similar statement of principles, perhaps an "Earth Charter," would be an important step in the global response to the integrated crisis of environment and development; so would the several agreements that it is hoped will be signed at the Earth Summit to buttress the global partnership for human survival. These range from a program of action on many fronts, Agenda 21 (an agenda for the twenty-first century drawn up by the Preparatory Committee for the Earth Summit), to conventions on such specific matters as global warming and biodiversity. To quote Maurice Strong again, this time speaking to the Preparatory Committee of the Earth Summit:

> Economic change is imperative, indeed critical. But, in the final analysis, economic factors, like other aspects of human behavior, are deeply rooted in the human, cultural, spiritual, social and ethical values which are the fundamental sources of motivation of the behavior of people and nations. Technocratic measures can facilitate, but not motivate solutions to the basic issues that will face the Earth Summit. The practical solutions we devise, the concrete measures we propose will be of little effect if they are not accompanied by a deep and profound stirring of the human spirit. Our common future is literally in our hands. To secure that future at Rio will require a unique and united act of statesmanship that reflects human values and the human spirit at their highest and best.

T H A T we urgently need a new universal ethic and a reordering of global priorities appears no longer to be in doubt. Above all, the new ethic must facilitate a global shift from today's pursuit of super-affluence to the elimination of poverty. It must make the stabilization of human numbers a world objective. It must promote movement toward a society in which national borders do not impede the progress of all humans. The new ethic must inspire action to uphold the primacy of these changes and to ensure their achievement.

Does it matter if we fail? In cosmic terms, perhaps not. Whether we go up in a nuclear bang or with an environmental whimper, Earth will heal her wounds, however grievous; our planet's flora and fauna, however transfigured by the manner of our going, will have a better chance to survive and flourish because we have gone. Having made ourselves the planet's greediest predator, we may not be missed. But surely that cannot be our conclusion. What of our duty to humanity itself, to our own worthiest qualities and the highest purpose of human existence, to the generations that should succeed us? Our species has a duty to sustain life that transcends our capacity to destroy it.

The ethic of human survival requires us to recognize how we have ravaged the planet and endangered its life forms, including our species. It requires us to acknowledge that we could nullify all of humanity's incomparable achievements unless we change course. It requires us to consider how we stand poised between a new globalism, heralding a more civilized society governed by the rule of enforceable law world-wide, and a return to old instincts of power, arbitrariness, and self-centered nationalism.

But the ethic of survival also helps to shape our responses and to lead us to the right choices. It encourages us to rise to the challenge that faces us, accepting that all must care for Earth if the future is to be secure for any. There is a spirit of solidarity abroad; many have recognized that the duty of care applies to everyone on Earth. The younger generation is increasingly willing to act to ensure that they inherit a habitable world. The ethic of survival is evolving in manifold ways. We need to nourish it and let it guide us. The concluding chapters explore the prospects of our doing so.

NINE

⚔

Muddling Through or Worse

Nobody heard him, the dead man
But still he lay moaning:
I was much further out than you thought
And not waving but drowning.
                    — *Stevie Smith*

"T H E end of history," "the end of nature," "the end of geography"—
expressions of conceit, of warning, and of opportunity, respectively,
all heard in the first years of the 1990s. They are a mark of the
momentous times heralding the third millennium. Francis Fukuyama
coined the phrase "the end of history," and as it implies, the epic
changes marking the end of the twentieth century are not confined to
our relations with nature. Even more dramatic, and almost as significant, are the changes in the political and economic relations among
nations: the end of the cold war, the triumph of capitalism, the ascendancy of the democratic ethic within states. History will continue to
unfold in its inexorable way, but within new frameworks of political,
economic, and military power. What will our new relations with each
other mean for our collective relations with nature? In particular, will
preoccupation with the fortunes of our separate nations continue to
obscure our view of the needs of our country the planet?

As we have seen, the Brandt Commission called for a world "based
less on power and status, more on justice and contract; less discretionary, more governed by fair and open rules." That in part at least was

the vision at San Francisco when the UN Charter was signed in 1945, a vision the cold war first obscured, then obliterated. In the era now unfolding, we should be spurred to create that world by the premonitions of environmental distress articulated by the American writer Bill McKibben from his retreat in the Adirondack Mountains. He is the one who warned of "the end of nature." And we should be encouraged by the chief economist for the Amex Bank in Britain, Richard O'Brien, when he speaks of the "end of geography," that is, the end of frontiers. We should return to the UN Charter's vision of one world. However gradually, we should begin to see each other in new ways, not as aliens from different countries but as compatriots of one world.

Perhaps now there is a better chance that this crisis of human survival will receive the attention its gravity demands. It would be a tragic irony if a sense of complacency were to so cloud our judgment that we settled in the end for oblivion masquerading as eternity. The lines of Byron (reflecting Tacitus) in "The Bride of Abydos" on the victory of the Roman superpower long ago would then be all too apposite:

> Mark! where his carnage and his conquests cease!
> He makes a solitude, and calls it—peace!

T H E nature and quality of the human response to current environmental damage will be determined by many factors. To an overwhelming degree, however, both will turn on the answers to three questions. First, how far will ideas of environmental sustainability influence policy-making and individual behavior? Secondly, how will North-South issues of global poverty and inequality—issues of equity—be addressed? Thirdly, to what extent will governments agree to global governance?

The answer to the first question is likely to influence responses to the other two. If, for example, the view prevails that environmental problems do not require any fundamental changes in human activity, that the concept of sustainable living is either overblown rhetoric or a panic response to ecological fears, chances are that neither issues of equity nor those of global governance will receive much attention. On the other hand, if the need for sustainability is taken more seriously, then equity and governance issues will, at least, find a place on the agenda. This outturn will shape the scenarios of our response to the crisis.

Three other factors will strongly influence these scenarios. The first is the process of globalization that is unfolding ineluctably; the second the role of science and technology as an engine of growth; and the third post–cold war global politics. The three together are seen by the Council of the Club of Rome in its 1991 book *The First Global Revolution* as ushering in a new type of world society.

B E T W E E N the 1950s and the 1990s the post-industrial era took shape and began integrating human activity on a global scale in the areas of economics, technology, and environment. This is the process referred to as globalization. Globalization of the world economy has moved forward on many fronts. Growth in foreign investment flows now exceed growth in trade by far. During the 1980s, companies from the five leading industrial countries expanded their assets through direct overseas investment from $50 billion to $1 trillion, 75 percent of this increase occurring in one another's countries. Much of the growth of international trade is taking place within networks created by multi-national corporations. National sovereignty in a traditional sense is being rapidly eroded by this diffusion of ownership and control.

Internationally, despite many frictions, growth in trade has consistently outpaced growth in production as a result of improved transport—bulk carriers, containers, and air freight—and trade liberalization at least among OECD countries. Interdependence has reached a point where a breakdown in the global trading system would have devastating effects on the economies of many countries.

Financial integration has created global markets, hence "the end of geography." One specialized component of world financial markets alone, "swaps," now accounts for trillions of dollars' worth of business. The opening up of financial markets through deregulation and the removal of exchange controls—particularly the incorporation of emerging markets in developing countries and Eastern Europe—together with improved communications are creating wider possibilities and also greater systemic risk.

Modern communications—cable, VHF, and satellite systems, telex, fax, and telematics—has enabled business and other institutions to operate virtually instantaneously and at rapidly falling cost across the world. We are still in the early stages of what is now called "techno-globalism." Electronic networks have reportedly been spreading 30 percent a month, creating a communications infrastructure crossing national frontiers to a degree that increasingly makes those frontiers invisible or irrelevant.

Ecological issues have moved swiftly from being local concerns to issues of regional and global significance. Since the mid-1980s, as we have seen, global environmental interdependence has made its mark even more decisively through the threat of global warming, with its wide-ranging implications, and the accelerating depletion of the ozone layer.

Additionally, cultures are converging through the internationalization of news and entertainment, travel, the growing dominance of English, and the spread of education and training in common systems. In London at a press conference on February 28, 1985, New Zealand's prime minister, David Lange, spoke of his differences with the United States over defense arrangements, yet described his country as being, in many ways, uncritically pro-American. He said, by way of comment rather than criticism, that New Zealanders were brought up on a diet of American images and saw the world through American camera lenses. If America wanted to attack New Zealand, he said, an effective way would be to bar "Dallas," "The A-Team," and Country and Western music.

Cultural penetration of this kind is possibly less damaging to a society than such domestic evils as censorship of the media and control of information. But it does carry danger, not least that images of unattainable lifestyles and all too imitable violence will reach deep into the psyches of societies worldwide. In the Caribbean some countries, including several with low per capita incomes, now receive over twelve channels of American television twenty-four hours a day. The social, economic, cultural, and political implications of this are incalculable, and ultimately there will be environmental consequences as well.

The process of cultural convergence is, however, far from inexorable. There is a counterassertion of local identity through religion, as in the Islamic revival, and through tribal, racial, and linguistic movements. And the inequalities in our world place their own limits on the progress of cultural globalization. In the 1980s the International Telecommunications Union (ITU) appointed a commission chaired by Sir Donald Maitland to consider how best to expand telecommunications in developing countries. In its report "The Missing Link" issued in 1985, the commission found that two out of three developing countries had virtually no telecommunications system and that three-quarters of the world's 600 million telephones were located in nine industrial countries. The whole of Africa had fewer telephones than the city of Tokyo. The number of telephones in the world has certainly gone up since then, but their distribution is not any more even. Just because the telecommunications revolution has a global reach does not mean it has touched the lives of all the world's people. Far from it.

It is not predetermined that all the forces of global integration will prevail. We do well to remember, as David Henderson, head of the economics department of the OECD secretariat, pointed out in a talk in London in April 1991, that the world has only just about recaptured the level of trade and investment interdependence that existed in 1913, before it was destroyed by slump, nationalism, and war (granted, much of that interdependence was the forced outcome of colonialism). The forces of nationalism and separatism remain strong. Nor can it be asserted that global integration will necessarily create a better world. It can serve as a vehicle for instability as well as for better living standards; for fraud and criminality as much as for legitimate business; for contention (as between regional blocs or rich and poor countries) as well as for cooperation. Any notion of globalization resulting in one big happy family has been quickly deflated by the resurgence of ethnic identity, often expressed with brutal force. The tribal and factional bloodletting in Lebanon and Yugoslavia is emblematic of how globalization can coexist with manifestations of an earlier stage of human history. Yet, for good or ill, the balance of probability is toward an ever more integrated and interdependent human society. Already, the world is one in many more respects than it has ever been.

T H E R E are powerful forces sustaining economic growth: rapidly diffusing technology; the spread of ideas that emphasize entrepreneurial potential and the virtues of wealth creation; growing numbers of educated, many with scientific knowledge or skills; and the compulsive urge of growing numbers in poor countries to survive at more than subsistence level.

The advance and spread of technology create a particular dynamic. Technology has virtually banished the concerns of an earlier generation about limits to progress and, in the process, made fools of many who tried too earnestly to predict the future. From Malthus on, there have been prognostications about the inexorable pressure of a rising population on a finite land generating disaster. Agricultural technology, in recent years the green revolution in Asia, has kept these fears at bay. Nearly a century ago, in 1896, a gathering of leading British scientists solemnly proclaimed that electricity, while interesting, would never be usable commercially and on a large scale. Only a few years ago there was quite serious concern that the world was running out of oil; now, a mixture (emulsion) of heavy oil and water promises to create vast new reserves, heavily polluting, regrettably, out of what were hitherto considered useless deposits in Venezuela, Canada, and elsewhere.

That there are limits is indubitable—limits, in particular, to Earth's carrying capacity. Earlier warnings may have been premature, but they were aimed in the right direction. Science and technology have enlarged our options and postponed our arrival at those limits. And that delay has both cowed disquiet and encouraged its disparagement as "doom and gloom." A human civilization grown arrogant with its power over nature does not want to hear of limits to that power. But such obduracy gambles with human destiny.

The pace at which fundamental changes are taking place is quickening. The information-technology revolution, based on electronics, is comparable in importance to the industrial revolution. It originated with the transistor and has developed to near-maturity within little over half a lifetime, yet already it is being superseded by fiber-optic technology. It would be rash to predict which of today's technologies will be dominant in ten, let alone twenty, years' time. What can be predicted is that the technological push behind economic growth will persist and probably accelerate.

Some trends can be discerned from the way long-term technological change and economic growth are evolving. One is that a vast multiplication of material production is bound to occur. Even if the world does no more than match the rate of growth of the 1980s—by common consent, a decade of missed economic opportunities and subpotential performance—by 2025 the world economy will be four times greater than it is today. If world growth were to equal that achieved by China and South Korea in the last decade, world output would multiply tenfold. But, with what impact on the environment?

Another trend is that while 75 percent of the world's population lives in developing countries, 95 percent of research and development is being carried out in technically advanced countries. The percentage is even higher for new technologies like electronics and information technology, new materials, and biotechnology. Rapid technological change does not therefore directly benefit the vast majority of humanity and, while it may indirectly be of some value, the basic thrust of technology—to satisfy rich consumer expectations, to improve temperate-zone agriculture, to save labor—may be irrelevant, inappropriate, or even damaging to those countries where the bulk of the world's people live.

Inexorably, these trends will widen the gap in living standards between rich and poor countries. If we take an uncontroversial set of numbers—allowing the economies of developed countries to grow at 2 percent per annum and of developing countries at the rate of the 1950s and 1960s, 6 percent per annum—by 2025, the center of gravity of the world economy will have shifted from the developed to what is now the developing world, but the gap in per capita income will be considerably wider than in the 1980s. The world will have become more, not less, unequal. Such extrapolations are, of course, not the whole story. They do not allow, for example, for the combined assault of greatly increased numbers of people and output, and of the heightened disparities in wealth, on ecological systems. Not only will the world have become more unequal; it may well have become less safe and almost certainly more unsustainable for human life.

T H E third factor controlling our response to the environmental crisis is the new global politics. The cold war is over. The Soviet Union as a state has disappeared, and communism as a system of values and social organization has suffered a severe, perhaps irreversible, setback. This defeat has been long in the making and must be frankly welcomed; but its abrupt and decisive culmination has now created great uncertainty and fluidity. Even so, beyond the present transitional period, new forces can be perceived coming into play. Multipolarity in global relations is surely one of them. However fashionable the image of a unipolar world with one supreme triumphant superpower, the reality is somewhat different. The economic, political, and military dominance of the United States is far from comprehensive, as its difficulty in paying for the Gulf war demonstrated. Other players—the European Community, Japan, Russia, and increasingly, China, India, and Brazil—will have key roles to play regionally and globally. Not even the developing countries, though buffeted by economic forces and political pressure, will meekly submit to the "pax Americana." In an inversion of roles, they will work for a more democratic world, sensing old dangers in a world ordered about as if by a Roman superpower.

Nonalignment, the policy through which so many countries refused to become the pawns of East or West, though some did, is widely assumed in the West to have no relevance in the post–cold war era. That may be too simplistic a conclusion. Nonalignment did develop its special character in a cold war context, with developing countries intent that they should not be drawn into the struggle between competing ideological blocs. For that reason it was disliked by East and West alike, but with rather more vehemence in the West. It needs to be remembered, however, that for most of its adherents, the basic tenet of nonalignment was a determination to protect their new sovereignty from being subsumed in either of the alliances and to guard against new dominion from whatever quarter. The existence of one superpower in place of two changes the global scene; it does not necessarily clear it of the dangers of overlordship. Nonalignment's old posture would be nothing short of quixotic in the 1990s; but a restructured (and renamed) movement of mainly, not exclusively, developing countries proclaiming the supremacy of internationalism and the authority of a UN system that is faithful to the Charter, itself possibly updated to conform better to the new era, may well find a place in the political constellation of that era. Whether that is the case or not, the urge for freedom from dominion will assert itself—and in the process, contribute to a multipolar world.

But such momentum could be checked not only by the national ambitions of the remaining superpower but also by the collective ambition being nurtured for "trilateralism," a power structure of North America, Japan, and Europe, both Western and Eastern. That ambition has come to the fore in the political vacuum left by the collapse of the Soviet bloc. Yielding to it can have serious consequences. The environmental crisis is pointing up the need, already arising in other contexts, for remodeling old-fashioned sovereignty to make it more appropriate to the modern world. Such reform has already begun to be explored. The 1991 Stockholm Initiative on Global Security and Governance was endorsed by three dozen heads or former heads of government, current or former foreign or finance ministers, leaders of international agencies, and respected internationalists. They were all acting in their personal capacities, but perhaps what they were saying was more important for that reason. Their memorandum, "Common Responsibility in the 1990s," spoke of the clear need for "a new concept of sovereignty":

> Given the interdependencies of today, the scope of sovereignty is in reality much more limited than either politicians or the public want to admit. For most nations this will be a difficult political transition—for the major powers as well as for many countries where nationhood is barely a generation old.
>
> The reality of the human neighborhood requires us urgently to seek a compact on establishing a strengthened system of global governance. That is not a new idea. Its necessity has been recognized by farsighted world leaders, from the founders of the United Nations in the 1940s to the members of the independent Commissions in the 1980s. We believe that the time now is ripe to move forward. The cessation of the Cold War removes the greatest obstacle that has hindered global cooperation. The transformed relations between East and West have created unprecedented opportunities to realize what was set out in the Charter of the United Nations and to establish a new order of global governance.

A balance between national sovereignty and common global responsibility can only be achieved in a climate of confidence that encourages countries—especially the developing countries, for whom independence and sovereignty are relatively new and in some cases the product of long struggle—to trade sovereignty for improvements in global governance. If what we are entering is an essentially hegemonistic world, those who make it so will have set back the prospects for managing human survival through genuinely global action in a genuinely democratic world. On the other hand, if Western countries are faithful to their own principles, they can help to establish a new, more enlightened, more internationalist, more equitable world order. Only such change will make possible the kind of global responses to the crisis of environment and development that are urgently needed in the long-term interests of all—victors, vanquished, and the great majority who were never part of the contest for primacy.

Against the backdrop of these controlling factors, it is possible to offer three scenarios of what humanity's response could be to the crisis of environment and development. These might be categorized as

"muddling through," "an ordered world," and "enlightened change."
The rest of this chapter will address the first two scenarios.

MUDDLING through is a continuation of the present pattern of
inadequate ad hoc responses to developments as they become critical.
The dominant spirit is one of well-intentioned but usually limited
action; firefighting rather than fire prevention; crisis and disaster management rather than avoidance; reacting rather than leading. In rich
countries, governments find it easier to improvise and disengage from
problems that are not right at the doorstep.

In this scenario, policy for environmental management almost everywhere remains a matter of dealing with effects rather than causes,
with cleaning up past damage rather than preventing future damage.
Only lip service is paid to the "precautionary principle" of minimizing,
and wherever possible preventing, discharges of substances that could
be harmful and of ensuring that products and processes are nonpollut-
ing. A proliferation of environmental agencies and ministries continues, all well meaning, but usually peripheral to the main economic
policy-making arms of government. A few countries, and several large
corporations, seek to make the integration of environment and development a central thrust of their operations, but these are exceptions.

As a consequence of these factors, the big global environment issues
are not effectively addressed. Little is done to reduce carbon-dioxide
emissions. Despite steadily enlarging scientific consensus on global
warming and the availability of resources, for example the "peace
dividend," residual scientific uncertainty and the cost of making adjustments to existing energy systems are made the excuse for inactivity.
Little is done to give concrete expression to the conclusions reached at
the Earth Summit in Rio in 1992. There is no consensus about the
global commons, and there are a growing number of conflicts over
fishing rights. Oil rigs appear in Antarctica, in breach of international
agreements to the contrary, and there is a disastrous spill. Several local
wars are fought in the Middle East over water supplies.

In the short run, growth is reasonably brisk in the OECD countries,
helped by technological advance and piecemeal cooperation over the
most pressing problems. Those developing countries in Asia and Latin
America that adapt to the needs of international competition, even on
unequal terms, do reasonably well. The big Asian countries (China,
India) have their own internal political preoccupations but despite

some turbulence make steady economic progress. Environmental damage is cleaned up by rich countries that can afford it, is left for future generations to tackle by those that cannot, or is seen as a reasonable price to pay for present progress. A global conference on environment and development in ten years' time, at the start of the third millennium, addresses much the same agenda as in 1992; it is able to report a few successes (for example, on CFCs) amid signs of aggravated environmental pressure on several fronts leading to economic and political stress. There is an emphasis on national or regional, rather than global, action. This approach has few immediate consequences for industrial countries and their blocs (the European Community and the U.S./Canada/Mexico trading group), but it steadily erodes multilateral rules and institutions.

Energy issues are not addressed systematically, and although there is general improvement in energy efficiency, economic growth and decreasing oil supplies collide to produce another oil shock in the late 1990s. The developed world and some NICs can cope with this crisis after a fashion, but Eastern Europe and many oil-importing Third World countries come under severe pressure.

GATT staggers through the 1990s, held together by tenuous compromises after missing the opportunity for comprehensive renewal presented by the Uruguay Round. Globalization proceeds because large businesses find ways of evading proliferating restrictions and the "trade management" governments put in their way, but weaker developing and East European countries are often ensnared in the controls. Multilateral institutions like the World Bank are marginalized. The bank loses its way as a development institution after coming under pressure to be an agency for enforcing environmental standards on developing countries and being denied imaginative support by the major industrial countries, which turn away from multilateralism. The heavy commitment to structural adjustment in the 1980s has left these institutions with a few successes, many failures, and particularly in Africa, large sums in unpaid loans. The retreat of communism promised more fertile ground, but the process of converting East Europeans to capitalism proves more difficult than at first thought.

The debt problem continues to be a classic illustration of muddling through. More than a decade after the crisis came to a head, a few debtors like Mexico emerge, blinking, from the darkness of prolonged stagnation and painful adjustment. Most face the 1990s with debt-servicing profiles not greatly improved from 1982; few can borrow on capital markets; and a majority continue to make net transfers of resources to creditors at the expense of domestic investment and living standards. By thus muddling through, the banking system does not collapse and most debtors adopt more realistic, market-oriented policies; but these could have been pursued at the outset in a systematic way, sparing many developing countries a decade and more of lost development from which some have still to recover.

Development is treated as a peripheral concern, and serious help is given only to those developing countries that are seen as crucially important in other contexts, for example, Mexico and Egypt. Others are told to help themselves, which some, mainly in Asia, manage to do. Africa slides off the map of Western attention. Its oil and minerals attract patchy interest and are developed on an enclave basis. In a climate of benign neglect, a few countries rich in resources and sufficiently organized to exploit them—Zimbabwe, Ghana, Nigeria, for example—make some headway. Many others continue slipping back. The rich world sits up and takes notice only when famine and political unrest generate large movements of population, some of which spill into Europe, and when military potential in a few countries sets off alarm bells. By then, Africa's forests have virtually disappeared outside the Zaire basin, and much of the currently marginal land has been made useless. Cities like Nairobi become immense and, though squalid, a source of considerable economic power. Latin America has mixed fortunes. Although considerable areas of the Amazon forest remain, the destruction of large areas brings signs of a changing local climate. The areas safeguarded as nature theme parks and scientific research centers prove too small to guarantee the survival of the region's immense biodiversity. Brazil, Argentina, Mexico, and Chile make partially successful efforts to join the "First World," as Spain and Portugal did in the 1980s; but there are enormous areas of poverty, racial tensions intensify, and the environment of the megacities deteriorates badly.

Poverty persists. So do high population growth rates, which some countries continue to sideline because of religious sensitivities. And some Western governments, taking the line of least resistance, avoid offending domestic interest groups to the extent of withholding support from global family planning programs and reducing support under bilateral programs. The assumption is that the population problem will solve itself. Some advances are nevertheless made; the sharpest reductions in birth rates are in Muslim countries in east Asia and Catholic countries in Latin America and southern Europe. This progress, a continuation of trends already evident, occurs where the interlocking problems of poverty, female illiteracy, and child mortality are tackled along with the provision of family planning services.

Overall, the world is in the kind of situation pictured by Riccardo Petrella, head of the Forecasting and Assessment of Science and Technology division of the European Community, in the *New Perspectives Quarterly* (fall 1991):

> Obviously, committing the vast majority of the world's population to a global underclass is not only unjust but unsustainable in a well-armed world that is ecologically interdependent and exposed to unstoppable waves of mass migration.
>
> Absent a strategy to use science and technology constructively in the global interest—rather than in the competitive interest of becoming Number One—the future, I fear, will be characterized by a prosperous network of transnational firms and revitalized capitals of innovation that will grow dynamically together in what is basically a G-7 club, leaving behind the great mass of humanity that doesn't qualify as customers.
>
> By absurdly redefining humanity as *customers*, the population of the planet in such a new world order would be conveniently reduced from an order of eight to one! Imagine how this order would redraw . . . the world map: on one side we would see a dynamic, tightly linked, fast-developing archipelago of technopoles comprising less than one-eighth of the world's population; on the other side would be a vast, disconnected and disintegrating wasteland which is home to seven out of every eight inhabitants of the earth. (p. 61)

Come the year 2000, the world has muddled through, but not through to safety. Evidence appears in some countries of a rise in the death rate, and the quality of life has declined markedly. People are increasingly impatient with cosmetic or halfhearted responses to green issues. They are by now more enlightened than their governments, and more frightened, and with good reason. Muddling through has led to something much more serious than a muddle.

IN MUDDLING through without any comprehensive effort to respond to looming environmental calamities, we cross the thresholds of sustainability. In the World Bank's environment working paper referred to earlier, "Building on Brundtland," Robert Goodland makes it clear how such a policy has brought rapid deterioration to an already endangered environment:

> The economic subsystem has reached or exceeded important source and sink limits. . . . We have already fouled our nest: practically nowhere in this earth are signs of the human economy absent. From the center of Antarctica to Mount Everest human wastes are obvious and increasing. It is not possible to find a sample of ocean water with no sign of the 20 billion tons of human wastes added annually. . . . Persistent toxic chemicals like DDT and heavy metal compounds have already accumulated throughout the marine ecosystem. One-fifth of the world's population breathes air more poisonous than WHO standards recommend, and an entire generation of Mexico City children may be intellectually stunted by lead poisoning. (p. 6)

Such accounts of universal and increasing human impact show us what we can expect if we continue along this path:

- Despite Japan's marked success in increasing output while using the same amount of energy, and smaller improvements in energy efficiency in such countries as the United States and Sweden, carbon-dioxide emissions continue to rise. Meanwhile, the transition to renewable energy sources—biomass, solar, hydro—is pitifully slow, largely because of lack of support for the intensive research and development that our situation requires and that could make large-scale use feasible by lowering costs.

- Global warming, through greenhouse gas accumulation, continues apace. The year 1990 was already the warmest in more than a century, and seven of the hottest years on record were all within the decade of the 1980s. The 1980s were over 0.5° Celsius warmer than the 1880s, and 1990 was nearly 0.75° warmer. In the last seven thousand years, the global climate never moved more than around 1.2° from today's. By the year 2000 it becomes clear how foolish and costly it has been for the world not to act on the greenhouse hypothesis. Increasingly, scientists differ only about the rate of warming. By the time there is irrefutable evidence that warming has taken place, however, it will be too late to avert the consequences. These will include the influx of millions of refugees from low-lying coastal areas (55 percent of the world's population live on coasts or estuaries), damage to ports and coastal cities, increased storm intensity in vulnerable areas, and worst of all, damage to agriculture. Muddling through on the whole promotes global warming.

- Without global agreements on such matters as pricing to take account of the environmental cost of natural resource products or compensation for forgone income from unexploited forests, deforestation, while slowing slightly in response to public sentiment, continues in many tropical countries, as more people needing land to grow food push back forest frontiers.

- The ozone hole discovered over Antarctica, more extensive than the area of the United States, continues to expand and deepen. In 1991, the U.S. Environmental Protection Agency increased its estimate of deaths from cancer caused by ultraviolet radiation by a multiple of twenty; there could be as many as a billion additional skin cancers, many of them fatal, among people alive today. As we muddle through, fears grow that a thinning ozone shield will reduce crop yields and marine fisheries and upset normal balances in vegetation. But humanity has been condemned already to that fate: The million tons of CFCs dumped each year in the biosphere continue on their ten-year journey to the ozone layer to destroy it further and linger for another century. Present damage reflects only the relatively low levels of CFCs released in the early 1980s; worse is to come. If CFC use is completely stopped now, the world can return to predamage levels over a period of one hundred years or more. The Montreal Protocol was a move in the right direction. But the unimaginatively modest level of funding it provided for large developing countries like China and India to switch to alternatives impaired its effectiveness from the outset. As much as 85 percent of CFCs are released by the rich countries. If in this matter they can only adjust to the degree that is painless, the prospects of adequate responses to other environmental problems are bleak indeed.

- As we muddle through, land degradation (soil erosion, salination, and desertification) continues, even accelerating in some areas. With 97 percent of food coming from the land rather than the sea, and 35 percent of Earth's land already degraded, the consequence of continuing in this direction is fearful and unavoidable. Food prices rise, worsening income inequality, and the number of malnourished people multiplies beyond the one billion who had too little to eat in 1990. With a third of the population of developing countries short of fuel, people turn to crop residues and dung, whose diversion from agriculture intensifies land degradation, poverty, and hunger.

- With the world's richest habitat for species, the tropical forests, already 45 percent destroyed, species continue to become extinct at the rate of more than five thousand a year, ten thousand times faster than before humans appeared on the planet. Estimates vary, with some experts putting the loss much higher, at 100,000 species a year. As arguments continue about the intellectual property rights of the biochemical industry, we court the disaster of so great a loss of biodiversity that there will soon be no more property rights to acquire.

- Poverty entraps more people; as it does, population growth rates remain unsustainably high in many poor countries. As developing countries follow the fossil fuel path to economic growth in a world in which muddling through fails to provide acceptable alternatives, enlarging populations add to the pressure on Earth's carrying capacity in almost all directions.

- Perhaps most disturbing of all is an implication of muddling through illuminated by Peter Vitousek and others in their 1986 study, "Human Appropriation of the Products of Photosynthesis." The authors showed that people worldwide make use of about 40 percent of the life-sustaining product of photosynthesis on land. That is, they use up 40 percent of the carbohydrates that green plants produce through the conversion of carbon dioxide and water. A simple extrapolation of Vitousek's analysis would suggest that a doubling of the world's population, which is expected in about forty years, would lead humans to use up 80 percent of the material that sustains all life on land. So great an appropriation is probably impossible, and even if it were achieved in, say, 2025, a demand for a 100 percent would not be far away. We would then have run out of "life."

IN SOME respects this last projection leads to a more terrifying prognosis than even global warming or ozone depletion. Photosynthesis is nature's solar-powered food-making process. It is carried out by trees, vines, grasses, algae, seaweed, green plants of every kind on the land and in the water. Its product is the year's growth of leaves, stems, flowers, fruits, seeds, roots, and tubers. In a balanced ecosystem, this annual gain is offset by more or less equal loss through, for example, dying plants, decomposition, shedding leaves, and grazing animals. Soil nutrients are constantly recycled. Only seventy years ago human requirements took about 10 percent of annual growth. Hence the prevailing belief, then and long afterward, that nature was limitless and inexhaustible.

Taking the annual mass of harvested crops, forage grasses maintained for livestock, timber and other forest products extracted (prorated for the years of growth involved), and houseplants cultivated, Vitousek calculates that the five billion people on Earth today have raised appropriation to 40 percent. In forty years, as our numbers double to over ten billion, it may be impossible for human appropriation to double to 80 percent. In other words, it may not be possible for us to continue on our present wasteful consumption path. If we were to succeed in doing so, we would have preempted in the process other animal life in our desperate scramble to enlarge land cultivation and corner its product for ourselves. Science and technology may increase the solar-powered productivity of nature's plants, but they are also cutting back production as desertification, urban growth, soil erosion, and pollution all steadily decrease the extent of Earth's green cover.

After taking 80 percent around 2025, humankind would not be far from the absolute limit of 100 percent. Like a plague of locusts we would have eaten ourselves out of our house and home. Like locusts we would move on, but the only thing left for us would be aquatic plant life. Our processing technologies would turn them to human use, but most likely they would provide nothing but fractional relief. Of course, well before our continental food stores ran out, men and women would flock to coastal areas in an internecine struggle for survival. The scene was sketched in the context not of Vitousek's projection but of the wider issues of people, poverty, and pollution in the September 1991 issue of *Panoscope*, the magazine on the environment and development published by the Panos Institute:

As the spaceship approached earth, the continents looked as if outlined with a heavy black pen. On closer inspection, the shaded area turned out to be a long line of sun-burned men, women and children crowded along the shores struggling for a scrap of the algae that carpeted the sea. Their very lives depended on that algae. Behind them the land was barren. Only the eldest among them could vaguely remember a time when vegetation peppered the never-ending dunes. (p. 14)

Science fiction, certainly. In real life before that extreme state could be reached, regions suffering shortages of food would have succumbed to pestilence and famine. In other areas, people would not allow such a fate to overtake them lying down. Political disarray would sweep over peoples and regions, local groups, families, and ultimately individuals in the scramble for advantage and at length personal survival. Civilization would evaporate before tooth-and-claw horror.

For the most part, present complacency is rooted in our faith in science. But scientists are also telling us bad news. If we listened, surely the Vitousek projection would jolt us out of our present state of contentment.

M U D D L I N G through is essentially a refusal by governments to face up to the implications of maltreatment of the planet that is our life source and habitation. This failure cannot be attributed to ignorance of the implications: The matters discussed in earlier chapters are known to those who make the relevant decisions. Muddling through reflects instead inertia and optimism, a dangerous mixture by which one can sacrifice one's own interests as well as the interests of others. Slavery was at its height when, in 1759, Voltaire wrote *Candide*, his satirical commentary on the philosophy of complacency and acquiescence. In one of many unforgettable incidents, the innocent hero encounters a Negro slave lying on the ground as he is about to enter Surinam. The slave, who has lost both a hand and a leg, tells Candide that this is the "price paid for the sugar you eat in Europe." "Oh Pangloss!" cries Candide to his valet, "this is an abomination you had not guessed; this is too much. In the end I shall have to renounce optimism." "What is this optimism?" asks the valet. "Alas," says Candide, "it is the mania of maintaining that all is good when all is bad." (pp. 84–86) And Candide weeps as he enters Surinam.

We know in our minds the thresholds we are crossing in our abuse of the planet, yet we press on, maintaining, for the most part, that all is good when much is bad. Our refusal to change course, to admit that complacency is ill-advised, signifies an aversion to change on the part of those who prosper. Muddling through is a process of perpetual deferment of hard choices, the kind of irresponsible refusal to adjust to changed circumstances with which the IMF is accustomed to charging developing countries. On environmental issues, however, it is the industrial countries that most need to adjust and that most defer action. Will knowledge of the probable consequences of muddling through tempt the strong to respond to the need for change by compelling adjustment on the part of the weak?

T H E September 28, 1991 issue of *The Economist* carried an article, "A New World Order: To the Victors, the Spoils—and the Headaches," which among other things said the following:

> Yet with those—substantial—caveats (*political will and public support*), the West has the power to win almost any battle it chooses to fight.
>
> Unsurprisingly, many people want to use that strength to encourage the spread of Western ideas. Dictators, it is argued, should no longer be able to stamp insouciantly on their people's rights while insisting that outsiders keep out; the democracies should assert a right of at least occasional intervention, to ensure the possibility of self-determination, a minimum of basic liberties and even, some add, of care for the environment. This notion has obvious risks. But it has attracted much support in the democratic world, from both right and left. Handled with care it could turn out to be the biggest by-product of the events of 1991. (p. 25)

Some of the support cited later in the article turned out to be statements asserting the right of "the world" to be more interventionist. It is a sign of the times how readily the world's right is equated with the right of the West to be more interventionist.

Six weeks later (November 9, 1991) *The Economist* sounded an editorial caution against moving "too fast" toward "new ways to run the world." Adducing reasons for "treading warily," it said it would be a pity to allow the new ways to be portrayed as "a neo-colonialist scheme imposed by the rich upon the poor." The caution counseled by *The Economist* does not, of course, eliminate the danger of the West assuming that ideological, political, and economic victories over its cold war adversaries give it the right to police the entire world. The temptation to do so may be strong, and there are many supremacists willing to urge the democracies on. But the strength of democracy lies in its values and in staying true to them. Any attempt to embark on a new imperialism under its banner would give rise to massive contradictions and therefore to resistance from within Western societies themselves. But can an arrogation of authority by Western governments be ruled out?

The Economist was not the first to raise the possibility that Western countries might be tempted to force developing countries to fall in line on environmental matters. David Adamson's *Defending the World*, published in 1990, discussed what the industrialized countries could do to get the Third World to limit carbon-dioxide emissions. It explained the path of dictation: "If persuasion does not work, 'green conditionality' might be the answer in some cases, unpopular though it would be; and for the really hard cases, sanctions, provided there is sufficient of a consensus to back them and the industrial world has not sunk into a mood of profound fatalism about the impossibility of stemming the greenhouse gases." (p. 210) This was written about the emission of greenhouse gases for which the main culprits to date have been the industrial countries.

Prudence may suggest caution about the pace, as *The Economist* has done, but there can be little doubt about the path some would like to follow. "An ordered world" is a scenario that cannot be excluded from the list of possibilities. Underlying it is a mixture of self-interest, idealism, and ideological fervor that leads their governments to try and tackle the problems of global insecurity and environmental threat directly and on their own terms. Intervention becomes a central feature of a new style of governance: If Third World governments do not meet decreed norms, the "international community," in other words, a small number of industrial countries, will come in and dictate solutions. "Sovereignty be damned" will be the righteous cry—but only the sovereignty of others.

An ordered world, unlike the world of muddling through, sees economic control increasingly wielded through the international finance institutions based in Washington, the IMF and the World Bank. Western governments, exercising tighter rein over these institutions, use them as mouthpieces and instruments. Environmentalism is encouraged both globally and nationally. The Antarctic Treaty is put forward as a model for global commons management by selected countries. Developing countries that agree to manage their forests the way the industrial countries want them to receive additional aid and debt swaps.

"Environmental conditionality" emerges as a key lever for ensuring that developing countries conform to standards that industrial countries—or powerful pressure groups in their legislatures—consider appropriate. Plans for forestry development or dam construction or coal-burning power stations, criticized as unsuitable by green activists in Washington or Berlin, have to be abandoned or slowed because of threats to withdraw aid or impose trade restrictions. Those countries that fail to sign or abide by the Montreal Protocol on ozone-destroying gases are reminded that GATT sanctions apply.

An ordered world scenario could develop easily from present circumstances. In the first phase it might even seem successful. The spread of pluralistic, democratic politics continues apace and the remaining recalcitrants move quickly to install liberal political systems, at least superficially. There is similar movement in the economic field. With the Soviet Union divided into several capitalist states, India locked into a medium-term program of market-oriented reforms under IMF supervision, and the regime in China returning to the economic liberalization of the 1980s, there is no longer any serious challenge to the prevailing economic orthodoxy. The multinationals are tempted back into Africa and Latin America and are everywhere greeted by malleable governments offering generous incentives.

All this gives a major injection of demand into the world economy, and the 1990s recapture for business the optimism of the long boom of the 1950s and 1960s. Western countries, having learned the habits and benefits of collaboration in their responses to the Gulf war and to the changes in the Soviet bloc, are able to work together more effectively, overcoming regional rivalries. A meaningful GATT agreement is signed, and this reinforces confidence.

An ordered world seems too good to be true, and it is. The contradictions start to appear as the decade progresses. The economic success stories, however real, still leave pervasive poverty; in many countries the adjustment process is long and painful and there are many victims of austerity. Those leaders promising salvation through free markets and liberal democracy find themselves under growing attack from old-style nationalists and populists and have to give ground. In countries where the advent of democracy has brought few tangible benefits, the military emerges from the barracks.

What starts initially as localized reaction develops into broader anti-Western sentiment as increased communications and travel expose the contrasts in quality of life and the double standard, "Do as we say, not as we do." Migrants from poor countries are unwelcome in rich countries and often harshly treated. Western companies, initially well received, become less popular when evidence mounts that expectations of what they can contribute to development have been exaggerated and the behavior of some raises old ghosts about exploitation.

Where there is a strong rallying point for alternative values, as in the Islamic world, resentment builds. And unresolved problems like that of a Palestinian homeland and the increasingly casual intervention by Western countries in the internal affairs of weaker countries fuel resentment. More substantial Third World countries like China and India, cut off from external arms supplies, build their own military-industrial complexes. Dictation and intervention breed animosity and a spirit of confrontation, which in turn harden the resolve of those who espouse the path of compulsion. As the decade unfolds, it becomes clear that an ordered world is not going to be any more durable than the old imperialisms. Large sections of public opinion in the West, always uneasy about the authoritarian styles their governments adopt abroad, become vocal in opposition and call for dialogue, not dictation. Others simply recoil from involvement in seemingly intractable global problems and exert strong pressures on governments to "de-link," to retreat behind barricades.

An ordered world does not offer a reliable way out of world problems, and its most glaring failure is in tackling global environmental issues. These prove far too complex to be solved by twisting arms in poor countries. They worsen as rich countries, under no compulsion themselves save that of enlightenment, fail to find the political will to turn their own societies away from unsustainable ways of living. The outcome for environment and development is much the same as it is with muddling through: Ecological limits are crossed, with fearful and inescapable consequences.

Yet even in an ordered world there are some in the directorate of power more ready than others to follow the path of sustainability. OECD countries, for example, made important moves to curb greenhouse gas emissions at the start of the 1990s. The United States initially blocked agreement on stabilizing emissions at 1990 levels by the year 2000, but the European Community decided to go ahead and made the commitment. Within the community, however, Britain resisted proposals for implementing that commitment, claiming that the measures envisaged would impose "a disproportionate cost and effect to the consumer"—an explanation that had already led the British Association for the Conservation of Energy to ask, "How on earth are we going to meet our obligations if we won't agree on any of the measures which are going to cut back greenhouse gases?" How indeed? The problem with an ordered world is that those who need most to conform are giving the orders.

Perverse though it is, underpinning an ordered world on the ecological front is the premise, no longer unspoken, that it is much harder for rich countries to accept a fall in living standards—wrongly but widely assumed to be the result of moderating consumption—than for poor ones to avoid causing ecological harm through unsustainable development. The main response, therefore, must come from developing countries. Even though their contribution to present environmental stress is minimal, their future development can be the ecological bridge too far; they must be prevented from crossing it. That will allow the industrial countries the longest time possible to continue on a business as usual path while science finds the inevitable answers. So, for example, there can be more power generation stations using fossil fuel in industrialized countries to provide the energy for uninterrupted economic growth. The moral contradictions are resolved by paying for enough trees to be planted, in poor countries, to absorb as much carbon dioxide as the power plants will add to the stock of global warming gases. One such arrangement has actually been made: Trees are to be grown in Guatemala to offset the greenhouse emissions of a new coal-burning power station in the United States. In an ordered world, securing agreements of this kind will be no problem, nor will policing them. In this and in other fields—the disposal of hazardous waste is one—developing countries will act as sinks to absorb the effluents and pollutants of industrial countries, a role that will come to be recast as a duty.

But an ordered world will fail for another reason, namely, its imposition of external values and methods on human communities that often in fact have more understanding about how to manage their own resources than outsiders do. Development assistance has often failed because of the assumption of superior wisdom by foreign experts who have not spent enough time with local communities. The ordered world scenario is the antithesis of all that experience teaches us. Experience indicates that solutions have a better chance when local communities are given the support they need in health care, education, employment, economic growth, and family planning, and when sustainability is built at the local level, modifying central policies to permit that process. The ordered world philosophy is as much a delusion as the dogma imposed on Eastern Europe by the Soviets was. An ordered world is not just a problem of North/South neocolonialism in the name of environment. It arises from a strong human proclivity to choose what appears to be the simple and straightforward way out of a dilemma. It will fail, mainly because it is founded on oversimplification, intolerance, a "mother knows best" attitude, and ignores the crucial role of individuals and local communities in the care of the environment.

In an ordered world there are, of course, no negotiations. An environmental security council is established as an adjunct to the Group of Seven's economic management process, not by an amendment to the UN Charter or by an agreement with developing countries. This becomes the instrument for dealing with the handful of developing countries—China, India, Brazil, and a few others—whose support is considered desirable. Capital flows are the main lever for securing their acquiescence, but these are kept to a minimum and related strictly to the concerns of industrial countries—the conservation of tropical forests, for example, and the phasing out of CFCs. Perhaps the most damaging consequence of an ordered world is its deferment of the rule of enforceable law worldwide, law that binds the strong and the weak, the rich and the poor, law for one and all, with none above the law; law that does not accept that any country, however mighty, or any group of countries, however united, can be accuser, policeman, judge, jury, and prison warder all in one.

DEVELOPING countries must act to minimize the chances of an ordered world being imposed on them. They can do so in diverse ways, not least by opting not to offer hostages to fortune as Saddam Hussein did by his militarism and oppression and eventual aggression. They must enhance their development prospects by policy reforms of the kind recommended by the South Commission, including drastic curtailment of military expenditure. They must help to bring about a nuclear weapons–free world, at least by not themselves entering the race of proliferation. If developing countries are to take the high ground against authoritarianism in international relations, they must be above reproach in their own domestic and regional policies. They must make serious efforts to moderate high rates of population growth and show a readiness to share responsibility for securing global survival through programs of sustainable living.

This may seem to be asking the poor and weak to pay a penalty for the malfeasance of the rich and strong. It is not. It is acknowledging the realities of international life and suggesting to developing countries that prudence and self-interest no less than morality require them to provide no excuses for external intervention. That they should fully uphold the norms of civil society is in their interest. The closer Third World conduct is to this ideal, the stronger the hand will be of the many citizens of industrial democracies whose instinct is to argue against a world ordered by the strong and in favor of one rooted in negotiation and partnership.

In the context of environment alone, the scenario of an ordered world seems absurd, so palpable is the need for genuine cooperation to secure a common future of sustainable living. But the scenario is of much wider import. It conjures up a world in which international relations have seriously regressed. Yet who can doubt that this scenario is indeed being conjured up? The discussion in *The Economist* of the new world order specifically raised the possibility of the "victors" intervening beyond their borders in the interest of caring for the environment. This would be like arsonists putting out small fires while around them the larger fire raged.

TEN

Enlightened Change

> We need each others'
> breathing, warmth, surviving
> is the only war
> we can afford.
> — *Margaret Atwood*

MUDDLING through would be collectively inducing a disastrous end through separately persisting with unsustainable living. An ordered world would be a return to an outmoded and ultimately unworkable imperialism leading similarly to disaster. Neither offers a worthy or viable response to the crisis of environment and development. The world must choose another way, the path of shared responsibility for our common future. Although still largely untrodden, it is in fact the kind of path we have been trying to chart, however haphazardly, since the 1920s in our search for a working internationalism, first through the League of Nations and later, after its failure and the disastrous war that followed, through the United Nations.

That our efforts have been haphazard is testimony to the human tendency not to sustain enlightened change once the crisis that inspires it seems to recede. Enlightened change is easily disparaged as visionary thinking. But there have been times when enlightened change seemed the only road to take. There is no better example, perhaps, than the ideas that stirred men like Churchill and Roosevelt in the 1940s as they looked to peace and took up the challenge to build a world secure against the scourge of war. As we face again the need to turn aside from old ways in order to secure our future, it is instructive to remember the part played by those two very different men, both seasoned practitioners of the politics of war and peace.

Churchill was unapologetically a man of empire, but his internationalism, shaped by a long crusade against the weakness of the League of Nations and a campaign to avert the war he had foreseen, overrode imperialist ambition. The lessons of the 1930s never left him. On September 6, 1943, with the war at its turning point, Churchill received an honorary degree from Harvard University. He spoke of Anglo-American unity and his vision of the future. The Atlantic Alliance and the Commonwealth association, he said, offered "far better prizes than taking away other people's provinces or land or grinding them down in exploitation. The empires of the future are the empires of the mind." But he also envisaged new global arrangements: "We have learned from hard experience that stronger, more efficient, more rigorous world institutions must be created to preserve peace and to forestall the causes of future wars." A central task was to work out the "form a system of world security may take," a task that included coming to grips with "derogations . . . from national sovereignty for the sake of a larger synthesis." Churchill complained that if the League of Nations had failed, it was "largely because it was abandoned, and later on betrayed." And, he counseled the youth of America and Britain, "there is no halting-place at this port. We have now reached a stage in the journey where there can be no pause. We must go on. It must be world anarchy or world order."

Roosevelt fully shared Churchill's vision that led, two years later, to the founding of the UN, an event Roosevelt did not live to see. It was his successor, Harry Truman, who spoke at the founding conference in San Francisco on April 25, 1945: "We still have a choice between the alternatives: the continuation of international chaos . . . or establishment of a world organization for the enforcement of peace." He added, almost in self-fulfilling prophecy, "If we should pay merely lip-service to the inspiring ideals and then later do violence to simple justice, we would draw down upon us the bitter wrath of generations yet unborn."

We have indeed paid lip service to the ideals of the UN Charter and done violence to simple justice. Like the League of Nations before it, the UN was betrayed throughout the era of the cold war. Yet there is no denying the enlightenment of the vision and effort that went into the establishment of the UN as "a world organization for the enforcement of peace." Times have changed, but the priority remains human survival; we still need to save succeeding generations, this time from the scourge of our onslaught on the environment. We need again the enlightened approaches that briefly gave hope in those anxious times, and we need the courage of those who urged them. We need their vision and their refusal to settle for little plans if we are to pursue the path of enlightened change.

It is, therefore, useful to recapture some of the other creative ideas that the mood of that time helped to generate. These could have changed our postwar experience in significant ways. There were proposals, for instance, for the global management of nuclear power that might just have spared us the risks of the nuclear arms race, the horror of Chernobyl, and the threat of global warming.

I F W E were to write an energy policy for the world on a clean sheet, its primary objective would have to be to diminish reliance on fossil fuels. Fossil fuels are a nonrenewable asset. At current rates of consumption, the known resources of oil, gas, and coal could be exhausted for all practical purposes within the next hundred years, oil very probably sooner. An immensely more compelling reason is that the world environment cannot stand the impact of increasing carbon-dioxide emissions from the continued use of fossil fuels.

We would have to examine whether in a nuclear weapons–free world nuclear energy—under rigorous international control in respect of power generation, waste disposal, and security against military uses—offered humanity a practical way to avoid the greenhouse effect and other disasters to which continued reliance on fossil fuels would inexorably lead. Today's nuclear energy production, based on fission— a technology involving the splitting of uranium or plutonium atoms— poses serious problems. It inevitably gives rise to other radioactive materials that take centuries to decay and hence threaten life forms with which they come into contact. The risk of accidents like Chernobyl aside, no country has yet been able to solve satisfactorily the problem of disposal of high- and intermediate-level radioactive waste. Where waste lasts for thousands of years, total safety would mean shielding it against the possible impact of an ice age or other similar environmental upheaval, something that it is difficult to guarantee.

Nuclear scientists have for decades held out the hope of creating energy from fusion, that is, by combining atoms of hydrogen to make helium, the same process that powers the sun. If it could be achieved, fusion would provide almost limitless energy from basic and widely available raw materials and without the grave safety and waste problems associated with nuclear fission. A small breakthrough in this process was achieved in October 1991 in a joint European research center in Britain. But the successful management of fusion reactions—they require immensely high temperatures, several times that of the sun—as a source of everyday commercial energy is many decades off and calls for solutions to the problems of safe plant design and operation.

Against the uncertainties of nuclear power must be set the attractions of what are called renewable sources of energy. These include solar, wind, wave, and tidal power. The largest renewable of all is simply efficiency in use, or energy conservation. A number of calculations suggest that many developed countries could halve their per capita emissions of carbon dioxide without increasing their electricity-generating capacity if they introduced more efficient techniques. The output of carbon dioxide from road vehicles could be halved by achieving fuel-economy targets already technically possible and for which leading motor manufacturers have designs. Among the other renewables, solar power, tapped in the world's deserts and semiarid regions, could make a valuable contribution, harnessing the energies of that great fusion reactor, the sun, safely insulated from us by some 93 million miles of high-vacuum space. Wind, wave, and tidal power are less easily harnessed on a large scale, but there are many devices that promise to use such sources on a small scale in various parts of the world. Cost has been a deterrent to the use of renewables, but cost equations would be transformed if the pricing of fossil fuels were to include the full cost of greenhouse warming.

There are several arguments for nuclear power, particularly that based on fusion. It would avoid the greenhouse and pollution hazards posed by fossil fuels. It would make it possible for energy consumption to be enlarged in developing countries, the precondition of economic growth and of the elimination of chronic poverty, which coupled with population expansion is now a major contributor to environmental stress. Unlike fossil fuels, nuclear energy is renewable.

It offers, in short, the prospect of an energy source that sustains life and enhances living standards worldwide without the risk of global warming.

But before the world can embark on a major expansion in nuclear power generation, the big questions have first to be answered. How do we overcome the problems of safety, waste, and security attendant on nuclear fission? How do we pursue on a global basis the possibilities of fusion? Justifiably appalled by the nuclear arms race and by the safety and waste problems of nuclear power generation, we have been reluctant to develop nuclear energy. But it is worth noting that France relies on it for three-fourths of its electrical power, and that nuclear plants now also provide from a third to a half of the power used in Belgium, Finland, Spain, Sweden, and Switzerland in Western Europe, in Bulgaria and Hungary in Eastern Europe, and in Taiwan and South Korea in Asia. So, with the first moves toward a world free of nuclear weapons, should we now contemplate assigning the responsibility for all nuclear matters, including the development of fusion technology, to a truly international authority?

F E W recall that this is exactly where we were in 1946 before the nuclear arms race began. As we contemplate its end, and the conclusion of the IPCC that the world must reduce carbon-dioxide emissions by at least 60 percent if the global warming process is to be checked, it is worth revisiting that missed opportunity. Not surprisingly after the horror and trauma and guilt following the dropping of two atomic bombs on Japan in 1945, the very first resolution adopted, unanimously, by the General Assembly of the UN pledged member states to total nuclear disarmament and to the use of nuclear energy for peaceful purposes only. The resolution was moved by Britain (where Atlee had succeeded Churchill) and cosponsored by the United States, the Soviet Union, and France. However, as Nobel Peace Prize winner Philip Noel-Baker was to recall much later in *Disarm or Die*, it "proved a long and weary task to find a plan to carry out Resolution I." It was never to be carried out, but there was a chance. In 1946 the United States, through its delegate on the Atomic Energy Commission, Bernard M. Baruch, proposed what came to be known as the Baruch Plan, though it appears that many others were involved in its architecture, including J. Robert Oppenheimer, who led the team that made the first atom bomb, and Dean Acheson and David Lilienthal, who had drafted a similar plan in 1945.

As Noel-Baker described it, the Baruch Plan called for "a vast international agency, to be created and controlled by the United Nations, which will own and operate the whole nuclear industry of the world, including everything from mining of uranium to the operation of civil reactors for the production of electric power." The authority would exercise a monopoly over the ownership, production, and research for peaceful purposes of all atomic material and operate the entire enterprise from mine to product. It would prohibit the manufacture of any type of atomic weapon, inspect all nuclear activities, and impose severe penalties on any violator by veto-free Security Council action. With provision for an adequate system of inspection and control, the plan called for the cessation of all atomic weapons production, the destruction of the U.S. stockpile of atomic weapons, and the transfer of U.S. scientific information on atomic processes to the international authority.

The Baruch Plan, endorsed by the great majority of the UN General Assembly, was bitterly opposed by the Soviet Union, which feared it would be consigned permanently to second-rank status as a non-nuclear power, leaving the United States with a monopoly of knowledge in nuclear science and weapons. Discussions on the proposal in the Atomic Energy Commission reached a deadlock. Three years later, in 1949, the Soviet Union tested its first atomic weapon. The nuclear arms race had begun.

Had the International Atomic Development Authority (IADA) proposed by Baruch come into being, had the United States destroyed its still minimal stockpile of atomic weapons and transferred its nuclear information to the IADA, had the Soviet Union used its position not to veto the plan but to ensure that the IADA was genuinely international and independent of Western control, had it not gone on to develop its own nuclear weapons—how different the world would have been in so many ways. How greatly strengthened postwar internationalism and the UN system would have been. It is too late for all that; but are we not at a point in history when such a plan deserves another chance?

The irony is that today it is from the heirs to a broken Soviet Union that support for such a plan might come, while the West might voice opposition. The West should heed the fact that in 1945 it was a victor, and that then wisdom pointed the way through internationalism. Now along with the need for security there is environmental need demanding that we direct the science of nuclear fission—and even more so, fusion—to the betterment of the planet. In a scenario of enlightened change dictated by the imperative of human survival, one that inspires confidence in internationalism and is not diminished by the politics of dominance, one in which the weak see their sovereignty made real by the instruments of global governance and in which the strong see gains for stability—in such a scenario, creative ideas unacceptable at other times may well find a propitious climate.

T H E third scenario stretches the limits of current policy approaches to encompass a significant degree of multilateral commitment to the environment and to development. It envisages the ascendancy of democratic values within states assisting the emergence of democracy within the global state and thereby promoting enlightened change worldwide. At heart, it acknowledges humanity's need for mutual sustenance. Enlightened change is an updated version of the kind of global order to which the victors aspired in the middle of this century. The UN system, the Bretton Woods institutions, and the Marshall Plan in Europe are elements of early postwar experience suggesting that almost fifty years later humanity can indeed rise to the new challenges.

Enlightened change is not the blueprint of an ideal world. Mass poverty will take years, even decades, to eradicate. Demographic trends cannot be reversed in the short run. Given the interests of governments, and the world's many distinct national, linguistic, ethnic, and religious groups, there will be no dramatic switch to internationalist thinking. But it is not fanciful to envisage, as this scenario does, a modest but definite swing toward longer-term and more internationally cooperative modes of decision-making. Now that the transformation of relations between East and West has ended the cold war, we should free minds long locked in sterile confrontation and resources tied to military consumption. An important challenge of the 1990s and the first years of the new century will be to develop concepts of global order based not on ideas of deterrence or dictation but of collective security and common responsibility.

Divided Europe leads the way, ambitious in extending cooperation and seeking integration. Visions of a peaceful continent with no boundaries dividing its peoples are already being translated into practical decisions through the Conference on Cooperation and Security in Europe (CCSE), which has risen to the challenge of overseeing the difficult transition in central and Eastern Europe. The Treaty on Conventional Forces in Europe (CFE), signed in Paris by thirty-four heads of state and government in November 1990, was the most substantial disarmament treaty ever. It was the result of a process of dialogue reaching back to the first summit at Helsinki in 1975. And the CCSE process has extended beyond security in the conventional sense to such other issues as economic and environmental relations and human rights. It could be the prototype for other regional security arrangements beyond Europe. Already, it helps to create an international climate receptive to enlightened change.

In the area of nuclear disarmament, recent developments between the United States and the former Soviet Union, particularly the START treaty and the Bush initiative for unilateral cuts, which has to some extent overtaken START, are moves in the same positive direction. Despite limitations in respect of retained nuclear capability and sustained military spending, there is a logic to these events that may prove more compelling than their authors envisioned. Certainly millions of people the world over, including many in the nuclear power countries themselves, will continue to insist that the dream of a world free of nuclear weapons become a reality before its absence leads us to a world in which they proliferate.

The scenario of enlightened change holds an enlarged role for internationalism and for the UN in particular. Efforts are already being made to strengthen the UN as the principal instrument for peace and security in their truest meaning. The Stockholm Initiative on Global Security and Governance has called for a world summit on global governance similar to the meetings in San Francisco and Bretton Woods in the 1940s. That initiative taken in 1991 by thirty-six international figures looked to 1995, the fiftieth anniversary of the signing of the UN Charter, as a time for revisiting human hopes and plans for a peaceful, just, and habitable world. We must look in two directions, back to the vision of 1945 and forward to its translation into new machinery relevant to present realities. Prominent among these is the irresistible urge for democracy within world society and the pressing need to save succeeding generations from the scourge of environmental degradation.

O N E O F the earliest signs of enlightened change would be the way issues are discussed. Not only in a small number of European countries (Holland and Norway, for example), but also in the more powerful industrial countries and in many developing countries, governments would start to talk about sustainable development in ways that implied more than token gestures to potentially troublesome green groups. This would happen as governments felt politically threatened by an environmental movement beginning to transcend some of its earlier weaknesses: parochialism (the "not in my backyard" syndrome); otherworldliness, an antigrowth and antibusiness philosophy; and a lack of organization for disciplined campaigning. With its growing maturity and broader base, it becomes a people's movement building coalitions within and among countries, and its message is reinforced by growing evidence of environmental stress.

In this context, the tone of political debate undergoes discernible changes. In industrial countries, environmental issues begin to be given greater priority by policy-makers. Governments and local authorities that fail to maintain environmental standards, to ensure that national accounts and budgets capture environmental costs and benefits, and to support global action on both environment and development find themselves in trouble with the press, during elections, and sometimes because of judicial intervention following action by community groups. There is general recognition that some aspects of existing lifestyles have to change. Transportation policy, in particular, is reviewed, and those pressing for improved public transport, urban road-user charges, and less-polluting cars gain ground.

The environmental movement moves toward a politically attractive middle path on lifestyle issues, between ascetic self-denial and complacent self-indulgence. A crucial element is the link between environment and development. A mixture of altruism, fear (of mass migration from developing countries and of the global consequences of environmental neglect), and commercial self-interest puts the question of poverty and development higher up the global agenda. The availability of a peace dividend from the end of the cold war creates more favorable conditions—despite the claims of Eastern Europe—for finding additional resources for development. As the economic progress of Third World countries is seen to be in the mutual interest of rich and poor, aid comes to be perceived more as investment, less as philanthropy.

In developing countries, too, there is change. Besides the democratization of Eastern Europe, political progress in Latin America, southern Asia, and increasingly, Africa, is eloquent testimony to the speed and effectiveness with which powerful ideas can spread in certain parts of the world. In the 1990s, the strong tide of democracy and market economics is augmented by another: the idea of empowerment. This is the belief that everyone is entitled to certain minimum standards achieved less through decisions made on high than through opportunities for self-improvement: the right to land ownership, to work, to education (especially for women), and to structures of genuine local decision-making. And these ideas are connected to environmental consciousness, since empowerment gives the poor a bigger stake in the management of common resources such as local watersheds, woods, irrigation systems, and grazing areas. Improved and more equitable tenure stimulates better management of the land. Improvements in education and health facilities create a more receptive base for campaigns to popularize family planning. Such changes are often slow in coming and uneven when they do come, but democratic elections and the near-universal diffusion of ideas through radio and television are powerful catalysts. Successful experiments, like the Indian food-for-work programs developed in the state of Maharashtra, cease to be isolated examples and are more widely copied and improved upon.

A CENTRAL feature of the enlightened change scenario is that certain dominant ideas—the enthusiasm for democratic political systems, for liberal-market economics, and for sustainable development—reinforce each other, providing powerful synergies in both developed and developing countries. In developed countries, environmental awareness combines with the preference for market economics to push new forms of energy taxation. These are designed not to augment government revenue but rather to achieve a less polluting, especially less carbon-intensive, energy mix and to encourage business and households to pay more attention to energy conservation and efficiency. The Canadians, Japanese, and Scandinavians lead the way, followed by other Europeans. Eventually, even in the United States, where the idea of something like a carbon tax is initially anathema, political pressure mounts for change. Changes produce results in less energy-intensive forms of growth; and this, in turn, enables the rich world to adopt a less hectoring approach toward developing nations on preventive measures against global warming, and to more willingly shoulder the bulk of the burden of reducing carbon-dioxide emissions.

Other problems too become more tractable. Popular disgust at economically wasteful and environmentally damaging agricultural protection and overproduction in the European Community at last produces real reform of CAP and opens the way to multilateral agreement over trade in which Third World access to markets is safeguarded. Discriminatory tariffs against processed products and manufactured goods from developing countries are relaxed, removing pressure for bulk export of raw materials and for the unsustainable exploitation of forests.

In developing countries the same chemistry works to advantage. In Asian and African societies where there is meaningful democracy, it is the rural poor who become politically influential; the resulting emphasis on the development of farming and on rural areas reduces interest in energy-intensive and inefficient forms of industrialization. Market-oriented approaches to development offer better rewards to peasant farmers who find it increasingly possible to invest in sustainable forms of agriculture. Similarly, realistic pricing for energy (whether as electricity or petrol), timber, fertilizer, and water leads to a reduction of waste, especially by the rich, and encourages conservation. It is in the former communist world, where democracy, markets, and environmental sustainability are all revolutionary ideas, that the most striking changes take place.

In this scenario, the more cooperative mood brings developed and developing countries together to achieve strong conventions to protect the world from manmade climate change and to prevent species or biodiversity loss through programs for conserving tropical forests. Conventions could be vacuous expressions of goodwill committing no one to anything, or agreements with no prospect of ratification. But NGOs successfully press for quantitative, time-bound undertakings, country by country, that turn conventions into firm pledges of action.

Agreement between rich and poor countries on the conventions signifies their acceptance of ground rules for negotiated agreements on big international environmental and development issues. In essence, the developing countries undertake to play a full, committed role in tackling global issues like greenhouse warming and tropical forest conservation on the clear understanding that the industrial world will support their development, through trade—principally by improving access to markets—and through flows of resources that recognize the costs of sustainable development. That rich countries should meet the targets for development aid internationally agreed upon is an old, almost ritual, demand; but their response is now influenced by the availability of a peace dividend, by the knowledge that many developing countries are now following market-oriented strategies, and by the fact that there is now a mutually understood tradeoff. The bargain is not narrowly conceived. It is not a matter of providing a little more aid for environmentally sound projects. It is a broad compact based on the shared understanding that mobilizing resources to overcome poverty is as important an environmental objective as direct action to reduce carbon-dioxide emissions.

A vital part of the scenario is the setting up of a multilateral fund to support sustainable development, financed by an international tax based on countries' ability to pay as measured by their GNP. This tax is an old idea, previously damned as impractical. In this context, however, it reflects universal recognition that the most critical environmental problems are global in their impact, that they do not respect national sovereignty, and that they require global solutions and global institutions to apply solutions. How such a levy is charged is seen as less important than the question of who manages the resources involved. Much unnecessary time was spent in the past debating the merits of new versus old institutions for realizing global objectives. The World Bank, one of the old ones, has a generally credible record in promoting development, and, particularly because of its new openness to democratic systems of management and governance and its sensitivity to environmental issues, all countries agree that it can handle the operations of the new fund.

AN IMPORTANT element of the scenario is a set of guidelines for governments on implementing sustainable development. The Brundtland Commission put forward the concept of sustainable development in its report but did not attempt to elaborate with detailed proposals. Its task was to mobilize international opinion to meet the challenges confronting our common future. That the report did, creating a global constituency for enlightened change. From that constituency concrete proposals for action are emerging.

Ultimately, the most comprehensive set of proposals will come from the preparatory process leading to the Earth Summit in June 1992, but that process itself will be informed and assisted by a wide range of suggestions that have emanated from a variety of sources. Many of these have been sensitively described in *Beyond Interdependence: The Meshing of the World's Economy and the Earth's Ecology*, a Trilateral Commission book by Jim MacNeill, Pieter Winsemius, and Taizo Yakushiji. Particularly important is their discussion on the financing of action to prevent global warming, which illustrates one of the major elements of all negotiations that lie ahead. If satisfactory funding arrangements cannot be agreed upon in the area of global warming, it bodes ill for the prospects of enlightened change across the wider field of environment and development.

The secretary-general of the Earth Summit, Maurice Strong, has called for an imaginative response to this need for financial resources to achieve sustainability. The "Caring for the Earth" report has priced its strategy for sustainable living in the years from 1992 to 2001 at a total of $1,288 billion, with expenditure rising from $77 billion in 1992 to $161 billion in 2001. This covers energy conservation, including developing renewable sources ($417 billion), retiring Third World debt ($300), moderating population growth, including improvements in education and health ($270), protecting topsoil on croplands ($189), reducing deforestation and conserving biodiversity ($52), and forest and tree planting ($60). Many of the actions leading to sustainable living will pay for themselves by increasing efficiency and prosperity while costing no more than inherently wasteful current practices. But some actions will require more money, hence the total over the decade. Arresting and reversing environmental degradation will be costly. Measures to deal with the range of threats to human survival detailed in earlier chapters will call for sustained expenditures. Climate change, ozone depletion, and pollution of the air, rivers, and seas are worldwide threats; so is the pollution of poverty. Facilitating development, reversing desertification, reducing deforestation, conserving biodiversity—all these require considerable financial resources. What is at stake is survival, or at the very least, survival of civilization as we know it.

In the UNCED preparatory process, it has been estimated that the cost of implementing Agenda 21 could be $125 billion a year until the end of the century. It helps to place these additional resources in perspective by recalling that in 1990 developing countries transferred

$140 billion in debt service payments, capital and interest, to creditor nations. But there is more.

Over the next decade world military expenditure, even by conservative estimates, is expected to total some $9 trillion, all in the name of security. Securing sustainable living on planet Earth, the precondition of security in the conventional sense, will require expenditures that are a small fraction of this amount. If military expenditure were to be reduced progressively, starting with a cut of 5 percent in 1991 and rising to 18 percent by the end of the century, it could yield nearly $1,300 billion over the decade toward making the planet secure against environmental disaster. Diversions from military budgets are, of course, only one possible source of funds for investment in environmental security. There are many avenues that could be explored, including forms of global taxation. As important as locating sources of additional finance for developing countries is creating conditions in which they are better able to earn their way so that they can themselves afford to care for the environment. The barriers to their exports should be removed, their primary products should receive fairer returns, and their burden of debt should be lightened. It is against such a backdrop that our response to the crisis of environment and development must be formulated. The conclusions of *Beyond Interdependence* are inescapable:

> The negotiations leading up to Rio will force governments to decide—and leaders to reveal—the extent to which they are really prepared to go beyond rhetoric and make the difficult decisions that are now needed. Western leaders must demonstrate enlightened leadership. Only they command the economic resources, the technologies, and the political resilience to accommodate significant change. Only they can initiate the restructuring of international economic and political relations needed to reverse the tragic flow of capital from the poorer to the richer countries and to ensure that developing countries get equitable access to the technologies needed to support sustainable development. A breakthrough in these two areas will be the key to the success of the Earth Summit. Failure would be an enormous setback to North-South relations and would likely cripple prospects for a new global alliance to secure the future of our planet. (p. 127)

IMPORTANT roles have already been played by ad hoc high-level consultations like the Hague Conference in 1989, the Bergen Conference in 1990, and the Beijing Conference in 1991, all of which advanced creative proposals. The conference at the Hague was attended by heads of government from a significant sample of developed and developing countries. Their "Declaration of the Hague" described environmental problems as "vital, urgent and global," and as requiring not only the implementation of existing principles but also a new approach involving the development of principles of international law and more effective decision-making and enforcement mechanisms. The leaders agreed that most of the emissions that affect the atmosphere at present originate in the industrialized countries, and that it is in these countries that there is the greatest room for change and the most resources to deal with problems effectively.

The declaration expressed unanimous support for developing institutional authority within the UN, by either strengthening existing institutions or creating a new one, for combating global warming. This institution should have the authority to make decisions even if, on occasion, there was not unanimity. Countries that found the protection of the atmosphere to be an abnormal or excessive burden, in view, inter alia, of their level of development and actual responsibility for the deterioration of the atmosphere, should receive fair and equitable compensation. The Hague Conference was breaking new ground and doing so on the basis of North-South consensus at the highest political level.

Ministers from thirty-four countries took part in the Bergen Conference, convened by the government of Norway and the UN Economic Commission for Europe as part of an international follow-up to the report of the Brundtland Commission and preparations for the Earth Summit. In the Bergen Ministerial Declaration, they acknowledged that unsustainable patterns of production and consumption, particularly in industrialized countries, were the root of numerous environmental problems that were foreclosing options for future generations. Environmental measures must "anticipate, prevent and attack" the causes of environmental degradation, they declared. Where there were threats of serious or irreversible damage, lack of full scientific certainty should not be used as a reason for postponing preventive measures.

The conference expressed support for policies to make prices, particularly of energy, reflect environmental costs and benefits more fully. It also encouraged policies that would increase the flow of capital and environmentally sound technology to developing and

Eastern European countries, assisting them on resource and environmental management projects and helping them to meet their international obligations to protect the environment. Delegates agreed to accelerate international dialogue on the links between trade and environmental policies so as to ensure that trade does not ultimately harm the environment. Detailed recommendations were made in respect of energy, industrial activities, and raising public awareness of environmental matters. All ECE countries were urged to take action to reduce the emission of carbon dioxide and other greenhouse gases, with the declaration noting that in the view of most ECE countries the stabilization of emissions at present levels, at the latest by 2000, must be the first step.

The Conference on Environment and Development held in Beijing in June 1991 was attended by ministers from forty-one developing countries. In their Beijing Declaration, they affirmed the developing nations' intent to participate to the best of their ability in global efforts to protect the environment, while pointing out that steady economic growth was needed to break the cycle of poverty and environmental degradation in poor countries. Since poverty is at the root of the developing world's environmental problems, they saw the Earth Summit as an opportunity to launch a global program against poverty and its effects on the environment. They declared that the success of efforts to protect the environment requires the broadest possible international participation and therefore depends on the availability of adequate additional resources and the transfer of technology on preferential terms to developing countries.

In stressing the importance of action on long-standing problems of immediate concern to developing countries—including desertification, land degradation and soil loss, deterioration in freshwater resources, deforestation, and coastal pollution—the conference proposed a "Green Fund" to assist developing countries in tackling these problems, which are still not covered by existing international arrangements. On climate change, the declaration maintained that developed countries should take immediate action to stabilize and reduce emissions given their historic and present role in producing greenhouse gases. Developing countries, which have growing energy needs, cannot be expected to accept such obligations in the near future; they should be helped to undertake measures that contribute both to their development and to their efforts to tackle global warming.

Third World commitment to the protection of the environment was also voiced by the leaders of major developing countries at the second summit of the Group of 15 in Caracas in November 1991. They said that the prime need of developing countries was to revitalize their economies, end poverty, and achieve growth that was sustainable both in economic and environmental terms. International cooperation should enable them to realize their objectives. The developed countries, they stressed, had the greatest responsibility for establishing environmentally sustainable development in the world. The Group of 15 saw the Earth Summit as an occasion to address environmental and development issues in an "integrated, comprehensive, and balanced manner" and said that "a concrete program for the greening of the world would meet the needs of all countries, safeguard the global environment, and ensure the full participation of the international community."

A short time before that Caracas Summit in September 1991, a working group convened by the South Center—set up to promote action on the recommendations of the South Commission—and chaired by a former secretary-general of UNCTAD, Gamani Corea, urged developing countries to pool their efforts to achieve two primary objectives. First, to provide adequate environmental space for their development and, second, to support changes in global economic relations that would assist them in achieving growth that is sound environmentally and robust enough to provide for essential needs. The group declared that developed countries must improve commodity prices, access to markets, debt relief, and resource flows if the Third World was to follow a path of sustainable development. It called for a global program to alleviate poverty and to protect or rehabilitate the environment. On climate change, the group supported the principle that a "country['s] emission entitlements [should be] based on an equal distribution of emission rights among the world's inhabitants." On biodiversity, the group called for a mechanism to compensate developing nations for the biological resources they provide and to give them access to biotechnologies developed by using their genetic material.

OTHER proposals have begun to come from many quarters in the international community. In October 1991 the World Conservation Union (IUCN), UNEP, and the World Wide Fund for Nature

(WWF)—the major world environmental agencies—launched their joint report "Caring for the Earth" referred to earlier. Both an analysis and a plan of action, a broadly oriented but practical guide to policies and programs, it is designed to meet two fundamental needs:

> One is to secure a widespread and deeply-held commitment to a new ethic, the ethic of sustainable living, and to translate its principles into practice. The other is to integrate conservation and development: conservation to keep our actions within the Earth's capacity, and development to enable people everywhere to enjoy long, healthy and fulfilling lives. (p. 3)

It defines, for example, the principles for a sustainable society and recommends 132 specific actions to be taken by governments and people. The principles are clear enough, and in a world committed to enlightened change should find broad acceptance. They enjoin us to do the following:

- Respect and care for the community of life
- Improve the quality of human life
- Conserve the Earth's vitality and diversity
- Keep within Earth's carrying capacity
- Change personal attitudes and practices
- Enable communities to care for their own environments
- Provide a national framework for integrating development and conservation
- Create a global alliance for sustainability

Among specific measures recommended are the following:

- Energy consumption: Countries with per capita energy consumption above 80 gigajoules should reduce their consumption by 1 percent a year until 2000, and 2 percent a year after that. (Canada is now at 291, the United States at 280, and the Netherlands at 213; Japan, by contrast, is at 110 and France 109.) Those with consumption around or below 80 gigajoules should not exceed it. (Greece is at 72 and Spain at 62; China, by contrast, is at 22 and India at 8.)
- Pollution: By the year 2000, high-income countries should reduce sulphur-dioxide emissions by 90 percent from 1980 levels, cut

nitrogen-oxide emissions by 75 percent from 1985 levels, and cease the manufacture and use of CFCs. By 2005, carbon-dioxide emissions from high-income countries should have been cut by 20 percent from 1990 levels. CFC use should stop everywhere by 2010.

• Forests: By the year 2010, net global forest depletion should have ceased, and a comprehensive genetic conservation system should be in place.

• Poverty: By the year 2000, per capita income should be increasing by 2 to 3 percent annually in low-income developing countries. All children should have been immunized against the main childhood diseases, and basic malnutrition and child mortality should be reduced by half. Everyone should have access to safe water; at least four in five people should have sanitation. All children of primary school age should be enrolled in school, and dropout rates should have fallen by half. Adult illiteracy should also be halved by 2000.

• Population: Countries should bring their fertility rates down to 2.1 births per woman (stable replacement level) as rapidly as practicable, most by 2010 at the latest.

• Legal regimes: By 1995, a comprehensive conservation regime for Antarctica should be in force. By the year 2000, adherence to conventions on natural resources such as endangered species, wetlands, and migratory animals, should rise to 75 percent of the world's nations. New conventions on climate change and the conservation of biological diversity should have been adopted and implemented by 50 percent of nations, and the UN Convention of the Law of the Sea (UNCLOS) should be in force.

"Caring for the Earth" makes a series of additional recommendations for action to implement the principles of a sustainable society in specific sectors like energy, business, industry and commerce, human settlement, and farming.

A s w e have seen, earlier, in August 1990, the Latin American and Caribbean Commission on Development and Environment produced the report "Our Own Agenda." It pointed out the impossibility of conceiving a strategy for sustainable development in the region separated from events in the industrialized world. Such a strategy would be viable only if there were important changes in developed countries themselves and in the "factors underlying their international relations with us." The report called for dialogue to achieve a new pact of solidarity between North and South:

> It will be necessary to inspire an ethic that allows the common interests of nations to prevail over those of individuals; that affords a more objective appreciation of the great risks faced by humankind unless we resolve situations which, like the rampant poverty or changes in climate, compromise global stability; that starts with the premise that progress is not viable in the long term if it is not conceived as a process enabling all countries—not just a group of countries—to realize their development aspirations in an equitable and egalitarian manner, and lets us address the problems that affect us from the vantage point of the longer term. (p. 83)

"Our Own Agenda" emphasized the link between underdevelopment and environmental degradation: Without economic growth, there would be no development and hence no transition to sustainable development. The debt problem, which had ground economic growth to a halt, would have to be resolved for the region's countries to come to grips with impoverishment. There were other global mechanisms that were generating poverty and therefore needed correction; these included the reduction in the prices of raw materials produced in developing countries and the export to these countries of capital-intensive, labor-saving technologies, as well as the structural adjustment measures that had deepened the social crisis in debt-ridden countries.

Western economic policies that constrained sustainable development in Third World countries were pinpointed in the report. These included discriminatory trade policies that interfered with access to markets, farm subsidies that similarly harmed the interests of producers in developing countries, the export of toxic wastes, and the export of products whose sale was banned within developed countries themselves. The commission outlined a number of other issues along with these as ripe for negotiation: conditions for the control of deforestation, the cost to developing countries of complying with such environmental measures as the Montreal Protocol on phasing out CFCs, and conditions for the use of Third World genetic material in biotechnologies developed in industrial countries.

The report underlined the importance of peace for sustained development. While observing that the main threat to peace lay in the nuclear arsenals of the great powers, the commission said developing countries should eliminate regional tensions and lower their own military expenditure to what was needed for internal security. In other recommendations addressed to developing countries, the report called for a more equitable distribution of income so that poverty could be rooted out. The commission recognized that excessive population growth is an obstacle to the region's development and said that a cutback in population growth could be achieved only "by dint of the minimum economic growth indispensable for improving education and the quality of life to levels compatible with human dignity." (p. 85)

Carrying out sustainable development strategies in Latin America and the Caribbean would require financing that was beyond the savings capacity of the region, which was estimated to have an annual investment deficit of some $80 billion, partly because of the debt crisis and low terms of trade. The commission called for an international environmental fund to assist a variety of investment projects. It pointed out that the World Bank's GEF could not address such problems as those related to the urban environment and water and soil problems, which required urgent attention in the region. The report noted that various mechanisms such as a tax on carbon-dioxide emissions or on the use of fossil fuels had been identified for mobilizing resources for such an international fund.

In August 1991, another set of proposals emerged from the New World Dialogue, which was sponsored by the World Resources Institute in Washington and brought together eminent public figures from the United States, Canada, Latin America, and the Caribbean. Their proposals, from "Compact for a New World," called for a number of initiatives to promote sustainable development. The following paragraph indicates its essential approach:

> The initiatives are closely linked, and must be negotiated as a package. Enduring progress cannot be made on some fronts unless it is also made on the others. Without alleviating poverty, for example, it will not be possible to reduce pressures that degrade natural resources. Without gains in energy efficiency, long-term economic development will be threatened. Without more resources from the hemisphere's richer countries, governments of the poorer ones will be hard-pressed to keep their environmental commitments and to maintain their progress toward more responsive democratic rule. Without environmental commitments, the global environment and the

natural resources needed for economic development will continue to deteriorate, further impoverishing generations to come. (p. 8)

Specific elements of the compact follow:

- A forestry initiative aimed at reversing deforestation and protecting biological resources, and applying to both temperate zone and tropical forests.

- An energy initiative directed at providing energy for development and reducing greenhouse gas emissions. It calls on Canada and the United States to reduce their per capita emissions of carbon dioxide by 30 percent by the year 2005.

- A pollution prevention initiative seeking changes in tariffs that protect polluting industries, in subsidies for commercial fertilizer and pesticide, and in policies that keep gasoline prices low and otherwise encourage profligate use of automobiles.

- An antipoverty initiative calling for action by all governments to achieve the minimum target of eliminating hunger by the year 2000 and eradicating poverty by the year 2020 throughout the western hemisphere.

- A population initiative to stabilize population within the region by 2050, with the United States restoring and increasing its annual contribution to the UNFPA.

- A science and technology initiative to develop and diffuse technologies for sustainable development, including a new discipline of "ecological economics" enabling public policy-making to take account of both the positive and negative consequences of development.

- A trade and investment initiative designed to promote sustainable development through enlarging free trade areas and encouraging international investment in the hemisphere while protecting the environment. Control over the traffic in hazardous substances, the migration of polluting industries, and the sale of such products as DDT whose use has been prohibited in exporting countries is also envisaged.

- Financial initiatives to secure additional funds for sustainable development from new and existing sources, including funds raised from domestic resources, reduced military expenditures, a solution to the debt problem, and international assistance. Significant funding should come from a new "ecofund," with resources raised on the polluter-pays principle through a tax on fossil fuels. A tax of one dollar per barrel of oil would produce $1 billion annually (calculated on the basis of consumption in the western hemisphere in 1989).

In the context of the 500th anniversary of Columbus's arrival in the region, the New World Dialogue calls on the western hemisphere to set an example by producing this compact for a new world at the Earth Summit in Rio. The proposal clearly has significance beyond the western hemisphere. It could help us to forge a global partnership for survival.

B E S I D E S such wide-ranging proposals from international and regional sources, there have been significant institutional proposals focused on greenhouse gases. Global warming is a key issue, and it arouses strong feelings about responsibility and response. A study by Anil Agarwal and Sunita Narain of New Delhi's Center for Science and Environment (CSE), a leading Third World research institution, has attracted wide attention. Entitled "Global Warming in an Unequal World: A Case of Environmental Colonialism," it addresses not only the question of what we must do collectively but the prior issue of how to assess responsibility on a basis of equity.

Not all the carbon dioxide and other warming gases we produce accumulate in the atmosphere to add to the greenhouse effect. Some of our output of these gases—apart from CFCs—is absorbed by nature's own cleaning process, with land, sea, and vegetation acting as sinks. It is what we produce in excess of what these natural sinks take in that contributes to global warming. How should Earth's sink capacity be allocated among countries? This is clearly more than a technical question. As we consider human responses to the threat of global warming, the issue of responsibility becomes unavoidable, and how we measure its extent becomes a crucial factor. To that is closely allied the question of entitlement. How much, for example, is each one of us as an Earth-dweller entitled to release by way of greenhouse gases into the atmosphere? The answer must surely derive from the premise that every human being, in whatever part of the world, is as entitled as any other to a share of Earth's sink, which is part of the global commons. Given that the planet's absorptive capacity for greenhouse gases is limited, must not human beings everywhere have an equal claim on that capacity and be equally responsible for not exceeding their share of it?

The view strongly pressed by Agarwal and Narain in the CSE study is that Earth's sink capacity should be divided in equal shares among the world's people and therefore allotted to countries according to population. Each country's allocation is its permissible level of emissions, or quota, and each country is responsible if it surpasses that level. The CSE study thus questions the basis for allocation used by established sources of environmental data like the World Resources Institute of Washington (WRI). WRI's approach is to apportion global sink capacity to countries according to their share of total emissions. Agarwal and Narain argue that this method benefits high-emission countries at the expense of the Third World. China and India together account for less than 0.5 percent of global net emissions of greenhouse gases, according to CSE calculations, against 10 percent according to WRI calculations. The U.S. contribution goes up from 17.4 percent to 27.4 percent. The CSE method does not show every industrial country as being responsible for a share of net emissions larger than that suggested by WRI. Nor do all developing countries fare better under the CSE method. But the share of industrial countries as a group does go up from 53 percent to 67 percent.

The principle of the entitlement of individuals as opposed to countries receives support from another study, "Allocating Responsibility for Global Warming: The Natural Debt Index," by Kirk Smith of the Environment and Policy Institute of the East-West Center in Honolulu. Smith points out that "to allocate by country is, at the absurd extreme, to imply that Singapore's 3 million people should be able to emit as much [in the way of greenhouse gases] as all of China's 1100 million." (pp. 95–96)

The CSE study has raised two further points that are pertinent in determining responsibility for contributions to greenhouse warming. One relates to the rates at which forests are being destroyed. This information is critical in calculating the total output of carbon dioxide for many countries. Data on forest loss remains poor, and the study questions the accuracy of statistics used by WRI and others. There is clearly a need both for better information and for caution in relying on the available data. The other point concerns the role of Third World rice fields and cattle in producing methane, one of the greenhouse gases. Here again the information is far from reliable. An equally important matter, one of principle, is whether the "survival emissions" from subsistence farming in poor countries should be judged on the same basis as the luxury emissions of automobiles used by the rich.

The Indian study and others have also proposed a system of tradeable permits under which a country emitting less than its quota of greenhouse gases could sell the unused share, at a fixed rate, to a country with excess emissions. It also suggests that countries emitting gases in excess of their own quota (plus any purchases) be fined at a higher rate. The fines would go to a global fund to help countries harmed by climate destabilization and to develop technologies to reduce greenhouse emissions. Such a system would have important benefits. Income from traded quotas would be a strong incentive to developing countries to keep their greenhouse emissions down. The liability for fines would encourage developed countries also to hold down their emissions. To the extent that countries are excessive in their output of greenhouse gases, their obligatory contributions to a global climate fund would serve a worthy purpose. The system would therefore promote environmentally sound behavior worldwide. Clearly, innovative approaches of this kind need to be explored if we are to pursue a path to sustainable development that takes account of fairness and equity and provides incentives to mend environmentally unsustainable ways. The important point is that these issues are now on the table.

T H E S E are by no means the only ideas to have been advanced, but they are sufficient to indicate that there is no shortage of proposals, many of them dispassionately developed, authoritatively analyzed, and sensitively assembled. That does not mean that there is nothing to negotiate, nor that these ideas and proposals are comprehensive. Others will emerge in preparation for the Earth Summit, from the summit itself and in the negotiations that follow it. We are now approaching a stage, however, where decisions can be made and where their postponement cannot be defended on the ground of inadequate analysis, or a lack of imaginative or even realistic ideas, the old alibis for inaction. In the whole of human history, no process leading to global decision-making has been as comprehensive in its reach and as supported by a universal acknowledgment of the need for urgent, practical action in the interest of human survival. Not even the founding of the United Nations in 1945 matches this effort. Enlightened change is within our grasp.

By the end of the twentieth century newly discovered horrors may jolt us into collective action to save ourselves. Already, however, there are enough threats to compel us in the direction of enlightened change. How we respond to these threats depends in large measure on how we allot responsibility for them; but how we are disposed to respond will influence the manner in which we define responsibility. Inevitably, self-interest will lead different groups to strike different postures. This has already begun. The great contribution that professionals can make, particularly from the nongovernmental positions many of them occupy, is not to be blinded by national self-interest.

In this context, it is a great pity that so little of the early intellectual work on environmental issues has been done in the developing world, Brazil and India being notable exceptions. In one respect this is understandable: Development, not environment, was the preoccupation in developing countries. On the other hand environment, not development, was of great concern to thoughtful people in the industrial world: The quality of life, rather than life itself, was what mattered at their level of economic security. Both groups were to find that the two issues were merely aspects of a single issue, the pathway to sustainable living on Earth. Much will now depend on the degree to which the developing countries occupy their intellectual space and lay the professional foundations for negotiating our common future. And much will depend, as well, on whether the professionals of the world—scientists, economists, ecologists, and the many others involved with these inseparable issues in developed and developing countries—establish broad consensus among themselves on environmental threats, on responsibility for them, and on what the response should be.

If humanity is to take the path of enlightened change it has to do so on the basis of partnership and compact. That means negotiation, and the best negotiations are intellectually rigorous. Only through rigorous encounter can we achieve enduring accord. Nothing will contribute more to that outcome than professional consensus building. The process has started, the IPCC having given it an auspicious launch, but there is a long way to go. The reality of environmental stress will exert its own compulsions. But what we do, how we respond, will depend on many impulses, not all of them rational. It is therefore important that responses not be allowed to run down the blind alley of irrationality for want of a clear lead from international professional opinion.

The goal is to preserve and sustain life on Earth for ourselves, all of us, and for the generations to come. At the very least we must leave opportunities for those who follow us to sustain life for themselves and the generations that succeed them. Others besides professionals will be involved in elaborating the elements of enlightened change. As with development, so with environment: Concerned people will flock together in global constituencies. They are already doing so in, for example, the substantial nongovernmental networks that are now so active on environmental issues. And it is fitting that these networks reach out to the world's indigenous people, not only as victims whose interests must be protected but also as the preservers of bodies of traditional knowledge vital to protection of the environment. But these movements still embrace a minute percentage of the world's people, the mass of whom tend to follow the lead of governments that in turn do as little or as much as is demanded of them by public opinion. There is a role therefore for everyone, in every country. All are affected; all must be involved.

F o R all the reasons already elaborated, the UN Conference on Environment and Development in Rio de Janeiro in June 1992—the Earth Summit—comes not a moment too soon; our concern should be whether in at least some areas of environmental stress it comes too late. But, just as it is senseless to postpone remedial action on a hope-for-the-best basis, so it is unworthy of us to abstain from effort by succumbing to a sense of hopelessness. The Earth Summit is a call to reject despondency and to affirm our resolve to stave off disaster. It is a global lifesaving effort to which we must commit our capacity for both caring and courage.

We now have to ensure that that congregation of Earth's political leadership, supported by an enlightened global community of people, seizes the opportunity to move action for survival up to a higher plane of performance. The community of people is, on the whole, better informed than governments; it is global in its reach and its links are interdisciplinary. It understands intuitively that human fate is collective, that belonging to the planet makes us all kin. Equally important is the passion for protecting life that stirs nonformal representatives of the world's people. Too easily disparaged as frenetic, the passion for life—for raging "against the dying of the light," as Dylan Thomas once put it—is a necessary antidote to the inertia not only of bureaucracies but also of formal politics, which eschews populism but lives by its instincts. At and beyond Rio, the world will need to heed these insistent voices.

From the high-profile occasion in Rio will not come all the decisions that will guide us to a safer and better future. But Rio must represent a point of departure in the direction of sustainable living. It must signal the sort of commitment to enlightened change that is being sought through the proposed Earth Charter and Agenda 21, an agenda for the twenty-first century. The Preparatory Committee for the Earth Summit has invested much effort in drawing up the charter and the agenda. Their endorsement by the summit can make them powerful instruments in humanity's quest for a secure future.

Agenda 21 is a comprehensive plan of action by governments, intergovernmental, and nongovernmental organizations designed to bring about the transition to sustainable development. Agenda 21 draws upon the experience, insights, and capacities of all these actors, including the other reports and initiatives referred to in this chapter, and it provides the global framework in which these actions must be pursued to secure our common future. It is a program of action premised on all nations sharing responsibility, but which recognizes that responsibilities and priorities differ, particularly between developed and developing countries. It accepts that habitat cannot be protected in the absence of development and therefore envisages that development and environment issues be addressed simultaneously in a new climate of international cooperation.

The progressive reduction and ultimate eradication of poverty is a crucial aim of Agenda 21, as is the removal of international obstacles to the progress of Third World countries through action on such issues as protectionism and market access, commodity prices, debt, and resource flows. It accepts that consumption patterns, particularly in industrial countries, must be changed and that high rates of population growth, particularly in developing countries, must be moderated in order to bring both into balance with the Earth's capacity. It recognizes that a transition to sustainable consumption requires countries to avoid unsustainable levels of resource exploitation at home or abroad. Similarly, it envisages responsible and fair use of shared resources, like the atmosphere and the high seas, that are part of the global commons. As we have seen, detailed proposals for achieving these and related objectives have been developed in the preparatory process leading up to the conference in Rio. They add up to an ambitious, wide-ranging program of national action and international cooperation to transform global prospects.

Rio must be a turning point for human society, the beginning of a more resolute stage in the process of retrieving our heritage of life on Earth. Because that effort has been delayed so long, we may not be able to succeed if we let the present opportunity slip. Even if we could renew the effort later in a last desperate lunge for life, we might find the chances of securing a global compact for survival no longer there, the climate for partnership itself having been fouled beyond repair in the scramble for survival.

Governments must therefore approach the Earth Summit with the kind of determination to save human civilization that characterized the meetings in San Francisco in 1945. There the world was responding to a disaster already encountered; the evidence was palpable that another such large-scale conflict would put human existence itself at risk. Now we foresee the disaster—we know that human existence will be at risk unless we act in time to prevent it. We forfeit our species' claim to higher intelligence if, made aware of that risk, we fail to summon up the will to save ourselves and other species in the process.

It is in such a light that we must view ideas and initiatives of the kind mentioned in this chapter. They are all on offer to the UNCED process. They are part of the the journey to Rio, the summit at Rio, and the continuing search beyond Rio. We know what can be done. We have the means to do it. Can we muster the will, all governments, all societies, all people, to take the path of enlightened change?

T H E war for human survival is unlike other wars. It is not a matter of winners and losers. Each must lose so all may win. Only to the extent that individual nations accept limits and thresholds can there be collective victory. It is not a war of man against man, nation against nation, but rather a war of humanity against unsustainable living. It is the only war we can afford. Only through enlightened change can humanity hope to triumph.

Bibliography

Adamson, David. *Defending the World.* London: I. B. Tauris, 1990.

Agarwal, Anil, and Sunita Narain. "Global Warming in an Unequal World: A Case of Environmental Colonialism." New Delhi: Center for Science and Environment, 1991.

Angell, David J. R., et al., ed. *Sustaining Earth: Response to the Environmental Threats.* London: Macmillan, 1990.

Aristotle. *Politics.* Book I. Translated by H. Rackham. London: Heinemann, 1932.

Bates, Marston. *The Forest and the Sea.* New York: Vintage Books, 1960.

Böll, Heinrich. *The Thrower-Away.* In *Absent Without Leave and Other Stories.* London: Weidenfeld and Nicholson, 1966.

Borges, Jorge Luis. *Historia de la Eternidad.* Buenos Aires: Emece Editories, 1953.

Brown, Arthur, et al. "Change for the Better: Global Change and Economic Development." A report by a Commonwealth Group of Experts. London: Commonwealth Secretariat, 1991.

Brown, Lester R., et al. *State of the World, 1990.* Worldwatch Institute publication. New York: Norton, 1990.

Brown, Lester R., Christopher Flavin, and Sandra Postel. *Saving the Planet: How to Shape an Environmentally Sustainable Global Economy.* New York: Norton, 1991.

Chateaubriand, Francois-Renë. Mémoires d'oute-tombe. Book 6. Paris: Garner, 1924.

Chinery-Hesse, Mary, et al. "Engendering Adjustment for the 1990s." A report by a Commonwealth Group of Experts. London: Commonwealth Secretariat, 1989.

Commission on International Development. "Partners in Development." New York: Praeger, 1969.

Deger, Saadat, and Somnath Sen. *Military Expenditure: The Political Economy of International Security.* Oxford: Oxford University Press, 1990.

Eckholm, Erik. *Down to Earth: Environment and Human Need.* London: Pluto Press, 1982.

Ehrlich, Paul, and Anne Ehrlich. *The Population Explosion.* New York: Simon and Schuster, 1991.

Fukuyama, Francis. "Are We at the End of History?" *Fortune* 121, no. 2 (1990): pp. 33–36.

Goldsmith, Oliver. *The Vicar of Wakefield*. Oxford English Novel Series. Oxford: Oxford University Press, 1974.

Goliber, Thomas J. "Africa's Expanding Population: Old Problems, New Policies." *Population Bulletin* 44, no. 3 (November 1989): 39.

Goodland, Robert, et al. "Environmentally Sustainable Economic Development: Building on Brundtland." Paris: UNESCO, 1991.

Goodland, Robert, and Howard Irwin. *Amazon Jungle: Green Hell to Red Desert*. New York: Elsevier, 1975.

Gordon, Anita, and David Suzuki. *It's a Matter of Survival*. Toronto: Stoddart, 1990.

Grainger, Alan. *The Threatening Desert*. London: Earthscan, 1990.

Grigg, David. *Population Growth and Agrarian Change*. Cambridge: Cambridge University Press, 1980.

Harris, Wilson. *The Four Banks of the River of Space*. London: Faber and Faber, 1990.

Harrison, Paul. *The Greening of Africa*. Windsor: Palladian Publications, 1987.

Harth, Erich. *Dawn of a Millennium*. Harmondsworth: Penguin, 1991.

Head, Ivan. *On a Hinge of History: The Mutual Vulnerability of South and North*. Toronto: Toronto University Press, 1991.

Hobhouse, Henry. *Seeds of Change*. London: Sidgwick and Jackson, 1985.

Hobsbawm, Eric. *Nations and Nationalism since 1780*. Cambridge: Cambridge University Press, 1990.

Holdgate, Martin, et al. "Climate Change: Meeting the Challenge." A report by a Commonwealth Group of Experts. London: Commonwealth Secretariat, 1989.

Ince, Martin. *The Rising Seas*. London: Earthscan, 1990.

Independent Commission on Disarmament and Security Issues. "Common Security: A Program for Disarmament." London: Pan, 1982.

Independent Commission on International Development Issues. "North-South: A Program for Survival." London: Pan, 1980.

_____. "Common Crisis North-South: Co-operation for World Recovery." London: Pan, 1983.

Independent Commission on International Humanitarian Issues. *Famine: A Manmade Disaster?* London: Pan, 1985.

_____. "The Encroaching Desert." A report for the Commission. London: Zed Books, 1986.

_____. "The Vanishing Forest: The Human Consequences of Deforestation." A report for the Commission. London: Zed Books, 1986.

_____. "Winning the Human Race." London: Zed Books, 1988.

Indira Gandhi Institute of Development Research. "Consumption Patterns: The Driving Force of Environmental Stress." A report prepared for United Nations Commission on Environment and Development. Bombay: IGIDR.

Intergovernmental Panel on Climate Change. "Climate Change: The IPCC Scientific Assessment." Report of Working Group 1. Cambridge: Cambridge University Press, 1990.

_____. "Potential Impacts of Climate Change." Report of Working Group 2.

Geneva: World Meteorological Organization and United Nations Environment Program, 1990.

————. "Formulation of Response Strategies." Report of Working Group 3. Washington, D.C.: Island Press, 1990.

King, Alexander, and Bertrand Schneider. "The First Global Revolution." A report by the Council of the Club of Rome. New York: Pantheon Books, 1991.

Latin American and Caribbean Commission on Development and Environment. "Our Own Agenda." Washington, D.C.: Inter-American Development Bank, 1991.

Lean, Geoffrey, Don Hinrichsen, and Adam Markham, eds. *The World Wide Fund for Nature Atlas of the Environment*. London: Arrow Books, 1990.

MacKenzie, James J., and Michael P. Walsh. *Driving Forces*. New York: World Resources Institute, 1990.

MacNeill, Jim, Pieter Winsemius, and Taizo Yakushiji. *Beyond Interdependence: The Meshing of the World's Economy and the Earth's Ecology*. A Trilateral Commission Book. Oxford: Oxford University Press, 1991.

Malthus, Thomas Robert. *Essay on the Principle of Population*. London: J M Dent & Sons, 1914.

Marstrand, Pauline K, et al. "Sustainable Development: An Imperative for Environmental Protection." A report by a Commonwealth Group of Experts. London: Commonwealth Secretariat, 1991.

McKibben, Bill. *The End of Nature*. London: Viking, 1990.

Miller, Kenton, and Laura Tangley. *Trees of Life: Saving Tropical Forests and Their Biological Wealth*. Boston: Beacon Press, 1991.

Mungall, Constance, and Digby J. McLaren, eds. *Planet Under Stress*. Toronto: Oxford University Press, 1990.

Myers, Norman, et al. *The Gaia Atlas of Planet Management*. London: Pan Books, 1985.

Naipaul, Vidia S. *India: A Wounded Civilization*. London: André Deutsch, 1977.

New World Dialogue. *Compact for a New World*. Washington, D.C.: World Resources Institute, 1991.

Non-Partisan Fund for World Disarmament and Development. *Disarm or Die*. London: Taylor and Francis, 1978.

Organization for Economic Cooperation and Development. *The State of the Environment*. Paris: OECD, 1991.

Parry, Martin. *Climate Change and World Agriculture*. London: Earthscan, 1990.

Pearce, David, ed. *Blueprint 2: Greening the World Economy*. London: Earthscan, 1991.

Petrella, Riccardo. "World City-States of the Future." *New Perspectives Quarterly* 8 no. 4 (1991): 61.

Plutarch. *Parallel Lives*. Translated by B. Perrin. London: Heinemann, 1914.

Prescott-Allen, Robert, and Christine Prescott-Allen. *Genes from the Wild: Using Wild Genetic Resources for Food and Raw Materials*. London: Earthscan, 1988.

Reijnen, G. C. M. and W. de Graff. *The Pollution of Outer Space, in Particular of the Geostationary Orbit*. Dordrecht: Martinus Nijhoff, 1989.

Repetto, Robert. "Population, Resources, Environment: An Uncertain Future."
    Population Bulletin 42 no. 2 (1987): p. 3.
Rodgers, Gerry. *Poverty and Population.* Geneva: ILO, 1984.
Rodway, James. *In the Guiana Forest: Studies of Nature in Relation to the
    Struggle for Life.* London: Fisher Unwin, 1985.
Royston, Michael. *Pollution Prevention Pays.* London: Pergamon, 1987.
Sadiq, Nafis, ed. *Population Policies and Programs: Lessons from Two Decades
    of Experience.* New York: New York University Press for the United Nations
    Population Fund, 1991.
Seth, Vikram. *The Golden Gate.* London: Faber and Faber, 1986.
Seymour, John, and Herbert Girardet. *Far From Paradise: The Story of Human
    Impact on the Environment.* London: Green Print, 1990.
Sivard, Ruth. *World Military and Social Expenditures, 1991.* Washington D.C.:
    World Priorities Inc., 1991.
Smith, Kirk. "Allocating Responsibility for Global Warming: The National Debt
    Index." *Ambio* 20 no. 2 (April 1991): 95–96.
South Commission. "The Challenge to the South." Oxford: Oxford University
    Press, 1990.
Starr, Joyce. "Water Wars." *Foreign Policy* 820 (1991): pp. 17–36.
Stockholm Initiative on Global Security and Governance. "Common Respon-
    sibility in the 1990s." Stockholm: Prime Minister's Office, 1991.
Stockholm International Peace Research Institute. *SIPRI Yearbook 1990: World
    Armaments and Disarmament.* Oxford: Oxford University Press, 1990.
Tinbergen, Jan, co-ordinator. "RIO: Reshaping the International Order." A re-
    port to the Club of Rome. New York: Dutton, 1976.
Tobin, Richard. *The Expendable Future.* Durham: Duke University Press,
    1990.
United Nations Development Program. "Human Development Report, 1991."
    Oxford: Oxford University Press, 1991.
United Nations Population Fund. "State of the World Population, 1991." New
    York: UNFPA, 1991.
Urdang, Stephanie. *And Still They Danced.* London: Earthscan, 1989.
Vitousek, P. M., et al. "Human Appropriation of the Products of Photosynthesis."
    BioScience 36 no. 6 (1986): pp. 368–373.
Voltaire. *Candide.* Translated by John Butt. Penguin Classics series. London:
    Penguin, 1987.
von Weizsacker, C. F. *Strategies for Peace: The Seventh Corbishley Lecture.*
    London: Wyndham Place Trust, 1983.
Walgate, Robert. *Miracle or Menace? Biotechnology and the Third World.* Lon-
    don: Panos Institute, 1990.
Ward, Barbara, and René Dubos. *Only One Earth: The Care and Maintenance of
    a Small Planet.* Harmondsworth: Penguin, 1972.
World Bank. *World Development Report, 1990.* Oxford: Oxford University
    Press, 1990.
———. *World Development Report, 1991.* Oxford: Oxford University Press,
    1991.

World Commission on Environment and Development. "Energy 2000: A Global Strategy for Sustainable Development." London: Zed Books, 1987.

――――――. "Food 2000: Global Policies for Sustainable Agriculture." A report to the Commission. London: Zed Books, 1987.

――――――. *Our Common Future*. Oxford: Oxford University Press, 1987.

World Conservation Union, United Nations Environment Program, and Worldwide Fund. "Caring for the Earth: A Strategy for Sustainable Living." Gland, Switzerland: IUCN, UNEP, WWF, 1991.

World Resources Institute. "World Resources: A Guide to the Global Environment, 1990–91." A report by WRI in collaboration with the UN Environment Program and the UN Development Program. Oxford: Oxford University Press, 1990.

Further Reading

Abrahamson, D. E. *The Challenge of Global Warming*. Washington D.C.: Island Press, 1989.

Alexandratos, N., ed. "World Agriculture Towards 2000." A report by UN Food and Agriculture Organization. London: Pinter, 1988.

Allaby, Michael. *Into Harmony with the Planet: The Delicate Balance between Industry and the Environment*. London: Bloomsbury, 1990.

Allen, Robert. *Waste Not, Want Not: The Production and Dumping of Toxic Waste*. London: Earthscan, 1991.

Anderson, D. *International Aid and the Environment*. London: Overseas Development Institute, 1991.

Anderson, D, and R. Fishwick. *Fuelwood Consumption and Deforestation in African Countries: A Review*. Washington D.C.: World Bank, 1991.

"Antarctica: The Next Decade." A report of a study group chaired by Sir Anthony Parsons. Cambridge: Cambridge University Press, 1987.

Asian Development Bank. *Economic Policies for Sustainable Development*. Manila: ADB, 1990.

Barrow, C. J. *Land Degradation: Development and Breakdown of Terrestrial Environments*. Cambridge: Cambridge University Press, 1991.

Batstone, R., J. E. Smith, and D. Wilson, eds. *Safe Disposal of Hazardous Wastes: The Special Needs and Problems of Developing Countries*. 3 Vol. Washington D.C.: World Bank, 1989.

Benedick, Richard E. *Ozone Diplomacy: New Directions in Safeguarding the Planet*. Cambridge: Harvard University Press, 1991.

Bridgman, Howard. *Global Air Pollution: Problems for the 1990s*. London: Pinter, 1990.

Bruce, J. P. *The Atmosphere of the Living Planet Earth*. World Meteorological Organization no. 735. Geneva: WMO, 1990.

Cairncross, Alec, et al. *Protectionism: Threat to International Order*. A report by a Commonwealth Experts Group. London: Commonwealth Secretariat, 1982.

Cairncross, Frances. *Costing the Earth*. London: Economist Books, 1991.

Carroll, John E., ed. *International Environmental Diplomacy: The Management and Resolution of Transfrontier Environmental Problems*. Cambridge: Cambridge University Press, 1990.

Cassen, Robert, et al. *Does Aid Work?* Oxford: Oxford University Press, 1987.

Clark, R. B. *Marine Pollution.* second edition. Oxford: Oxford University Press, 1989.

Clarke, Robin. *Water: The International Crisis.* London: Earthscan, 1991.

Cleveland, Harland. *The Third Try at World Order: U.S. Policy for an Interdependent World.* New York: Aspen Institute, 1976.

Clive, William R., ed. *Policy Alternatives for a New International Order.* New York: Praeger, 1979.

Collins, Mark, ed. *The Last Rainforests.* London: Mitchell Beazley, 1990.

Conway, Gordon R., and Edward B. Barbier. *After the Green Revolution: Sustainable Agriculture for Development.* London: Earthscan, 1990.

Conway, Gordon R., and Jules N. Pretty. *Unwelcome Harvest: Agriculture and Pollution.* London: Earthscan, 1991.

Cook, G., ed. *The Future of Antarctica: Exploitation versus Preservation.* Manchester: Manchester University Press, 1990.

Creekmore, Charles, and Daniel Stiles. *Rolling Back the Desert: Ten Years after UNCOD.* Nairobi: UN Environment Program, 1987.

Crump, Andy. *Dictionary of Environment and Development: People, Places, Ideas, and Organizations.* London: Earthscan, 1991.

Cushing, D. H. *The Provident Sea.* Cambridge: Cambridge University Press, 1988.

Daly, Herman E., and John R. Cobb. *For the Common Good: Redirecting the Economy Toward Community, the Environment, and a Sustainable Future.* Boston: Beacon Press, 1989.

Dankelman, Irene, and Joan Davidson. *Women and Environment in the Third World: Alliance for the Future.* London: Earthscan, 1988.

Dasgupta, Partha, and Karl-Göran Mäler. *The Environment and Emerging Development Issues.* WIDER Studies in Development Economics. Oxford: Clarendon Press. In Press.

Dreze, Jean, and Amartya Sen, eds. *The Political Economy of Hunger.* Vols. 1 and 2. Oxford: Oxford University Press, 1991.

Durning, A. *Poverty and the Environment: Reversing the Downward Spiral.* Washington D.C.: Worldwatch Institute, 1989.

Ehrlich, Anne H., and John Birks, eds. *Hidden Dangers: Environmental Consequences of Preparing for War.* Nevada: Sierra Club Books, 1990.

El-Hinnawi, Essam. *Disarmament, Environment, and Sustainable Development: A Time for Action.* Nairobi: UN Environment Program, 1986.

El-Hinnawi, Essam. ed. *Environmental Impact of Production and Use of Energy.* Natural Resources and Environment Series, no. 1. Nairobi: UN Environment Program, 1981.

Faber, Mike, and Stephanie Griffith-Jones. "Approaches to the Third World Debt Reduction." *IDS Bulletin* 21 (1990): 2.

Finger, Michael J., and Patrick A. Misserlin. *The Effects of Industrial Countries' Policies on Developing Countries.* Policy and Research Series 3. Washington D.C.: World Bank, 1989.

Fisher, D. ed. *Options for Reducing Greenhouse Gas Emissions.* Stockholm: Stockholm Environment Institute, 1990.

Fishlow, Albert, et al. *Rich and Poor Nations in the World Economy*. New York: McGraw-Hill, 1978.

Gauhar, Altaf. ed. *Talking about Development*. London: Third World Foundation, 1983.

————. ed. *The Rich and the Poor*. London: Third World Foundation, 1983.

————. *South-South Strategy*. London: Third World Foundation, 1983.

"Global Warming and Climate Change: Perspectives from Developing Countries." Papers presented at the 1989 International Conference on Global Warming and Climate Change, New Delhi.

Goldemberg, J., et al. *Energy for a Sustainable World*. Washington, D.C.: World Resources Institute, 1987.

Goodman, D., and M. Redcliff. *Refashioning Nature: Food, Ecology, and Culture*. London: Routledge, 1991.

Gourlay, K. A. *Poisoners of the Sea*. London: Zed Books, 1988.

Gribbin, J. *Hothouse Earth: The Greenhouse Effect and Gaia*. London: Bantam Books, 1990.

Griffin, Keith, and Jeffrey James. *The Transition to Egalitarian Development*. London: Macmillan, 1981.

Gupta, Avijit. *Ecology and Development in the Third World*. London: Routledge, 1988.

Gupta, J. *Toxic Terrorism: Dumping Hazardous Wastes*. London: Earthscan, 1990.

Gwynn, Richard. *Way of the Sea: The Use and Abuse of the Oceans*. London: Green Books, 1989.

Haq, Mahbub ul. *The Poverty Curtain: Choices for the Third World*. New York: Columbia University Press, 1976.

Haq, Khadija, ed. *Global Development: Issues and Choices*. Washington, D.C.: Society for International Development, 1983.

Hardoy, Jorge E., and David Satterthwaite. *Squatter Citizen: Life in the Urban Third World*. Earthscan, 1989.

Hardoy, Jorge E., Sandy Cairncross, and David Satterthwaite, eds. *The Poor Die Young: Housing and Health in Third World Cities*. London: Earthscan, 1990.

Harrison, Paul. *Inside the Third World*. Harmondsworth: Penguin, 1979.

Hecht, S., and A. Cockburn. *The Fate of the Forest: Developers, Destroyers, and Defenders of the Forest*. London: Penguin, 1989.

Helleiner, Gerald. *The New Global Economy and the Developing Countries*. Aldershot, England: Edward Elgar, 1990.

————. *International Economic Disorder: Essays in North-South Relations*. London: Macmillan, 1980.

Helleiner, Gerald K., et al. "Towards a New Bretton Woods." A report by a Commonwealth Group of Experts. London: Commonwealth Secretariat, 1983.

Hinrichsen, Don. *Our Common Seas: Coasts in Crisis*. London: Earthscan, 1990.

Holmberg, Johan, and Lloyd Timberlake. *Defending the Future: A Guide to Sustainable Development*. London: Earthscan, 1991.

International Institute for Environment and Development in co-operation with

UN Environment Program. *Action on the Environment: The Role of the United Nations*. London: IIED, 1989.

Jager, J., and H. Ferguson, eds. *Climate Change: Science, Impacts and Policy*. Cambridge: Cambridge University Press, 1991.

Jalan, B., ed. *Problems and Policies in Small Economies*. London: Croom Helm, 1982.

Jayawardena, Lal. *A Global Environmental Compact for Sustainable Development: Resource Requirements and Mechanisms*. Helsinki: World Institute for Development Economics Research, 1991.

Johnson, Lawrence E. *A Morally Deep World: An Essay on Moral Significance and Environmental Ethics*. Cambridge: Cambridge University Press, 1991.

Jones, Russell R., and T. Wigley, eds. *Ozone Depletion: Health and Environmental Consequences*. London: Wiley, 1989.

Juma, Calestous. *The Gene Hunters: Biotechnology and the Scramble for Seeds*. London: Zed Books, 1988.

Kemp, Ray. *The Politics of Radioactive Waste Disposal*. Manchester: Manchester University Press, 1991.

Kohr, Leopold. *The Overdeveloped Nations*. New York: Schocken Books, 1978.

Krause, Florentine. *Energy Policy in the Greenhouse: From Warming Fate to Warming Limit*. London: Earthscan, 1990.

Kristoferson, Lars, and V. Bokalders. *Renewable Energy Technologies: Their Application in Developing Countries*. London: Intermediate Technology Development Group, 1991.

Lappé, Frances Moore, and Rachel Schurman. *Taking Population Seriously: The Missing Piece in the Population Puzzle*. London: Earthscan, 1989.

Leach, Gerald, and Robin Mearns. *Beyond the Woodfuel Crisis: People, Land, and Trees in Africa*. London: Earthscan, 1989.

Leggett, Jeremy, ed. *Global Warming: The Greenpeace Report*. Oxford: Oxford University Press, 1990.

Leonard, Jeffrey H., et al. *Environment and the Poor: Development Strategies for a Common Agenda*. U.S.–Third World Policy Perspectives, no. 11. Washington, D.C.: Overseas Development Council, 1989.

Lever, Harold, et al. *The Debt Crisis and the World Economy*. A report by a Commonwealth Group of Experts. London: Commonwealth Secretariat, 1984.

Lewis, W. Arthur. *The Evolution of the International Economic Order*. Princeton: Princeton University Press, 1977.

Louis Harris and Associates. "Public and Leadership Attitudes to the Environment in Four Continents: A Report of a Survey in Fourteen Countries." New York: Louis Harris and Associates, 1988.

Lovelock, James. *The Ages of Gaia: A Biography of Our Living Earth*. London: Bantam Books, 1990.

Lowe, Marcia D. *Alternatives to the Automobile: Transport for Livable Cities*. Worldwatch paper no. 98. Washington, D.C.: Worldwatch Institute, 1990.

Markandya, Anil, and Julie Richardson. *Earthscan Reader in Environmental Economics*. London: Earthscan, 1991.

Mather, A. S. *Global Forest Resources*. London: Pinter, 1990.

McCormick, John. *Acid Earth: The Global Threat of Acid Pollution.* London: Earthscan, 1989.

McDonald, A., and D. Kay. *Water Resources: Issues and Strategies.* London: Longman, 1988.

McHale, John, and Magda Cordell McHale. "Basic Human Needs." A report to the UN Environment Program. New Brunswick: Transaction Books, 1978.

McIntyre, Alister, et al. "Towards a New International Economic Order." A report by a Commonwealth Group of Experts. London: Commonwealth Secretariat, 1977.

McNamara, Robert S. *One Hundred Countries, Two Billion People.* New York: Praeger, 1973.

McNeely, Jeffrey A., et al. *Conserving the World's Biological Diversity.* Geneva: IUCN, 1990.

Meybeck, Michael, Deborah Chapman, and Richard Helmer, eds. "Global Freshwater Quality: A First Assessment." A report for the UN Environment Program and the World Health Organization. Oxford: Blackwell, 1989.

Mintzer, I., W. R. Moomaw, and A. D. Miller. *Protecting the Ozone Shield: Strategies for Phasing out CFCs during the 1990s.* Washington, D.C.: World Resources Institute, 1990.

Moody, R., ed. *The Indigenous Voice: Visions and Realities.* Vols. 1 and 2. London: Zed Books, 1989.

Moyers, B., and Center for Investigative Reporting. *Global Dumping Ground: the International Trade in Hazardous Waste.* Kent: Butterworth, 1991.

Mpinga, James. *Regaining the Lost Decade: A Guide to Sustainable Development in Africa.* Nairobi: UN Environment Program, 1990.

Pachauri, R. K., L. Srivastava, and K. Thukral, eds. *Energy—Environment—Development.* Vols. 1 and 2. New Delhi: Vikas, 1991.

Panos Institute. *Greenwar: Environment and Conflict in the Sahel.* London: Panos Institute, 1991.

————. *Who Is Taking the Heat? Global Warming and the Third World.* London: Panos Institute, 1991.

Pearce, David, Edward Barbier, and Anil Markandya. *Sustainable Development: Economics and Environment in the Third World.* London: Earthscan, 1990.

Pereira, Winin, and Jeremy Seabrook. *Asking the Earth: Farms, Forestry, and Survival in India.* London: Earthscan, 1991.

Perlin, John. *A Forest Journey: The Role of Wood in the Development of Civilization.* Cambridge: Harvard University Press, 1991.

Peters, I., and L. Robert, eds. *Consequences of the Greenhouse Effect for Biological Diversity.* New Haven: Yale University Press, 1991.

Porritt, Jonathan. *Where on Earth Are We Going?* London: BBC Books, 1990.

Prins, Gwyn, and Robert Stamp. *Top Guns and Toxic Whales: The Environment and Global Security.* London: Earthscan, 1991.

Reid, Walter V. C., and Kenton R. Miller. *Keeping Options Alive: The Scientific Basis for the Conservation of Biodiversity.* Washington, D.C.: World Resources Institute, 1989.

Renner, Michael. "National Security: The Economic and Environmental Dimensions." Worldwatch Paper 89. Washington, D.C.: Worldwatch Institute, 1989.

Repetto, Robert. *The Forest for the Trees? Government Policies and Misuse of Forest Resources.* Washington, D.C.: World Resources Institute, 1988.

Richards, John F., and Richard P. Tucker, eds. *World Deforestation in the Twentieth Century.* Durham: Duke University Press, 1988.

Roan, S. *The Ozone Crisis: The Fifteen Year Evolution of a Sudden Global Emergency.* London: Wiley, 1989.

Sand, Peter H. *International Co-operation: The Environmental Experience.* Washington, D.C.: World Resources Institute, 1990.

_____. *Lessons Learned in Global Environmental Governance.* Washington, D.C.: World Resources Institute, 1990.

Sanger, Clyde. *Safe and Sound: Disarmament and Development in the Eighties.* Ottawa: Denean Publishers, 1982.

Sarkar, P., and Hans Singer. "Debt Crisis, Commodity Prices, Transfer Burden, and Debt Relief." Institute of Development Studies discussion paper. Sussex: IDS, 1991.

Sarre, Philip, Paul Smith, and Eleanor Morris. *One World for One Earth: Overcoming Environmental Degradation.* London: Earthscan, 1991.

Schramm, Gunter, and Jeremy J. Warford, eds. *Environmental Management and Economic Development.* Baltimore: Johns Hopkins University Press, 1989.

Sears, Paul B. *Deserts on the March.* Reprint. Washington, D.C.: Island Press, 1988.

Seymour, John. *Changing Lifestyles: Living as Though the World Mattered.* London: Gollancz, 1991.

Shea, Cynthia Pollock. *Renewable Energy: Today's Contribution, Tomorrow's Promise.* Washington, D.C.: Worldwatch Institute, 1989.

Shiva, Vandana. *Staying Alive.* London: Zed Books, 1989.

Singer, H. W. *The Strategy of International Development.* London: Macmillan, 1975.

Socialist International. *Global Challenge. From Crisis to Cooperation: Breaking the North-South Stalemate.* London: Pan, 1985.

Sontheimer, Sally. *Women and the Environment: A Reader.* London: Earthscan, 1991.

Sopiee, Noordin, B. A. Hamzah, and Leong Choon Heng, eds. *Crisis and Response: The Challenge to South-South Economic Co-operation.* Kuala Lumpur, Malaysia: Institute of Strategic Studies, 1988.

Starke, Linda. *Progress Towards Our Common Future.* Oxford: Oxford University Press, 1990.

Stewart, Frances, and Arjun Sengupta. *International Financial Cooperation.* London: Pinter, 1982.

Strauss, W., and S. Mainwaring. *Air Pollution.* Sevenoaks, England: Edward Arnold, 1984.

Sutton, Francis X., ed. *A World to Make: Development in Perspective.* New Brunswick: Transaction Publishers, 1990.

Swaminathan, M.S., and S. K. Sinha, eds. *Global Aspects of Food Production.* London: Tycooly, 1986.

Taylor, Lance. *Foreign Resource Flows for Developing Country Growth.* Helsinki: WIDER, 1991.

Tester, Jefferson W. *Energy and the Environment in the Twenty-first Century.* Cambridge: MIT Press, 1990.

Tévoédjrè, Albert. *Poverty: Wealth of Mankind.* Oxford: Pergamon, 1978.

Thanh, N. C., and A. K. Biswas, eds. *Environmentally-sound Water Management.* Oxford: Oxford University Press, 1991.

"The Nairobi Declaration on Climate Change." Adopted by the International Conference on Global Warming and Climate Change: African Perspectives, May 1990. Nairobi: African Center for Technology Studies.

Timberlake, Lloyd, and Laura Thomas. *Defending the Future: A Guide to Sustainable Development.* London: Earthscan, 1990.

UN Center for Human Settlements. "Global Report on Human Settlements." Nairobi: UNCHS, 1987.

United Nations. *The Consequences of Rapid Population Growth in Developing Countries.* London: Taylor and Francis, 1991.

————. "The State of the Marine Environment." A report by a Group of Experts on the Scientific Aspects of Marine Pollution. Oxford: Blackwell, 1991.

United Nations Children's Fund. *The State of the World's Children, 1991.* Oxford: Oxford University Press, 1990.

United Nations Department of Technical Co-operation for Development. *Energy Issues and Options for Developing Countries.* London: Taylor and Francis, 1989.

United Nations Environment Program. *Selected Multilateral Treaties in the Field of the Environment.* Vol. 1 (1983) and Vol. 2 (1991). London: Grotius Publications.

————. *Scientific Assessment of Atmospheric Ozone.* Nairobi: UN Environment Program, 1989.

————. *Sustainable Water Development and Management: A Synthesis.* Nairobi: UN Environment Program, 1989.

————. *Action on Ozone.* Nairobi: UN Environment Program, 1990.

————. *The State of Environment: Children and the Environment.* Nairobi: UN Environment Program, 1990.

UN Environment Program in co-operation with World Resources Institute and the UK Department of the Environment. "Environmental Data Report." Published every alternate year.

Vallega, A., and H. D. Smith. *The Development of Integrated Sea Use Management.* London: Routledge, 1991.

Ward, Barbara, and René Dubos. *Progress for a Small Planet.* New York: Norton, 1979.

Warrick, R. A., and T. M. L. Wigley, eds. *Climate and Sea Level Change: Observations, Projections, and Implications.* Cambridge: Cambridge University Press, 1991.

Weir, David. *The Bhopal Syndrome*. London: Earthscan, 1988.

Westing, Arthur H., ed. *Cultural Norms, War, and the Environment*. Oxford: Oxford University Press for UNEP and SIPRI, 1988.

Wilson, E. O., ed. *Biodiversity*. London: Wiley, 1988.

Winpenny, James T., ed. *Development Research: The Environmental Challenge*. London: Overseas Development Institute, 1991.

Winterbottom, Robert. *Taking Stock: The Tropical Forestry Plan After Five Years*. Washington, D.C.: World Resources Institute, 1990.

World Meteorological Organization and International Council of Scientific Unions, World Climate Research Program. *Global Climate Change*. Geneva: WMO, 1990.

World Rainforest Movement. *Rainforest Destruction: Causes, Effects, and False Solutions*. Malaysia: WRM, 1990.

World Resources Institute. *Natural Endowments: Financing Resource Conservation for Development*. Washington, D.C.: WRI, 1989.

Young, John E. "Discarding the Throwaway Society." Worldwatch Paper 101. Washington, D.C.: Worldwatch Institute, 1991.

Good-faith efforts have been made to get permission for the use of the following materials:

Index

About the Author

Sir Shridath Ramphal is a former foreign minister of Guyana and was secretary-general of the fifty-nation Commonwealth 1975-1990. He was a member of all the major international commissions that reported in the 1980s, including the Brandt Commission on International Development Issues and the Brundtland Commission on Environment and Development. Now president of the World Conservation Union (IUCN) and chairman of a commission looking into the future of the West Indies, he brings to his writing the views of a lifelong internationalist informed by the perspectives of developing nations.